W9-CMP-230

COLLECTED WORKS OF ERASMUS

VOLUME 71

Phillips

COLLECTED WORKS OF
ERASMUS

CONTROVERSIES

EPISTOLA AD DORPIUM

APOLOGIA CONTRA LATOMI DIALOGUM

APOLOGIA PRO DECLAMATIONE
MATRIMONII

ACTA ACADEMIAE LOVANIENSIS
CONTRA LUTHERUM

AXIOMATA ERASMI PRO CAUSA LUTHERI

CONSILIUM CUIUSDAM

MANIFESTA MENDACIA

edited by J.K. Sowards

University of Toronto Press

Toronto / Buffalo / London

The research and publication costs of the
Collected Works of Erasmus are supported by the
Social Sciences and Humanities Research Council of Canada.
The publication costs are also assisted by
University of Toronto Press.

© University of Toronto Press 1993
Toronto / Buffalo / London
Printed in Canada

ISBN 0-8020-2869-1

Printed on acid-free paper

Canadian Cataloguing in Publication Data
Erasmus, Desiderius, d. 1536
[Works]
Collected works of Erasmus

Partial contents: v. 71. Controversies / edited by
J.K. Sowards.
Includes bibliographical references.
ISBN 0-8020-2869-1 (v. 71)

1. Erasmus, Desiderius, d. 1536. I. Title.

PA8500 1974   876'.04   C74-006326-X

Collected Works of Erasmus

The aim of the Collected Works of Erasmus
is to make available an accurate, readable English text
of Erasmus' correspondence and his
other principal writings. The edition is planned
and directed by an Editorial Board, an Executive Committee,
and an Advisory Committee.

Contents

Introduction
by J.K. Sowards
ix

Letter to Dorp / *Epistola ad Dorpium*
translated by R.A.B. Mynors and D.F.S. Thomson,
annotated by James K. McConica,
and edited by J.K. Sowards
1

Apology against the Dialogue of Latomus
Apologia contra Latomi dialogum
translated and annotated by Martin Lowry
31

The Defence of the Declamation on Marriage
Apologia pro declamatione matrimonii
translated and annotated by Charles Fantazzi
85

Acts of the University of Louvain against Luther
Acta Academiae Lovaniensis contra Lutherum
translated and annotated by Martin Lowry
97

Brief Notes of Erasmus for the Cause of Luther
Axiomata Erasmi pro causa Lutheri
translated and annotated by Martin Lowry
106

Minute Composed for the Peace of the Church
Consilium pro christianae religionis tranquillitate
translated and annotated by Martin Lowry
108

Manifest Lies / *Manifesta mendacia*
translated and annotated by Erika Rummel
113
Notes
133
Works Frequently Cited
174
Short-title Forms for Erasmus' Works
176
Index
181

Introduction:
Erasmus and the Louvain Circle

I

Louvain was an ancient cloth town and one-time capital of Brabant. But it was more important as the site of the only university in the Low Countries. The university had been founded in 1426 and through the rest of the fifteenth and early sixteenth centuries was a magnet attracting intellectuals of every persuasion to Louvain. Erasmus arrived in the early fall of 1502 for his first prolonged period of residence there. He does not tell us specifically why he came to Louvain, except to escape the plague which had broken out in Saint-Omer where he had been staying as the guest of the abbot of St Bertin, Antoon van Bergen, the brother of his old patron, Hendrik van Bergen, the bishop of Cambrai (Ep 170). The abbot, who had connections with the university, may have suggested that Erasmus go there and may have sent letters of introduction with him, one perhaps to Adriaan Flori-zoon, the future Pope Adrian VI and already dean of St Peter's in Louvain and chancellor of the university. We do know that immediately upon Erasmus' arrival Adriaan persuaded the city magistrates to offer him a public lectureship at the university. Erasmus turned it down: his reason, 'the study of Greek absorbs me completely.'[1] This had been his preoccupation for the past two years.

These had been the hardest and most desperate years of Erasmus' life. He had at last resolved to be a theologian. His friendship with John Colet at Oxford in 1499 had wakened echoes of this purpose in him which had been muted by the difficulties and tribulations of his last few years at the University of Paris. Colet had invited him to stay at Oxford and join him in the exposition of the Bible. Erasmus declined, not because he failed to share Colet's vision but because he realized that if he wanted to discover the historical and theological basis of Christianity he must have Greek. Erasmus had been exposed to it from time to time since his schoolboy days at Deventer but never either seriously or intensively. It was to this deficiency that he referred in a letter to Colet, ironically by quoting in Greek the proverb to begin 'to learn pottery on the largest size of jar' (Ep 108:102–3). Colet, who had little or no Greek himself, did not share Erasmus' views in this matter. But to Erasmus it was as essential to return to the letter of the Scriptures as to their spirit. Many years later he would write, in the preface to the first edition of his Annotations on the New Testament, 'It is the least part of Scripture, what they call the letter; but this is the foundation on which rests the mystic meaning. This is only rubble; but rubble that carries the august weight of the whole marvellous edifice' (Ep 373:116–18).

At the end of January 1500 Erasmus left England for the continent, for Paris, and for study. He had his goal at last firmly fixed before him; he knew what he had to do. For that very reason, the poverty and illness, the frustrations and interruptions that dogged his steps were more intolerable than ever. His patrons were negligent. The bishop of Cambrai 'goes so far as to turn his back upon me.' The bishop's brother, the abbot of St Bertin, while not hostile to Erasmus, nevertheless put him off – 'the abbot bids me be of good hope.' The wealthy Anna van Borssele, the Lady of Veere, whom Erasmus had earlier courted so assiduously, remained evasive – 'my lady merely extends promises from day to day' (Ep 128:17–18). The generosity of his less exalted patrons and friends was soon exhausted as were their contacts with other possible benefactors. During these first months of his return to Paris he wrote to a friend in the Low Countries, 'My readings in Greek all but crush my spirit; but I have no spare time and no means to purchase books or employ the services of a tutor. And with all this commotion to endure I have hardly enough to live on; and this is what I owe to my studies!' (Ep 123:25–9).

It was in this desperate time and in these desperate circumstances that he was forced to find out what indeed he did owe to his studies. He turned to the printing press. He had gained some small reputation from his association with Gaguin's *Compendium de origine et gestis Francorum* and from the publication of his edition of Willem Hermans' poems. He had contacts with printers and booksellers through Gaguin and his other friends in Paris. He had, moreover, a valuable literary property in the facile, elegant, and fashionable Latin style that he had cultivated since boyhood. And he had a dozen projects – some in bits and pieces, some nearly complete, some only in mind. A few still unpublished poems, the manuscript of the *Antibarbari*, and copies of his letters had been circulated among his friends and were admired by them. Other pieces had grown out of his own study and his friends urged him to publish them. These were largely of the type of critical editions of standard classical authors for which the continuing popularity of the classics and the fashion of humanism created a profitable market. In the course of the year 1500 Erasmus prepared an edition of Cicero's *De officiis* for the press of Johannes Philippi in Paris. As his hard struggle with Greek progressed and he became able to handle the language with some ease, he turned his exercises and drills to the same sort of profit, preparing translations of Greek authors into Latin. As early as the winter of 1500 he was at work on Plato and had borrowed a Greek Homer from a friend (Epp 131, 138). Within two more years he was working on the translation of three declamations of Libanius (Ep 177) and shortly thereafter on the dialogues of the second-century Greek satirist Lucian, who was to remain his favourite Greek author.

Even as Erasmus began to publish his editions of the pagan classics, he had already turned to the classics of Christianity. In the winter of 1500 and through the next year there are scattered references to the work on St Jerome that was in time to produce his great, authoritative edition of Jerome's letters, to be followed by dozens of editions of and commentaries on the other church Fathers, both Latin and Greek.

Still other writing projects grew from Erasmus' own cultivation of style and from his earlier experience with the tutoring of private pupils in Paris. The first such project to be published was his *Adagia*. It was a collection of stock phrases, epigrams, maxims, proverbs – in short, 'adages' – culled from the literature of antiquity. He probably started it in some fashion or other before his visit to England. In the spring of 1500, after his return to Paris, he was hard at work on it and the book was printed by Philippi in June.[2] It was undoubtedly a by-product of Erasmus' intensified study at this time, of his re-reading of the classical writers and his busy schedule of editorial work, even of the beginning of his Greek studies, although the slim volume of the first edition contained only a handful of references to the new treasures of Greek learning among its 818 entries.

Following the publication of the *Adagia*, the search for patrons as well as sporadic outbreaks of the plague in Paris frequently forced Erasmus to be away from the city and his studies. In 1501–2 he travelled extensively in the Netherlands, trying without much success to regain the good will of the bishop of Cambrai and using every contact he could muster to find new patrons. But things did not improve much. In the fall of 1502 he wrote despairingly to his old friend Willem Hermans, 'Fortune has had a glorious fling at my expense this year!' Death had claimed François de Busleyden, the wealthy archbishop of Besançon whom Erasmus was courting as a patron. Anna van Borssele had remarried and the tutor of her son, Erasmus' faithful friend Jacob Batt, had died. His English patron Lord Mountjoy is 'cut off by the sea.' 'The plague puts France, England, and Germany all at once beyond my reach' (Ep 172). Within a month the bishop of Cambrai would also be dead.

This letter to Hermans was written from Louvain shortly after Erasmus arrived there. And, though he declined the opportunity that Adriaan Florizoon arranged for him to lecture at the university and complained mildly about the scarcity of Greek books and its general backwardness, nevertheless, he was shortly pulled into the circle of the university and his fortunes at last began to turn somewhat for the better. The friendship with Adriaan, which continued to blossom, was a source of important contacts. Perhaps through Adriaan, perhaps on his own initiative, he came to know Nicolas Ruistre, the former chancellor of the university, bishop of Arras, and councillor to Duke Philip of Burgundy. Erasmus dedicated his first Greek translation, of Libanius, to Ruistre. He had made friends with the learned and wealthy Jérôme de Busleyden, archdeacon of Cambrai and the brother of the dead archbishop of Besançon, whom he had earlier courted. He was the house guest of Jean Desmarez, a fellow poet and humanist and University Orator. Desmarez installed Erasmus comfortably in St Donatian's College, of which he was president, and introduced him to a group of humanist scholars at the Lily, the most advanced humanistic college of the university. He may have met Maarten van Dorp at this time, who was already a student there.[3] These contacts had begun to reach outside the university to touch the rich and cultivated Burgundian court. Jacob Mauritszoon, a fellow townsman of Erasmus from Gouda, a learned lawyer, and, like others of the Louvain circle, a councillor to the court, invited him to compose a Latin oration, a panegyric for Duke Philip upon his return to the Low Countries from a state visit to Spain. Desmarez also urged him to take on the task (Epp 176, 179). Through most of the fall of 1503 he worked intermittently on the panegyric, polishing its periods and fretting over its sentiments and protesting at the time it was taking him from more worthwhile labours.[4] In January 1504 Erasmus delivered his oration as part of the splendid occasion of the duke's return, held in the ducal palace in Brussels. He was given the princely sum of eleven livres.[5] The panegyric, further polished and expanded, was quickly given to the printer Dirk Martens to be printed while the occasion was still fresh in people's minds. In the course of his stay in Louvain Erasmus had also completed his first major devotional work, the *Enchiridion militis christiani*, which had been printed by Martens in February 1503, along with a number of lesser and related pieces under the title *Lucubratiunculae aliquot*.

In the course of the year 1504 Erasmus' reputation burgeoned and his fortunes improved dramatically. From Duke Philip he received an invitation to come to court as a member of his household: indeed, writes Erasmus, 'he promised me the earth' (Ep 180). But Erasmus declined. Then suddenly, in mid-winter 1504, he left Louvain. Why, we do not know. But he returned to Paris where he was staying with his English friend Christopher Fisher[6] when he wrote to Colet in England about some money owed to him that might sustain him for several months (Ep 181). He would not return to Louvain for another thirteen years.

It was a far different Erasmus who arrived in Louvain in the late summer of 1517. He had made his triumphant trip to Italy from 1506 to 1509. There he had received the doctor of theology degree from the University of Torino. He had met and been accepted by the humanists and the academic intelligentsia of Bologna. He had visited Rome and been befriended by some of the highest officials of the papal court, including Cardinals Riario and Grimani, and Giovanni Cardinal de' Medici, the future Pope Leo X. He had even been received by Pope Julius II. But most important of all, he had met the great Venetian scholar-printer Aldus Manutius who encouraged him to expand his earlier *Adagia*. Aldus and his circle entered enthusiastically into Erasmus' undertaking, making available to him from their own libraries books that had never been printed before, especially Greek books. The earlier version of the *Adagia* – Erasmus called it nothing but the raw material of the future book[7] – was transformed into a huge, heavy volume of over 3000 entries. The *Adagiorum chiliades*, when it appeared in 1508, immediately established Erasmus as one of the foremost classical scholars of his age, a reputation that would be burnished by every later, expanded edition of the work.

He returned from Italy to England, where he had been summoned by his English friends in anticipation of the lavish patronage of letters by the new young king Henry VIII – mountains of gold they promised! The promises, unfortunately, proved illusory. Erasmus stayed for a while with Thomas More in London. While there he wrote the most famous of all his books, *The Praise of Folly*. Then, with the hope of other preferment disappearing, in 1511 he accepted the invitation of his friend Bishop John Fisher to take up the Lady Margaret Beaufort professorship of divinity at Cambridge. For the next three years, though he found Cambridge a dreary place all the while, he worked through a long list of projects – a revision and still larger edition of the *Adagia*; a substantial textbook on rhetorical dilation entitled *De copia*, which he had promised Colet for his newly founded school, St Paul's, in London; an edition of the Roman philosopher Seneca; and a number of Greek translations, several works of Plutarch, several more of Lucian's dialogues, and the Greek Fathers Basil and Chrysostom. But his principal occupation was his work on St Jerome and the New Testament. Erasmus picked up this work on the New Testament once more at Cambridge, correcting and revising it. His letters are full of references to it. In the fall of 1512 he wrote his friend Pieter Gillis in Antwerp that he had completed the correction of the entire New Testament (Ep 264). Within the next year, perhaps sooner, he turned to the task of collecting as many manuscripts as he could find, both Greek and Latin, to produce yet further revision notes to the New Testament: 'I have annotated over a thousand places,' he wrote (Ep 296:165–6).

At the end of the first week in July 1514 Erasmus left England. As he wrote the prior of his monastery of Steyn, 'At present I am making for Germany, Basel in fact. There I intend to publish my writings' (Ep 296:241–2). On the way he stopped briefly at Louvain, probably to leave his manuscript of a number of minor works, including his edition of the *Disticha Catonis*, with the printer Dirk Martens. Maarten van Dorp, who was by this time a student of theology, hastened to renew his acquaintance with Erasmus and even undertook to see the book through the press (Ep 304:173–4).

In Basel, where Erasmus arrived in August 1514, he entered into his long association with Johann Froben and the Froben press. It was an association that had already begun. A year before, Froben had printed a pirated edition of the Aldine *Adagia* that elicited the grudging admiration even of Erasmus. More recently Froben had got hold of the manuscript of the *Adagia* that Erasmus had revised at Cambridge, along with most of the other works he had prepared there. Erasmus was compelled to make a virtue of necessity. What Froben had done was by no means unheard of in the cut-throat business of early commercial printing. The Froben press was a well-established house and Froben had Greek type. Moreover, the Froben press for some years had been engaged in publishing critical editions of the 'Doctors of the Latin church.' St Ambrose had appeared in 1492, Augustine in 1506. St Jerome was now under way. Erasmus' later friend Beatus Rhenanus actually says that it was the knowledge of the Jerome edition that brought him to Basel (Allen I 63).

Erasmus immediately became involved in the Jerome project, taking over the correspondence volumes and becoming senior editor of the entire enterprise. Even as he plunged into the work on Jerome, he and Froben came to an agreement on Erasmus' other great project, the Greek New Testament. What Erasmus actually had done on it at this stage is still somewhat problematic. We know that he had 'corrected' the entire New Testament. This undoubtedly referred to what would later be published as the Annotations. But it is now reasonably sure that he had not prepared either the text for a Greek version of the New Testament or done a Latin translation of his own.[8] The idea of printing an actual Greek text may very

well have originated with Froben, who was likely aware of the
Complutensian project in Spain and wanted to get his version into print
first. In any case it is first mentioned by Erasmus in a letter to Johann
Reuchlin, dated before 13 September 1514, at Basel, asking Reuchlin to lend
him a Greek manuscript of the New Testament for the work (Ep 300:31–8).
At this point Erasmus was still thinking of simply printing the Vulgate text
from which to append his annotations (Ep 421:46–7). But this changed in the
next few weeks. In a letter to Wimpfeling, dated 21 September 1514, he
refers to a version 'translated by me, with the Greek facing, and notes on
it by me' (Ep 305:229). This translation was only done after the printing on
the project had actually begun (Ep 421:50–1). And throughout the printing
he continued to add annotations. For the next year and a half Erasmus
worked furiously, collating, correcting, even composing as the book was
being printed.

Erasmus interrupted his work in the late spring of 1515 for a rapid trip
to England, for what precise reason we do not know. In any case, it was on
his return journey to Basel, as he stopped briefly in Antwerp, that Erasmus
became aware of a reproving letter Maarten van Dorp had written him from
Louvain almost a year before, sharply criticizing *The Praise of Folly* and
warning him darkly about continuing his radical and dangerous work on
the New Testament. Erasmus read a copy of the letter that a friend had and
wrote his defence, the *Epistola apologetica ad Dorpium*. He then went directly
on to Basel without either seeing Dorp or visiting Louvain.

In March 1516 the completed New Testament came off Froben's
presses, running to more than a thousand folio pages. And St Jerome was
not far behind. On 7 March Erasmus wrote to a friend, 'The New Testament
is published. Jerome is receiving the finishing touches' (Ep 394:38–9); a few
weeks later, to his German humanist friend Willibald Pirckheimer, 'the New
Testament for better or worse is finished. Jerome comes up breathless to the
finishing line and will soon be in the hands of the public' (Ep 407:5–7). The
printed New Testament had made the Frankfurt spring book fair and was
for sale everywhere. Erasmus was the most famous biblical scholar in the
world.

II

Later that spring Erasmus left Basel for the Netherlands. He had been
appointed a councillor to Prince Charles and, though it was largely an
honorific appointment (Epp 392, 1148), he nevertheless felt some obligation
to present himself at court.[9] For the occasion he had composed for the
sixteen-year-old prince his *Institutio principis christiani*, though its printing

by Froben had been delayed past his departure. He was courteously received by Charles' chancellor, Jean Le Sauvage, who promised a substantial income if Erasmus would come to court or at least remain in the Netherlands (Ep 436).

In the summer of 1516 he went briefly to England again, to see to the matter of a final dispensation from Leo x from the disability of his illegitimate birth, which was being handled for him by his friend Andrea Ammonio through his Italian-papal connections (Epp 517–18). Returning to the Low Countries he spent the rest of 1516 and the first half of 1517 in Antwerp, Brussels, and Ghent, most of the time staying with his friend Pieter Gillis in Antwerp.

In January 1517 Erasmus visited Louvain for a few days, perhaps to test his relations with the theologians there. He had heard a few weeks earlier that some of them had been working to secure a public decree stipulating that his writings be officially examined by the Universities of Louvain and Cologne (Ep 505:9–19). He was entertained at dinner by Dorp who had also invited not only Erasmus' host Jean Desmarez but several theologians including Jan Briart, the dean of the Louvain theological faculty and university vice-chancellor (Ep 509). The meeting seems to have gone well enough.

In the meantime Erasmus received an invitation from the French king to take up a lucrative benefice, which he turned down because of his responsibilities to 'our excellent Prince Charles' (Ep 529:48). In the spring of 1517 Erasmus paid another brief visit to England to receive his dispensation from Leo x at the hands of Ammonio. Back in the Netherlands he was drawn even closer to the Burgundian court, which he followed to Ghent and Bruges. Prince Charles was making plans to depart shortly for Spain to be invested with the crowns of Castile and Aragon. Erasmus was invited to accompany the court entourage. He declined courteously.

With his courtly patrons about to leave, Erasmus now had to find other means to live. He turned at long last, again, to Louvain and the university. It was a decision he made with some misgivings. Almost a year before he had speculated about moving there in a gossipy letter to Ammonio, 'I have turned somewhat against Louvain,' he wrote:

> If I were there, I should have to pay my own way and be the humble servant
> of the university people. The young men would be interrupting me all the
> time with their chatter: 'Do correct these verses, Just vet this letter for me';
> there would be constant demands for different authors; and there is no one
> there whom it would be any credit or any help for me to know. On top of all
> this I should have to listen sometimes to the chatter of the theologians, the

dreariest sort of men, and among them the egregious X has very nearly got me into trouble; it is a case with him of my having the wolf by the ears, unable either to hold on or let go. Face to face he is all smiles, and uses his teeth behind my back; writes letters full of honey but with more than a little gall mixed in; professes friendship and behaves like an enemy. I have left no stone unturned to cure the defect in that man's nature, for I admire his gifts and appreciate his style, which is elegant by local standards. As I see that this makes no progress, I am resolved to let him alone and leave him to himself until this drunken fit blows over. If only great Jupiter with his famous thunderbolt would plunge this whole race of men into Tartarus: they produce nothing that can make us better men or better scholars, and they are a perfect universal nuisance (Ep 475:17–34).

The unidentified theologian in the foregoing excerpt was certainly Dorp. But more recently Dorp's friendly overtures had somewhat reassured Erasmus, though 'he is more inconstant than any woman' (Ep 637:13). And he was further reassured by the other Louvain theologians. To his friend Pieter Gillis he wrote that Jan Briart 'is entirely on my side' (Ep 637:12). Moreover, Briart had taken the lead in proposing to co-opt Erasmus as a member of the theological faculty. He was duly registered on 30 August 1517 in the matriculation roll and listed as 'sacre theologie professor.'[10]

For the first few weeks Erasmus was again the guest of his old friend Jean Desmarez. But he was negotiating for more permanent quarters in the College of the Lily, which continued to be the most humanistic college in the university. Its headmaster was Jan de Neve of Hondschoote, a long-time friend of Erasmus to whom, in 1514, he had dedicated the *Opuscula aliquot*, containing the *Catonis praecepta* and a number of other works that would be useful 'with those pupils of yours whom you guard from any taint of barbarism in education or in character' (Ep 298:42–3). It was probably de Neve who made the arrangements for his accommodations. He was provided with a spacious upper-story chamber 'where I can have more room to spread out my books' (Ep 643:13–14). Erasmus would live here for the next four years. He had no regular academic duties but he did attend all the faculty meetings 'in which they do the same thing over and over again' (Ep 695:21–2). Because he was not on the instructional staff he had to pay for his room and meet his other normal expenses. But these costs were modest and by this time Erasmus enjoyed a reasonably good income: as he wrote to his Italian friend Paolo Bombace, 'I ... have over three hundred ducats a year of my own, besides what more I get from the generosity of my patrons and as the fruit of my own labours.'[11]

Even as Erasmus' amity with Dorp and fellow theologians continued there were ominous undercurrents of change. The Louvain faculty of theology was one of the most conservative in Europe (Ep 1111:28–32, 49–51). It had reacted vigorously as the ripples of the Reuchlin controversy spread from Cologne.[12] The Louvain theologians were as deeply offended by the raucous *Epistolae obscurorum virorum (Letters of Obscure Men)* as those of Cologne had been. Although Erasmus had avoided becoming involved in this business, he had, nevertheless, strongly defended Reuchlin (Ep 300). And he had himself, in *The Praise of Folly*, written just as wickedly about divines and theologians as had the authors of the *Epistolae obscurorum virorum*.

All this had led to Dorp's letter to Erasmus complaining about *The Praise of Folly* in 1514. And he had also warned him of the danger of his proposed Greek New Testament and his revision of the Vulgate (Ep 304). Erasmus had replied to Dorp's letter with an elaborate *Epistola apologetica* (Ep 337) in which he had suggested that Dorp was being used as 'a stalking horse' by others to further 'their own designs' (Ep 337:27–8). He was exactly right. Those others were the leading Louvain theologians, including especially Jan Briart.[13] Dorp was just on the point of finishing his doctorate in theology at this time and very much under the thumb of his professors. But the doubts and reservations in his letter to Erasmus were unquestionably genuine as well. He continued to express them in another long letter in August of 1515, his response to Erasmus' *Apologia* (Ep 347). Erasmus did not reply to this one. But his friend Thomas More did, in a long and blistering letter-tract, dated 15 October 1515.[14] Dorp was totally converted by More's arguments.[15]

By this time Dorp had received his doctorate, been appointed full professor, and given a lucrative prebend in St Peter's, the principal church in Louvain.[16] Despite his new enthusiasm for theology he had never entirely given up either his interest in humanistic letters or his connections with the humanist circle of Louvain, including Jean Desmarez, Adrianus Barlandus, Jan de Neve, and the printer Dirk Martens.

As an earnest of his commitment to the values of humanism, Dorp delivered an inaugural oration, on 6 July 1516, to a course of lectures on the Pauline Epistles. He emphasized that in the study of Scripture humanistic rhetoric is to be preferred to scholastic dialectic and that such study absolutely requires a thorough knowledge of Greek. Since he himself had no Greek he was glad to use the learned writings of Valla, Lefèvre, and most important of all, Erasmus. He even advocated the textual criticism of the Vulgate.[17] Erasmus, who was in Brussels at the time, heard of the oration from Desmarez and immediately wrote Dorp an enthusiastic note: 'Oh blessings on your brave spirit! Right on target! So men rise to the stars. You have bravely espoused a cause fully worthy of you: carry it through' (Ep 438:6–8).

Dorp had indeed done a brave thing. And he paid for it. On 30 September 1516 his colleagues in the theological faculty refused the yearly renewal of Dorp's certification as an academic teacher.[18] Notwithstanding the spitefulness of his fellow theologians, Dorp maintained his stance. He wrote Erasmus at the end of November that he intended to 'keep an open mind and behave like a true academic philosopher.' 'Whatever has passed between us, I should like to wipe off the slate, and be friends without reserve' (Ep 496:4–5, 20–1). By the beginning of the following year Dorp had managed somehow to get back in the good graces of his faculty colleagues, perhaps through the influence of the eminent Jan Briart who apparently continued to admire his talents. In any case, Dorp's reconciliation with his fellow theologians was completed in the following summer. He was not only reappointed as an academic teacher but elected dean of the faculty. He very well may have used his new-found acceptance to promote Erasmus' interests with the faculty and his co-optation to membership when he arrived in Louvain in the late summer of 1517.[19]

Erasmus' fragile peace with the Louvain theologians continued. The slights against theologians in The Praise of Folly seem to have been forgotten for the moment.[20] The Greek New Testament and the Latin version Erasmus had published in 1516 had not produced the dire consequences he had anticipated. In the spring of 1518, Erasmus could write, 'Between me and the theologians these are halcyon days, indeed there is a surprising degree of intimacy. They thank me openly for my Jerome, there are no complaints of my New Testament; in fact the leaders of the faculty heartily approve' (Ep 794:34–7). Briart, who had been one of the leaders of the opposition, seemed entirely won over (Ep 637:12). Erasmus was, after all, a renowned biblical scholar, a councillor to the archduke, now king, Charles, a familiar of the pope and other high-ranking churchmen – in short, a man who was clearly an ornament to the theological faculty. Briart himself seemed disposed to maintain amicable relations.

III

Then a fresh crisis appeared and Erasmus was in the very middle of it. It was a proposal for a radically new and innovative college for the University of Louvain, the Collegium Trilingue, for the teaching of the three biblical languages, Hebrew, Greek, and Latin.[21] It was a bequest in the will of Jérôme de Busleyden who, as a member of the ducal council, had accompanied Duke Charles to Spain, fell ill on the way at Bordeaux, and died on

27 August 1517. Erasmus had known Jérôme for many years, going back to his own student days in Paris and Orléans in 1498 (Ep 157:67–9). They had renewed acquaintances in 1502, during Erasmus' first extended stay in Louvain, when he was pursuing the patronage of Jérôme's older brother François, the archbishop of Besançon, who died on an earlier visit to Spain in the suite of the archduke Philip in 1502. In the fall of 1503 Erasmus wrote to Willem Hermans, from Louvain:

> I have made a friend of Jérôme de Busleyden, archdeacon of Cambrai; or rather he has made himself a friend to me. He is brother to the bishop, and he has a profound knowledge of both Latin and Greek. From time to time he repeats that, had that great man got back safe, my fortune would have been secure; certainly I reposed all my hopes in him (Ep 178:12–17).

From Italy Erasmus had sent Jérôme a literary gift of some of Lucian's dialogues he had translated (Ep 205:36–40).

Back in Louvain in the late summer of 1517, Erasmus renewed his friendship with Busleyden, among other things suggesting to him that he use his fortune to endow a college of the three languages.[22] He also proposed that the professors appointed to the respective chairs be accommodated in such a way that they could devote all their time and attention to their study and that, moreover, they be paid so well that the foremost experts would be attracted to the positions (de Vocht CTL I 13). He recommended that St Donatian's College, where he himself had resided many years before, be made the basis of the new foundation. It was now a moribund institution and its president, Jan Stercke, who had succeeded Erasmus' friend Desmarez in that post, entered enthusiastically into the planning for the new college for which he drafted the regulations that were then written into Busleyden's will. Busleyden himself had become almost obsessive about the plans for the college, all of which and in detail he had incorporated in his will, dated 23 June 1517, on the very eve of his departure for Spain.[23] Even on the day he died, later that summer in Bordeaux, he made a codicil to the will touching the college, providing additional executors to see to its implementation and specifying that the assistance of Erasmus be sought.

Erasmus was not slow to give his assistance. As the will was being carried into effect and even before Busleyden's goods had been disposed of, on 19 October 1517 Erasmus wrote to Gilles de Busleyden, the surviving brother and chief executor of the will, urging him to hire a Jewish physician who was in Louvain and available for the chair of Hebrew. His name was Matthaeus Adrianus and he was a Christian convert of long standing. But most important he was so skilled in the whole of Hebrew literature that in my opinion our age has no one else to show who could be compared with him. If my judgment in this matter does not carry enough weight with you, this is the unanimous testimony of everyone I know in Germany or Italy with any skill in the language. Not only has he a complete knowledge of the language, he has also deeply explored the recesses of the literature at first hand and has all the books at his fingertips (Ep 686:9–15).[24]

Gilles de Busleyden was quick to respond and Adrianus was promptly appointed, beginning his course of lectures in early December. Provision for the housing of the college had not yet been made and Adrianus lectured in rooms provided by the Augustinians.

Again on the recommendation of Erasmus, Adrianus Barlandus was appointed to the chair of Latin. He was a close friend of Erasmus and an enthusiast for the project of the new college. Further, he was well known in Louvain for the purity of his Latin style and his access to powerful nobles of the court. He had been tutor to the young Cardinal Guillaume de Croy and to the sons of the great Egmond family. He delivered the college's inaugural Latin lecture on 1 September 1518.[25]

By this time Erasmus was at work trying to arrange for a professor of Greek. He wrote to the distinguished emigré Greek scholar Janus Lascaris, whom he had known in Venice, telling him about the newly founded college, the appointment of the professors of Hebrew and Latin, and asking his recommendation for a person to fill the Greek chair, preferably a native-speaker of Greek. He may even have hoped to attract Lascaris himself (Ep 836). But he was not successful, either in interesting Lascaris or attracting any other native Greek, not even in attracting a well-known teacher of Greek. Instead, he settled for a young Dutchman named Rutgerus Rescius, who had studied Greek in Paris under Girolamo Aleandro. He had returned to Louvain where he worked for Dirk Martens' press, assisting with Greek texts. He had also matriculated in the law faculty of the university in anticipation of another career. He eagerly accepted the prestigious appointment to the Greek chair of the Collegium Trilingue (de Vocht CTL I 251, 294).

Erasmus was probably persuaded to recommend this rather marginal appointment to the Greek professorship, which he had earlier described in such exalted terms, largely because he wanted to get the new college established quickly. As he wrote to Jan Robijns, one of the executors of Busleyden's will, 'My own opinion is that the chairs should be got under way at once, that the thing may not cool off in the meantime, and to prevent any evil spirit from upsetting a scheme that will be so good for us all'

(Ep 805:31–4).[26] Indeed, there is a sense of urgency about all the measures he was taking for the college at this early point. For resistance was already beginning to form. The negotiations to set up the new college within the structure of St Donatian's dragged on and finally failed completely because of the degree of control demanded by the arts faculty of the university. But more was at issue than simply the jealousy or small-mindedness of faculty colleagues. There were important matters of substance. The proposal for the new college had revived the issues that the controversy with Dorp had first raised. As Erasmus later recalled, 'things were pretty tranquil for some time, until the rise of the College of the Three Tongues' (Ep 1225:34–6). Dorp himself was now a leading defender of the study of Greek and Hebrew. Erasmus called him, perhaps with some gentle irony, 'the leader of the Hebrew party' (Ep 794:84–5). Others on the faculty, however, remained unconvinced.

In the midst of these unsettling events, Erasmus had to leave Louvain temporarily and return to Basel to see to the second edition of his Greek New Testament. For, in spite of the adulation it had received, the 1516 edition was far from satisfactory. The book had been 'rushed into print,' as Erasmus confessed to Pirckheimer (Ep 694:18–21). And this haste had resulted in many errors that had 'slipped in here and there' (Ep 809:79). There were additional references that needed to be inserted which 'in my haste I formerly overlooked' (Ep 809:78–9). There were additional citations to authorities that needed to be made and additional manuscripts that needed to be consulted. And Erasmus wanted to do a fuller translation of the New Testament for the second edition.

In the preface to the reader in the first edition he had solicited suggestions and corrections (Ep 373:38–40). He wrote many of his scholar friends – Fisher, Colet, Latimer, Tunstall, Grocyn, Wentford, Glareanus, Budé (Epp 417, 422, 597, 707, 772, 784, 825, 833, 886) – asking for their ideas. And throughout 1517 and the early months of 1518 he was furiously busy with his own notes for the revision. In September 1517 he wrote to Wolsey, '... at present I am the slave of the New Testament so completely that I can do nothing else' (Ep 658:39–40); and a month later to Geldenhouwer, 'I am now devoted entirely to the New Testament, which has almost deprived me of my eyesight and my vital force' (Ep 682:5–6). The next month he wrote Hermann von Neuenahr, 'I am immersed in work, especially in the revision of the New Testament – I wish I had never touched it!' (Ep 722:15–16). But the work progressed. And he wrote to Pirckheimer earlier that same month that the first edition 'is now being taken to pieces and refashioned, so thoroughly that it will be a new book. It will be finished, I hope, within four months' (Ep 694:18–21). His estimate was about right. In the spring of

1518 he had apparently written Froben proposing the new edition. Froben eagerly accepted the proposal in a hastily written letter from the Frankfurt book fair. But he had doubts the book could be ready for the next fair, partly because of the shortage of time and partly because he still had nearly four hundred copies of the first edition to sell (Ep 801). Erasmus' letters through the rest of the spring of 1518 are full of his plans. And about 1 May he left for Basel. He expected to be gone only a few months and be back in Louvain by the early winter. He kept his room and left the care of his books and personal effects in the hands of friends.

Part of the reason for Erasmus' haste in getting the new edition ready had been his apprehension that opponents would seize on the many errors and try to discredit the whole undertaking. To his relief, as we have seen, the Louvain theologians seem to have accepted the work without complaint. 'Not a dog barks, except a few friars of some sort at Cologne, I hear, and Bruges, but in the distance and behind my back,' he wrote in March of 1518 (Ep 794:37–8). But this was not the case everywhere. A month earlier he had received a somewhat stiff letter from Johann Maier von Eck, the Ingolstadt theologian and later Luther's persistent antagonist. Eck objected to Erasmus' implication that the apostles possessed something short of perfect knowledge of Greek and reminded him that it was 'from the Holy Spirit that they learned their Greek' (Ep 769:81). Erasmus answered with a graceful and conciliatory letter but held his ground (Ep 844).

In the meantime a petty and annoying controversy had broken out not with an opponent but with a supporter and friend, Jacques Lefèvre d'Etaples. Lefèvre was the most eminent of the French biblical humanists and had for years been a warm friend of Erasmus. That friendship was now threatened over a trivial disagreement. In his annotations Erasmus had criticized Lefèvre for his interpretation of Hebrews 2:7 as 'Thou madest him a little lower than God' instead of 'a little lower than the angels.' In his second edition of the Epistles of Paul, Lefèvre not only maintained his reading of the passage but added a lengthy reply to Erasmus in which he seemed to be charging Erasmus with blasphemy. Erasmus promptly responded with the *Apologia ad Iacobum Fabrum Stapulensem*.[27] Neither man would let go of the matter. Erasmus constantly referred to it in his letters for more than a year before the quarrel was finally settled (Ep 814).[28]

IV

Just before leaving for Basel Erasmus had begun to become involved in what was to be one of the most lengthy and acrimonious of his controversies, with Edward Lee. Lee was a young Englishman who had studied theology at both Oxford and Cambridge and had come to Louvain to study Greek. Erasmus was quick to offer his aid, especially since Lee knew several of Erasmus' closest English friends: Thomas More sent him cordial greetings in a letter to Erasmus in 1517 (Ep 688). Naturally enough Erasmus shared with Lee his work in revising the New Testament and probably solicited his suggestions. Lee responded by collecting notes for the revision, 'which,' as Erasmus wrote to their mutual friend Cuthbert Tunstall, 'he thought of great importance, while to me they seemed just the opposite, except in one or two places' (Ep 887:58–60). Lee was offended by Erasmus' reaction and sent him, through another mutual friend, Maarten Lips, a collection of additional notes that went well beyond suggestions for revision to attack Erasmus' work itself and some of the theological bases on which it rested. Erasmus did not answer this attack until after he had arrived in Basel but he then responded in considerable detail and with withering effect to ninety-five of Lee's points (Ep 843). He immediately published the letter in a collection of his letters being prepared for the press, *Auctarium selectarum epistolarum*. For the moment the matter rested there. Erasmus turned to the more pressing matter of getting the second edition of the New Testament under way.

The first part of the task was the massively revised *Annotationes*, the second volume, which was ready for printing within three months. Then he turned to the text of the New Testament, volume one of the revised edition. By this time he had returned to Louvain, leaving the supervision of the printing in the hands of Beatus Rhenanus, one of Froben's house-editors and, as Erasmus tartly wrote to Froben, 'the only man of sense' in the entire operation (Ep 885:33). He also left one of his *famuli* (servant-pupils), Jacobus Nepos, to help with the proof-reading, along with the learned Amerbach brothers (Ep 886:27–8). In Louvain he continued to work at the revision and sent the remaining text of the New Testament to the press in October, along with head-note arguments to the apostolic books. He promised the prefaces and tail-pieces shortly (Epp 885, 886). In December the Pauline Epistles were being printed (Ep 904).

By this time Erasmus had scored another great coup in securing papal approval for the second edition. He had not had time to obtain it for the first edition, although he had dedicated the work to Leo x (Ep 384). But in preparation for the second edition he had approached the papal legate in Switzerland, Antonio Pucci, to help secure from the pope 'some brief to the effect that he welcomes this work of mine' (Ep 860:27–8). He also enlisted the aid of his old friends Cardinals Riario and Grimani (Epp 860:33, 865:22) and Paolo Bombace, now working at the curia. His efforts were successful and Leo x's enthusiastic note of approval, dated 10 September 1518 (Ep 864), arrived in Basel while the printing was still going on and was set up to be printed on the reverse of the title-page of the text volume. It was reprinted in all subsequent editions of the work. The second edition appeared in the early spring of 1519 (Epp 950, 971) and Erasmus reported that it was selling 'very successfully' (Ep 970:13–14). It was the most innovative and radically different of all the five editions that would appear in his lifetime.

Having returned to Louvain, he now had to deal with the continuing problems of the Collegium Trilingue. The effort to establish it within the legal framework of the College of St Donatian had come to nothing because of the obstructionism of the university arts faculty. Nevertheless, regular courses had been introduced in all three languages, and property in the city fish market was purchased in the spring of 1519 to house both students and teachers. It was not until the following spring that it was accepted by the university as an independent college with the right to appoint its own faculty – and then only after acrimonious debate and the intervention of the Council of Brabant (de Vocht CTL I and II *passim*).

In the meantime, the dispute with Lee had taken another turn. Lee had continued to collect the 'errors' in Erasmus' New Testament, both the earlier edition and the second edition, which had just appeared. He was circulating his manuscript among his friends and sympathizers and had declared his intention to publish it. Erasmus asked to see it: Lee refused (Ep 998:17–20). By this time Erasmus had become concerned about just what was in Lee's manuscript and left no stone unturned to get his hands on it. He later admitted,

> ... I tried every trick [*technis*] to hunt down the book. I left no manoeuvre [*insidias*] untried ... but all was in vain. For he was more circumspect in hiding the book than I was in tracking it down. I tried to get it by promising money to a scribe who had begun to copy the manuscript in Ath's house. I had already managed to intercept two short pages and could have had the rest, had I not given myself away in conversation ... As soon as Lee got wind of it, he asked for his book back ... I also tried friends in England. Snares were laid here and there, but nothing worked.[29]

Having failed to see the work, Erasmus next moved to prevent its being published. Lee had not even approached Martens with his proposal because of his close friendship with Erasmus. And the only other printers in the Netherlands who had Greek type were Michaël Hillen and Jean Thibault of Antwerp. Lee approached Thibault. Lee himself takes up the story at this point, in a letter to Erasmus later published as part of his book: 'When the printer already had the type of the first ready for me for the press, he told me that he did not dare proceed because the work contained an attack on you; and on the day before, in the evening, your servant was seen by one of mine going into the printing house' (Ep 1061:621–4). Lee went straight to the printer and asked him what had been said. 'The printer, not content merely to deny that your servant had been with him, swore to it as well' (Ep 1061:631–3). Later, Lee reported, he said that he would print the work, but changed the terms, 'for having promised ... to give me thirty free copies, he now tried to stipulate that I must take two hundred from him at my own expense' (Ep 1061:636–8). Lee was unwilling to trust the man further, 'for,' as he wrote to Erasmus, 'I had not failed to detect what you yourself were aiming at, namely that the quires should be shown you treacherously by the printer as they came off the press ... ' (Ep 1061:640–3).

Lee then took the book to Hillen, who accepted it, but 'scarcely an hour elapsed and he changed his mind, undoubtedly because you or your supporters had either bribed him or frightened him with threats' (Ep 1061:681–3). Erasmus denied that he had used threats, but he did not deny that he 'had hoped to bribe him ... to make available to me the printed pages' (Opuscula 253). At this point, Lee took his book to Paris where it was published as Annotationes Edouardi Lei in annotationes Novi Testamenti Desiderii Erasmi Roterodami by Gilles de Gourmont, in February 1520 (Ep 1037 introduction). Lee himself never returned to Louvain.

Both before and after the printing of Lee's book Erasmus had attacked him with his famous satiric wit. Lee complained that in a recent edition of the Colloquia, printed by Martens, Erasmus made one speaker say that such writings as Lee's were fit only for wiping the buttocks or wrapping mackerel. The other speaker responded that he knew a man whose tongue he would rather use for these purposes – obviously, Lee observed, himself.[30] Erasmus encouraged his humanist friends to attack Lee in the same way, writing to Justus Jonas in Erfurt:

> ... my friends are to write letters highly critical of Lee ... and him they are to laugh at as a foolish, boastful, deceitful little man, rather than attack him seriously. I should like to see many letters of this kind put together, so that he may be overwhelmed all the deeper. I should like them to be collected from the learned writers and sent to me by safe hand, and I will revise them and see to their publication. Great variety in them is desirable (Ep 1088:4–12).

The letters were dutifully sent, collected by Erasmus, and published by Hillen in Antwerp, April–May 1520, under the title Epistolae aliquot eruditorum, nunquam antehac excusae, multis nominibus dignae quae legantur a bonis omnibus, quo magis liqueat quanta sit insignis cuiusdam syconphantae *virulantia*. The volume was reissued in expanded form two months later and a much larger collection – twenty-eight pieces – was printed by Froben about the same time (Ep 1083 introduction). Earlier, in an entirely different vein but also at Erasmus' prompting, More and Fisher and several other English friends had written Lee, trying to mediate the quarrel. In exasperation Erasmus wrote to Fisher, 'The man of whom you wrote will never be other than himself; in fact at this moment he is exceptionally active in this purveying of slanders for which he seems to me to have a natural gift.'[31]

As to Lee's book itself, within three days of receiving it (Ep 1072:5–6) Erasmus wrote a long *Apologia ... qua respondet duabus invectivis Eduardi Lei* (*Opuscula* 225–303). Lee's book consisted not only of his annotations on Erasmus' Greek New Testament – 243 notes on the first edition and 25 on the second – but an apologia addressed to the students at Louvain, a short, ironic dedicatory letter to Erasmus (Ep 1037), and a second, very much longer apologetic letter to Erasmus (Ep 1061) in which he told his side of the controversy. In his response to Lee's book Erasmus told his side. Erasmus seems to have gotten somewhat the better of the exchange. Lee's account is full of contradictions, deceptive and self-serving. Erasmus' account is surprisingly moderate – 'replying to abuse without being abusive myself' (Ep 1072:6–7) – and 'on the whole much more consistent and convincing than that of Lee' (*Opuscula* 231). Erasmus' reply only touched on Lee's annotations. They were dealt with in two long *Responsiones*, published a few weeks later by Hillen.[32]

From this point the controversy declined rapidly. Detailed as Lee's notes had been they were not very significant and Erasmus had little difficulty in answering them. Erasmus, furthermore, made a conciliatory effort in encouraging Froben to reprint an edited version of their exchange, from which most of the venom had been removed (Ep 1100). But it was only partially successful and the differences between the two men remained fundamentally unresolved, surfacing later in Erasmus' controversy with Noël Béda (Epp 1581, 1606) and still later in his controversies with his Spanish critics (Epp 1747, 1828, 1831, 1861). Neither Lee nor Erasmus made many converts in the other's camp. The response of Wolfgang Capito from Basel is typical of the liberal humanists: 'It is best to forget the whole episode as a flash in the pan, and laugh it off with a light heart. There is no reason whatever to fear that a book so dull, not to say raving, can do any harm to your reputation with serious and learned men' (Ep 1083:6–8). On the other hand, conservative theologians, at Louvain and elsewhere, continued to approve of Lee, especially of his charge that Erasmus was in defiance of the church and orthodox dogma and that he thus gave support to 'the ravings of heretics.'[33] It is probably this continued support of Lee by the conservatives that, more than anything else, prolonged and embittered this otherwise trivial controversy.

Erasmus' explanation of the whispering campaign and of endless innuendos of the Louvain conservative theologians is expressed in this outburst in a letter to his English friend Thomas Lupset in December 1519:

> There are gangs of conspirators who have consigned themselves on oath to the infernal powers if they do not utterly destroy the humanities and classical theology; and they have sworn to hold forth against Erasmus everywhere: at drinking-parties, in markets, in committees, in druggists' shops, in carriages, at the barber's, in the brothels, in public and private classrooms, in university lectures and in sermons, in confidential conversations, in the privacy of the confessional, in bookshops, in the taverns of the poor, in the courts of the rich and in kings' palaces ... there is no place they cannot penetrate, no lie they will not tell, to make me, a general benefactor, into an object of general hatred.

He goes on to charge the mendicant orders in particular, 'to whom the world gives alms as beggars and whom it tolerates as bullies.'

> If anyone dares murmur a syllable against sophistical theologians or utter a word about the superstitions of Carmelites or Dominicans, at once all hell breaks loose. 'Christ's church is in danger,' they cry, and appeal to all the powers, above and below (Ep 1053:423–35, 440–1, 450–3).

One of the most persistent and troubling of these critics was Nicolaas Baechem of Egmond, a professor of theology and head of the Carmelite house of studies at Louvain. He had preached against Erasmus' Greek New Testament in the most extreme terms, as Erasmus recounts it, '... clamouring that a great crisis threatened the Christian religion and that the coming of Antichrist was at hand ... When it came to a discussion between us and I asked him with some urgency to produce what offended him in my New Testament, he replied in a simple-minded way that he had never read the book or even set eyes on it' (Ep 948:143–8). He nevertheless continued his denunciations of Erasmus and by 1520 was publicly charging that he was a supporter of Luther and a suborner of heresy (Ep 1144). At Erasmus' request, the rector of the university tried to settle his differences with Baechem; but the meeting between them – with the rector trying manfully to moderate – became a shouting match, Baechem doing most of the shouting (Ep 1162). The second edition of the Greek New Testament had done nothing to quiet Baechem's criticism. Erasmus directed two brief controversial apologiae against Baechem, in 1520 the Apologia de 'In principio erat

sermo' and in 1522 the *Apologia de loco 'Omnes quidem resurgemus,'* dealing
with readings he preferred to the Vulgate and had incorporated in his
Greek New Testament at respectively John 1:1 and 1 Cor 15:51 and with
which Baechem had violently disagreed. Neither had the slightest effect on
Baechem.[34]

Still another of his mendicant critics was Vincentius Theoderici, direc-
tor of studies for the Dominican house in Louvain and, like Baechem, a
member of the theological faculty. Erasmus called him 'a confounded
numbskull' and a 'blockhead' (Ep 1165:5–6, 13). He often complained of
Theoderici's attacks on him and, though he did not mention him by name,
voiced the suspicion 'that this man was entrusted by fellow spirits in his
order with the business of noting down out of all my books things they
could get their teeth into' (Ep 1126:283–5). Erasmus observed that the bull
against Luther, *Exsurge Domine,* had emboldened the Louvain mendicants
to 'couple me with Luther and defame me too in public': indeed, he said,
they 'hate me worse than they hate Luther himself' (Ep 1144:19–20, 26–7).
He was finally driven to respond to Theoderici and his 'fellow spirits' in a
long satirical letter, in mid-March 1521, to Theoderici, addressed as 'his
most obstinate opponent' (Ep 1196:1). In this letter Erasmus reviewed in
bitter detail the history of Theoderici's attacks on him, his own alleged
attacks on the mendicant orders, and ended with a long and sober entreaty
to Theoderici to cease his slandering in the name of common Christian
decency. But it did no good. Some three months later Erasmus addressed
a letter to the entire Louvain theological faculty, protesting against the
continuing slander of his critics, especially Theoderici and Baechem (Ep
1217). It did no good either.

V

In that same letter to the theological faculty Erasmus mentions a continuing
controversy with yet another Louvain theologian, Jacobus Latomus (Ep
1217:98–102), which had begun during the earlier controversy with Edward
Lee. It had actually started over an oration recently published by a young
German humanist, Petrus Mosellanus, *Oratio de variarum linguarum cognitione
paranda,* in which Mosellanus had enthusiastically advocated the study of
the three ancient languages as the fundamental basis of true theology.
Latomus had responded with a dialogue *De trium linguarum et studii theologici ratione,* promptly printed by Hillen in Antwerp in 1519. Mosellanus
was a friend of Erasmus who defended his oration warmly (Ep 948). But he
also suspected that he himself was as much a target of Latomus' dialogue
as Mosellanus. He further suspected that Latomus had been put up to it by

other colleagues in the theological faculty. Not only had they continued to oppose the Collegium Trilingue but the recent separate publication by Martens (Ep 745 introduction) of a revised and enlarged edition of Erasmus' *Ratio seu methodus verae theologiae*, one of the introductory pieces he had prepared for the first edition of the Greek New Testament, had made the same arguments for the study of the three ancient languages. This had caused the long-running dispute with the conservative Louvain theologians to heat up again. They had prevented a proposed lecture series on the *Ratio*, under the sponsorship of the Collegium Trilingue. It was probably this heightening of the dispute and Erasmus' suspicion of 'a sworn conspiracy' (Ep 948:30) that prompted him to respond to Latomus' dialogue. The two men were not open enemies. Indeed, Erasmus had an almost good-natured contempt for Latomus. He sarcastically characterized his dialogue as 'a scholarly and elegant performance' and noted that many suspected it was not 'his own unaided work' but put together by his fellow theologians 'and aimed at me.' 'My own view,' he wrote, 'is that it is good enough for Latomus but not good enough to look as though it had been passed by a majority vote of the theologians' (Ep 934:4–8). Moreover, Latomus' dialogue was reasonably moderate in tone. Erasmus notes in another letter that 'he has refrained from mentioning names and writes with very little venom.'[35] Erasmus responded in the same vein in his *Apologia contra Latomi dialogum*. The work was dated 28 March 1519 and quickly printed by Thibault in Antwerp.

The first book of Latomus' dialogue was a discussion between an advocate of the humanities named Peter – obviously representing Petrus Mosellanus – a theology student named John, and a new student named Albert, trying to decide upon a curriculum. The book is directed mainly at Mosellanus, and Erasmus, in his *Apologia*, makes no effort to refute the principal arguments. Rather he singles out those charges that he considered had been made against him.

He protests that he has not attacked the scholastic theologians, rather that he is criticizing them exactly as they do each other. Nor does he advocate the overthrow of the theological curriculum. Instead he urges that students of theology sample the patristic as well as the scholastic commentators. And he reproaches Latomus as 'too good a man even to want to use arguments like these against a friend who deserved no such treatment' and 'too sensible a man to want his intellectual development to start from this sort of a beginning' (39).

He protests that it is both easy and profitable to study the ancient languages and that it will not take undue time from the study of theology. He says that he was amused by Latomus' efforts to prove that 'to understand a craft, one does not have to understand the language in which it was first set out' (47). It is simply obvious that in such an exalted field as theology this kind of understanding is crucial. He flatly declares 'that no single subject is more dependent on languages than theology' (47). And as proof he cites the endless linguistic labours of the church Fathers, especially St Jerome.

In a related argument he says, 'Of course a linguist does not automatically acquire an intimate grasp of the divine mysteries: but it is equally true that, other things being equal, a man without knowledge of languages will be so much further from understanding those mysteries' (54).

In conclusion he says, 'Already I regret having to write this work: already, excellent reader, I feel sorry for you – if anyone is going to read this miserable stuff' (56). This tone of exasperated impatience continues to obtain. But he must press on and 'do the same thing with the second of Latomus' dialogues as we did with the first' (56).

In the second book Latomus' three speakers are replaced by 'a splendid old gentleman as his main speaker' (56). Erasmus' replies are addressed to him. The old man is never further identified. But his views clearly reflect those of the Louvain theological faculty. Erasmus refers to him both as a 'professor' and a 'theologian' in the course of the apologia. He may, in fact, be meant to represent Briart, whom Erasmus had come to suspect once more as a leading figure in the conspiracy against him.[36] He begins by deploring the behaviour of those conspirators and their slanders and falsehoods.

He ridicules the old man's objections to the pagan writers on moral grounds and returns to his defence of the ancient languages as necessary to the study of theology – at great length. He goes on then to criticize the traditional scholastic methods of training theologians, which Latomus had made his speaker defend and which, Erasmus responds, 'have not the slightest relevance to real theology' (77). He strikes again at the central position of Aristotle in the program of the scholastics, giving 'more weight to his authority than to that of the Gospels' (77). And, of course, he laments the dependence on the scholastic authorities from Peter Lombard, Thomas Aquinas, Scotus, and Bonaventure to Ockham, Gerson, and Pierre d'Ailly.

Erasmus denies that he is trying to create a new theology: 'I am trying, to the best of my ability, to restore an old theology which until now has been far too widely neglected' (80).

Erasmus hoped against hope that he had answered the complaints of the theologians against his linguistic approach to Scripture and to the study of theology. And he hoped that the moderate tone of both Latomus' *Dialogue* and his own *Apologia* would do something to lower the pitch of the controversy in which he seemed to be engaged on every hand. But his hopes were dashed. The *Apologia in Latomum* was dated 28 March 1519. Within four months there appeared in Louvain copies of a scurrilous and learned pamphlet, printed in Paris, and entitled *Dialogus bilinguium ac trilinguium* that mercilessly lampooned the leaders of the Louvain theological faculty.[37] Latomus, for example, is depicted as a 'huge pig,' 'descended from Gryllus.' One of the speakers of the dialogue asks, 'The one who disputed with Ulysses in Plutarch?' The other answers, 'The very one.' The first speaker objects, 'But that one spoke Greek and had some sense, and in fact he wasn't all that bad as a sophist.' To which the other replied, 'Circe long ago has taken away the human mind of this one. Instead of Greek he speaks French, or rather he grunts it. And he hasn't completely given up sophistry, except that what he retains is a crude type, worthy of a pig. All the rest of him is nothing but pig' (343–4). Even the entirely innocent Dorp is characterized as a smiling hypocrite who 'once wheedled his way into the company of the Muses, so that when he deserted them he could do them worse harm' (341). Dorp is further designated the alter ego of the leader of the motley procession of theologians, Ate. Ate is not only the ancient Greek goddess of destruction but a transparent allusion to Jan Briart, the vice-chancellor and leader of the Louvain faculty of theology, often called *Atensis* from his native city of Ath in Hainault.[38] Lest anyone miss the target of the pun, he is also called *magister noster* in the dialogue (341). He is depicted as feeble and doddering, dwarfish and pygmy-like, blear-eyed and squinting, and thoroughly venomous. His venom is distributed through his whole body 'as with a viper' but its power is particularly in his tongue. 'I wish I had that tongue,' says one of the speakers. 'What would you do with it?' asks the other. 'Wipe my arse,' he replies, to which the other says, 'To my mind you would be better off wiping it with a nettle than with such poison as that' (339).

The dialogue was available not only in Louvain and Paris, but elsewhere.[39] And everywhere the humanist liberals were enjoying the ridicule it heaped on the Louvain theologians. In Louvain there were howls of anguish. Lee was sure Erasmus had written it, as was Baechem. But this was not likely either on stylistic or strategic grounds. Quite the contrary: there is every reason to believe that Erasmus was embarrassed by the piece and that it was rather the work of an over-zealous supporter. The dialogue was attributed, in the title, to a learned young German named Conrad Nesen of Nastätten. But this attribution was only part of the free-swinging satire of the work. Conrad Nesen was by no means an 'eruditus adulescens': he was a beginning student, quite incapable of doing it. More likely it was the work of his older brother Wilhelm, already a learned humanist and friend of Erasmus who had visited him Louvain from Paris in the spring of 1519 and later moved to Louvain himself.[40] Under the circumstances he would not only have picked up the Erasmian views and turns of phrase that echo in the dialogue but would have had the opportunity to acquaint himself with Erasmus' adversaries. The dialogue was, on the other hand, clearly influenced by Erasmus and can be considered as another item in the well-orchestrated campaign of support he had solicited for his cause among his fellow humanists everywhere.

VI

The dialogue reflects, as we have seen, Erasmus' growing suspicion that Jan Briart had become one of the leaders of the campaign against him in Louvain. He had earlier been relieved to find Briart friendly toward him and more lately he had praised his impartiality in the heated disputes with Lee and Baechem. But he had become increasingly suspicious of him. He had darkly forecast the role assigned to Briart in the *Dialogus bilinguium ac trilinguium* in a letter of mid-summer 1519: 'One man is the principal source for all this flood of venom, and unless he lays off, he will soon be pilloried in all the writings of the learned and "famed in song the wide world o'er"' (Ep 993:58–60). A few months later he confided to his English friend Tunstall that it was Briart alone '... who originally egged Dorp on and started the whole melodrama' and who later 'set on foot the overtures for peace, when he realized the action I was threatening if they did not call it off' (Ep 1029:4–8).

His suspicions about Briart had already begun to be confirmed. In February 1519, when the controversy with Latomus was under way and the dispute with Lee still raging, Briart attacked Erasmus openly and quite gratuitously. The occasion was the awarding of the licentiate to a young Carmelite. Briart, as Erasmus later recalled, 'spoke powerfully against me publicly, in a crowded faculty meeting, and did not hesitate to refer to heresies.'[41] While, in fact, Erasmus' name was not mentioned in Briart's address, the heresies referred to had to do with marriage and clerical celibacy and clearly referred to a work of Erasmus, recently published, the *De laude matrimonii*,[42] which Briart did not mention either. But such charges, by so eminent a figure as Briart, could not be left unchallenged. As Erasmus wrote to him shortly, 'I will endure any misrepresentation, however false, provided I am not falsely maligned as a heretic' (Ep 946:15–16). A meeting was held between the two men, attended by Dorp and Gillis van Delft supporting Erasmus. They persuaded Briart that his charges were unfounded. But, since they had been made in a formal address at a public ceremony, it was agreed that Erasmus was entitled to make a public reply.[43] This was the *Apologia pro declamatione de laude matrimonii*, written within a few days, dated 1 March 1519, and published immediately by Martens, inserted in the *Paraphrasis in Corinthios*, already in press (Ep 916 introduction).

This apologia was a short, moderate, and respectful work, but a carefully crafted one. Erasmus takes two directions in his defence: first, that the work in question is not a serious theological treatise but rather a declamation; and second, that the charge of heresy that Briart had made was suggested to him by someone else against a book he had not read 'since he was occupied with more serious concerns' (90). Hence it was a disservice to Briart fully as much as to Erasmus. In short, as he wrote, 'I have seen fit by this apology to remove thoroughly every suspicion and protect at one and the same time the honour of the excellent theologian, Jan Briart' (89).

In the opening paragraph of the apologia Erasmus reviews the events, the occasion, the charges, and his own surprise at Briart's action: 'I certainly did not think that his integrity would allow him to sully the reputation of an innocent man in an important public address' or to charge 'with the heinous crime of heresy' (89) 'a friend who had implicit trust in him' especially since that friend was ready at hand and available to discuss the matter. He goes on to say that, according to Gillis van Delft, who was present, 'Briart had been falsely informed concerning my encomium of marriage because in some people's opinion I seem there to prefer matrimony to celibacy' (90).

From this point Erasmus goes straight to his argument to 'demonstrate by very clear proofs that I neither say nor believe anything of the kind' (90). He recalls that he wrote 'this insignificant little book' twenty-five years ago, 'if I am not mistaken,' 'to provide young men with a sample of my youthful writing so that in treating similar arguments they might exercise their writing ability and their inventiveness' (91). This is very likely the case, that he produced the first form of the work as a demonstration piece for his tutorial pupils in Paris in the late 1490s. Indeed the first manuscript version of the work was presented to one of them, Robert Fisher, in 1498 (Ep 71) and a slightly revised version to another, Lord Mountjoy, a year later (Ep 117). The work was then incorporated as an example of 'a letter of persuasion' in the manuscript version of a larger book on the art of letter-writing (91). This was widely known to his friends.[44]

In that book, he explains, the piece is not only presented as a 'suasoria' but the elements of a 'disuasoria' – an argument on the other side, against marriage – are also presented, not as fully developed but indicating 'in what ways that aspect of the question might be treated' (91). Because of the greater complexity of the topic, the fact that it is treated by many authors, and in the interest of time and space in a book that was already growing too long, 'it held no attraction for me' (91). Finally, the work had been recently published as one of four declamations. This was the version that Briart had attacked.

He goes on to defend himself, arguing that in praising marriage he is dealing with a subject often praised by others and directed, in this instance, to an imaginary recipient of the advice 'for whom marriage is more suitable than celibacy.' Certainly in such a case 'there would be no danger involved to faith and morals' (92). And certainly there is no basis to claim that Erasmus categorically prefers marriage to celibacy. He goes to considerable pains to point out that celibacy does not necessarily mean a chaste and pure life: it refers only to one's not having a lawful wife. The person who made the charge against him to Briart did not understand this, nor the Latin word *caelebs*. Nor did Briart himself 'who after delivering his oracular utterance in the Schools admitted to me that he thought of celibacy as a heavenly and chaste vocation, and considered a declamation equivalent to a sermon' (93).

He then lists the offending arguments and passages in the work, especially 'the passage which I suspect gives them most offence,' where he writes 'the holiest kind of life is wedlock, purely and chastely observed' (93). 'For here I seem clearly to prefer marriage to any other state of life' (93). He responds that this is not a categorical preference, that he is simply referring to 'a way of life' (93). Moreover, he continues, this is by way of contrast with those who conceal their vices behind the high-sounding name of chastity and who 'attach themselves to this way of life not so much through love of chastity as for the sake of gain or ease.' 'The hideous and wide-spread lusts which are found among them are known to those who have occasion to listen to the daily accounts of their secret transgressions.'[45]

In conclusion he argues that, while the preference of marriage to celibacy may be condemned, as Briart did condemn it, he should not be condemned since he had never categorically stated that preference. 'Briart condemned the belief, not me' (95). And he alleges that Briart had been made to see the distinction and had apologized to him (95). Further, he says, 'I don't think there is anything in my books by which anyone could be made worse. I acknowledge that I am a man. I have shown my sincere interest in furthering the cause of piety: I cannot guarantee the outcome' (95). He asks only for a fair and honest reader. And if that is lacking then no book is safe. He enjoins his critics to give up hatred and anger in favour of Christian civility, lest they themselves be similarly charged. 'For what mortal was ever wise all his days?' (95).

Despite the claims of friendship and the tone of respect for Briart that Erasmus expressed in his apologia, he was, as we have seen, convinced that

Briart had, in fact, again become an enemy, a leader among the 'gangs of conspirators' against him in Louvain. This was a view he continued to hold.

VII

Briart's death early in 1520 did nothing to dampen the increasing criticism of Erasmus in Louvain. For the hostility toward him had become blended with the growing clamour against Luther. Erasmus' most strident critics were already charging that he was the main source of Luther's heresies. Even more moderate men were convinced that he was sympathetic to Luther's views. If the former charge was false, the latter was at least partially true. And Erasmus himself had lent support to that perception, for he was equally convinced that the hostility toward Luther was only an extension of the conservatives' attack on good letters and humanistic theology.

The first of Luther's books to appear in Louvain was a hastily assembled collection of his writings, including his *Resolutiones disputationum de virtute indulgentiarum*, Luther's condemnation by the Roman theologian and Master of the Sacred Palace, Silvestro Prierias, and Luther's response, along with several of his sermons, printed by Froben in October 1518. Some of the Louvain theologians insisted that Erasmus had had a hand in this publication: it was published by his printer and they thought they recognized Erasmus' style in the elegantly phrased prefaces scattered through the work. Erasmus, of course, had not had a hand in it. It was his friend Capito who had edited the book for the press and probably also he who composed the elegant, humanistic prefaces.[46] Froben sent Erasmus a copy in early December (Ep 904). A few months later Erasmus wrote the papal legate Campeggi, 'I have not yet read the book through, yet from the outset they were saying it was mine, though I did not write a line of it' (Ep 961:36–8). He also claimed to know virtually nothing about Luther. This is probably true, but it is equally true that he had followed his career to date with considerable interest. A full year before his letter to Campeggi, in March 1518, he had sent More, in a bundle of other books, a printed copy of Luther's Ninety-five Theses, probably in the edition Froben had rushed into print in late 1517. Erasmus made no comment about the 'Conclusiones,' as the Ninety-five Theses had begun to be called (Ep 785:39). But half a year later he commented on Prierias' 'very ill-judged reply' to Luther's 'Conclusiones' and expressed disbelief that Johann Maier von Eck had issued his challenge to debate Luther: 'I cannot think what has come into Eck's head, that he should take up the cudgels against Eleutherius' (Ep 872:19, 25–6).

At the end of March 1519 Luther wrote directly to Erasmus. It was a brief letter, deferential and friendly, obviously seeking his support and implying that Erasmus approved of his writings:[47] he referred to himself as 'this younger brother of yours in Christ' (Ep 933:37).

After a decent interval, on 30 May 1519, Erasmus replied to Luther in a carefully written letter, cautiously distancing himself from 'the storm raised by your books' and 'the most groundless suspicion that your work is written with assistance from me and that I am, as they call it, a standard-bearer of this new movement.' On the contrary, he wrote, 'I assured them that you were quite unknown to me; that I had not yet read your books and could therefore neither disapprove nor approve anything' (Ep 980:4–7, 10–20).[48] It could hardly have been a surprise to Erasmus that this letter was promptly published. It appeared in the printed edition of the oration Petrus Mosellanus had given at the opening ceremony of the Leipzig debates, along with another letter Erasmus had written to Mosellanus (Ep 948), containing a scathing denunciation of the Louvain theologians for their attacks on the Greek New Testament.

In the fall of 1519 Jacob of Hoogstraten, the infamous Cologne inquisitor, arrived in Louvain carrying a copy of Froben's edition of Luther's 'Conclusiones' and their condemnation by the Cologne faculty of theology. On 12 October he appeared before the Louvain faculty of theology and requested that they too condemn the book. He had brought with him the printed version of Erasmus' letter to Luther to prove his association with Luther. The Louvain theologians condemned Luther's views on 7 November 1519 (de Vocht CTL I 425–7). And Hoogstraten joined the chorus of Erasmus' other enemies in Louvain, trying to link him with Luther. Erasmus called it a 'witch-hunt' (Ep 1070:5).

In the meantime the whole question of Luther had been elevated to another and more dangerous level. He had been protected, ironically, by the push and pull of political forces in the imperial election campaign following the death of Maximilian I in January 1519. But the election itself, which finally took place at the end of the following June, produced a unanimous vote for Prince Charles. Charles made what arrangements he could for the governing of his restive Spanish kingdom and he and his court sailed from the port of Corunna, bound for the Netherlands and the imperial coronation. He had been gone from the north of Europe for nearly four years.

Erasmus had kept track of events in Spain as best he could through letters to friends and patrons there (Epp 793, 853) and through contacts at the court in Brussels (cf Epp 886, 887, 893). But he was better informed about events closer at hand, the imperial election process among them (Epp 1001:58–90, 1009:15–55, 1030:54–71). He was aware of the candidacy of Francis I and the compromise candidacy of the elector Frederick the Wise of Saxony who 'was offered the imperial crown and nobly refused it' (Ep

1030:59). Erasmus clearly was not aware of the extent of the corruption and bribery that took place during the election. After Charles' election he wrote to the elector Albert of Brandenburg that 'the Empire has been given in trust, not sold' (Ep 1009:50). It had, in fact, been sold: and Erasmus may even have suspected as much. But, in any event, it was over: the grace of God had descended upon the assembled electors and they had chosen an emperor who would be 'useful to God Almighty, the Holy Empire, and us all.'[49]

It had been arranged that Charles, on his way to the Netherlands, should stop in England to meet Henry VIII, his queen Catherine of Aragon (Charles' aunt), Cardinal Wolsey, and the English court. This meeting duly took place on 27 May 1520, after the landing at Dover and a processional ride to Canterbury. The meeting was largely pomp and form with substantive matters deferred until a later meeting on the continent. Henry and Wolsey wanted first to test the intentions of Francis I and arrangements had already been made for Henry and Francis to meet immediately after the meeting with Charles. This was the occasion of the Field of the Cloth of Gold, the extravagance of which set the tone for the kingly posturing that was almost the only result of the meeting of the two monarchs, 7–24 June 1520. Thomas More and Archbishop Warham, who were in Henry's suite, urged Erasmus to attend. But he was ill and declined (Epp 1107:16, 1111:3, 1113:35, 1114:18–21, 1115:50–1).

In the meantime, on 1 June, Charles had landed at Flushing and travelled to Brussels. His travels promptly included another meeting with Henry VIII, which had been arranged when they had met the month before in England. They met at Calais, a few miles from the site of the meeting with Francis I. The failure of any substantial agreement with Francis made Henry somewhat more willing to seek a clearer rapprochement with Charles. They discussed a proposal of marriage between Charles and Henry's daughter Mary. But little else of consequence came out of this meeting. There were still too many major policy questions to be resolved and too much manoeuvring to be done by diplomats of both courts.

Erasmus did attend the meeting at Calais. He had probably joined the court at Brussels and was part of Charles' retinue. He wrote two graceful epigrams celebrating the concord this meeting of the two monarchs announced.[50] He met formally with Henry VIII who raised with him the ominous question of Luther and expressed the wish that Luther had written 'with more prudence and moderation': Erasmus could not have agreed more (Epp 1106 introduction, 1113 n10, 1127A:68–9). He was able to do no more than greet Wolsey and wrote the cardinal a follow-up letter some months later (Ep 1132). But he may have met, for the first time, Mercurino Gattinara, who had replaced his old friend and patron Jean Le Sauvage as chancellor to Charles, following Le Sauvage's death in 1518. Gattinara would become one of Erasmus' greatest defenders (see CEBR 'Gattinara'). And he also saw More. The two were able to travel together to Bruges where Charles and his court were going and where More was bound on diplomatic business.

Erasmus continued to attend the court off and on throughout the summer and fall of 1520. At the end of August he was in Brussels while the court was there (Ep 1136 introduction) and may have attended the sessions at Antwerp in late September (Ep 1146). Erasmus' appointment as councillor was and remained a strictly honorific one, with no formal obligation of attendance (Ep 1148:8–19). And he found the courtly life thoroughly distasteful: 'not for me to canvass the various factions, to thrust myself forward, and elbow some other man out of my way' (Ep 1148:11–13).

Early in October the court came to Louvain. And at this very moment the papal bull of condemnation against Luther, *Exsurge Domine*, arrived at the court, dated 15 June 1520. It had been long in preparation at the curia, much discussed, drafted and redrafted, and, of course, held up in any form until the imperial election had taken place. Now there was no longer any need for the pope to temporize. The elector Frederick the Wise and the other electoral princes no longer had to be placated. The candidacy of Francis I had failed. Charles had been elected. The bull had been anticipated for months. Erasmus had heard of it and it filled him with foreboding. To his friend Gerard Geldenhouwer he wrote in September, 'I'm afraid all this will end in serious disorder. The pope's advisers in this give him, in my opinion, counsel which may or may not be religious, but is certainly full of danger' (Ep 1141:26–8). Portions of the bull, in drafts purported to be genuine, had been circulated in the councils of the mendicant orders and among the conservative theologians at Louvain and elsewhere. The man who carried the bull as papal nuncio was Girolamo Aleandro. He had been carefully chosen for this task by the curia. He was a learned Italian, a well-respected humanist and doctor of theology. He was widely connected in the north both at Paris and in the Low Countries. And he was an old friend of Erasmus.

Years before, in Venice, they had shared a room at Aldus' house (Ep 2443:285–6) and Aleandro had been among those helpful scholars who supplied Erasmus with texts and citations for the Aldine *Adagia*.[51] Later Erasmus had recommended Aleandro to his humanist friends in Paris (Ep 256). But at some point and for reasons by no means clear, an estrangement between them had occurred which grew increasingly bitter. In the meantime Aleandro had attained notable success as a scholar and even more notable success as a place-seeker, rising to a high position in the curia. He was now the papal nuncio empowered to publish Pope Leo's bull against Luther and seek its implementation in Lower Germany and at the court of the new emperor.

VIII

Aleandro was able, apparently, to secure a hastily drafted royal edict in support of the bull just as the court was preparing to leave Louvain.[52] He proceeded immediately to a public burning of several of Luther's books (Ep 1157:7–8). And he approached the more than willing Louvain theologians to join in the condemnation and add their approbation of the bull. In the frenzy surrounding these events, Erasmus' old opponents took the occasion again to condemn him along with Luther – with the approval of Aleandro. All this caused Erasmus to dash off the short pamphlet, *Acta Academiae Lovaniensis contra Lutherum.* Although he did not put his name to it, in all likelihood he saw to its publication within two weeks in Cologne (*Opuscula* 311–15). It was directed to the general public, 'what I wanted you honest readers to know' (*Acta Academiae Lovaniensis* introductory letter, 101). It was one of the bitterest and most mean-spirited things Erasmus ever wrote, fully as frenzied and hysterical as the screechings of his enemies. His interest was to discredit both the bull and Aleandro, to strike again at his opponents in Louvain, to make again his now familiar argument that he was neither a supporter nor an alter ego of Luther, and to insist that Luther be given a fair hearing. The work clearly shows that Erasmus was playing for time. But to what purpose? Wallace Ferguson argues that it was part of 'a well organized campaign to keep the way open for the plan of arbitration which he was to propose in the *Consilium cuiusdam*' (*Opuscula* 311). Martin Lowry suggests that he hoped that time 'might give a more moderate faction at the curia the opportunity it needed' (*Acta Academiae Lovaniensis* introductory note, 99). Erasmus might equally well have hoped that his own arguments in the matter of Luther would eventually prevail at Charles' court. Or it may have been simply Erasmus' lashing out at his opponents – and Luther's – unwilling to let any of their charges go unchallenged, especially in the larger forum now created by the papal bull.

The work opens with an introductory letter, addressed 'to the honest reader.' But Erasmus is far from honest himself in the assault he launches against Aleandro, a vicious personal attack, charging him with vile habits, greed, lust, with being 'a total slave to his own self-advancement.' And he attributes his behaviour to his being a Jew and thus bent on 'celebrating his master Moses and darkening the glory of Christ.' There is not a shred of truth to the charge: Erasmus is simply retailing common gossip.[53]

He then, in the text of the piece, traces the course of recent events in Louvain – Aleandro's arrival, the public burning of Luther's books, and the 'acta' of the university 'solemnly assembled to hear proposals by the envoys of the pope' (102). The bull was read but without being examined or approved by the whole faculty. Within a few days, he continues, Baechem had taken up the cause in a sermon saying 'more against Erasmus ... than against Luther' (102). Baechem then secured a ruling from the rector authorizing him to add many points to the charges that were not in the bull itself. When the faculty of law raised procedural questions, the theologians boycotted the meeting.

Erasmus then attacks the validity of the bull itself. He charges that 'it is common knowledge that the matter was handled in Rome without proper procedure' (103) and that it 'was hatched at Cologne and Louvain, printed before it had even been distributed: and the printed version differs from the bull which Aleandro is bearing' (103). He even suggests that it is a forgery, emanating from the long-standing charges against Luther, and manipulated by Aleandro. Again he makes the charge that Aleandro is a Jew, 'the blood-brother of Judas,' 'set on betraying the future of the gospel.' 'It is fated for Christians to be plagued by Jews' (103). He continues that from such beginnings the charges were pushed along by Hoogstraten, Baechem, and his fellow mendicants, as well as other Louvain theologians with their own agendas. They have made no attempt to refute Luther's arguments.

And finally, he suggests that 'all this is being done without the pope's knowledge, or certainly without his being properly informed. Let Aleandro be questioned, and he will be proved a criminal and a Jew. Let the bull be examined, and it will be proved a forgery.' In any case, 'immediate action should not be taken. The pope should be given time to hear sounder advice: otherwise, there is a danger that this affair will provoke serious disorders throughout the Christian world' (105). Luther must be answered and answered with the evidence of Scripture.

Charles and the court had already departed Louvain for the coronation in Aachen. They delayed a few days in Brussels, waiting for the abatement of the plague, but on 22 October they pressed on to Charlemagne's ancient capital where the ceremony of coronation took place the next day. The court and many of the attendant princes immediately travelled on to Cologne where meetings and conversations were already scheduled. Erasmus chose not to attend the coronation.[54]

But he had already arranged to be in Cologne and arrived there shortly after the coronation was over for a meeting with Elector Albert of Brandenburg. He had written the elector over a year before (Ep 1033), thanking him for the gift of a cup and, more importantly, stating his own position on Luther – that he did not know him, nor had he read his books, nor did he support him; that he was distressed at the denunciations against him, largely by the mendicants, and at the damage such tumults were doing to the humanities. He had given the letter to Ulrich von Hutten, who was then in the elector's service, and instructed him to deliver it to the elector or, if he thought best, to destroy it. Hutten did neither; rather he rushed it into print, to the embarrassment of both the elector and Erasmus (Ep 1152:5–13). Now Erasmus needed to make amends.

Albert of Brandenburg was not the only electoral prince in Cologne who had Luther on his mind. Frederick the Wise of Saxony had come to Cologne several days before the coronation but fear of the plague and an attack of gout had prevented him from travelling on to Aachen for the coronation itself (Brecht 416). But when the imperial court moved on to Cologne, Aleandro sought Frederick out, presented his credentials to the elector, and demanded that all of Luther's books be burned and Luther himself imprisoned or delivered to Rome. He hinted darkly that the emperor and the other princes had already acceded to these demands. The next day, 5 November, Elector Frederick summoned Erasmus to an interview. They had not met before and perhaps Erasmus was somewhat taken aback by the bluntness of the old elector who asked him straight out to make a clear statement on the Luther affair. Erasmus replied, 'Luther has sinned in two things, by attacking the pope's crown and the monks' bellies.'[55] After dinner, Georgius Spalatinus, the elector's secretary, accompanied Erasmus back to his lodgings in the town house of his friend Count Hermann von Neuenahr. There he sat down and wrote out in more specific form, in twenty-two propositions, his views on the Luther question – *Axiomata Erasmi pro causa Martini Lutheri*. He gave the document to Spalatinus to convey to the elector but requested that it be returned to him.

The *Axiomata* repeat the by-now familiar litany of Erasmus' views on the Luther question. He charges that the entire matter really springs from hatred of the humanities and has been carried on in a spirit of wrangling, conspiracy, and libel. He questions the validity of the bull of condemnation as being out of character with the well-known gentleness of the pope. He questions the motives and character of those who are most critical of Luther. On the other hand, 'the best authorities and those closest to the doctrine of the Gospels are least offended by Luther.' Moreover, Luther in his willingness 'to submit himself to a public disputation before unbiased arbitrators seems to all reasonable observers to be making a reasonable request.' And, he notes, Luther has no personal ambition, unlike those critics of his 'trying to forward their own interests.' In conclusion Erasmus cites the 'profound importance of this issue,' the fact that here, at the beginning of Charles' reign, matters of state 'should not be shrouded by ghastly debates of this kind.' And finally he suggests that 'since the pope's reputation is under discussion, it seems best to settle the issue through the sane advice of unbiased and discreet persons' – the first hint of the proposal Erasmus would shortly make for a council of arbitration in the controversy.

Encouraged by Erasmus' advice, Elector Frederick met the papal legates the next day and refused their demands. While he himself was not convinced of the truth of Luther's views, he was convinced that neither Luther nor his views had been authoritatively condemned. On the contrary, Luther was approved by many good men (including Erasmus); he had indicated his willingness to defend his views publicly; and he would not give him up until he had been heard and condemned by an impartial tribunal of pious, learned, and unprejudiced judges. The elector may, by this time, already have obtained from the young emperor the assurance that Luther would not be condemned without such a hearing (Ep 1166:81–9). Erasmus' *Axiomata* certainly played a crucial role in defining the elector's position at this time. But they added further to the pro-Lutheran animus against Erasmus. For the document was not returned to him by Spalatinus, as he requested, but appeared in print at Leipzig within a matter of weeks (*Opuscula* 332–3).

The imperial court stayed on in Cologne, preparing for the meeting of the diet already scheduled for Worms in January 1521 – the meeting where Luther was to be summoned to present himself and his views. Erasmus returned to Louvain, to a confrontation of his own over the Lutheran matter, with Nicolaas Baechem, before the rector of the university. Of all Erasmus' hostile critics in Louvain the most strident, persistent, and annoy-ing had been Baechem. He had attacked him everywhere, in every forum available to him, and in the most outrageous terms. Finally, in mid-October 1520, on two occasions, Baechem had attacked him in public sermons 'saying to my face among many other things that I was a keen supporter of Luther' and threatening that Erasmus too 'will come to the stake one day' along with Luther (Ep 1153:23–4, 103). Erasmus had often complained about Baechem to university authorities. He did so again on this occasion, writing to the rector Godschalk Rosemondt and charging that this sort of misuse of the pulpit not only betrays the usage of the church but 'darkens the fair fame of this university' (Ep 1153:225). It was this matter that had detained Erasmus in Louvain when he might have been attending the imperial coronation. Yet all that Rosemondt would promise was an opportunity to confront Baechem in his own presence. It was for this meeting that Erasmus returned from Cologne. It took place in due course, but was a total failure. The red-faced, shouting Baechem stamped out of the meeting, having proclaimed 'as long as he refuses to write against Luther, we shall continue to regard him as a member of Luther's party.'[56] The rector neither could nor would take measures against Baechem, even though he deplored his behaviour (Ep 1173:36). The situation in Louvain remained unchanged. But the situation in the larger world could perhaps still be rescued.

For some months Erasmus had been ruminating on a scheme to bring an end to the Lutheran turmoil by impartial arbitration. He may have mentioned it to Henry VIII during their brief meeting in Bruges in July and urged Henry to act as a mediator.[57] He mentioned it in passing as part of the *Axiomata* for Elector Frederick. But even before that, in October 1520, he had the plan fully organized in his own mind. Now, with the Lutheran situation worsening and a hearing set for the early months of 1521 at the meeting of the diet at Worms, Erasmus wanted to get his plan before the emperor and the princes as a just and reasonable alternative to the solution that Aleandro plainly intended to propose.

In its final form it was entitled *Consilium cuiusdam ex animo cupientis esse consultum et Romani pontificis dignitati et christianae religionis tranquillitati.* And it was presented not by Erasmus but by Johannes Faber, a distinguished German Dominican prior and theologian, confessor and imperial councillor to the emperor Maximilian. The reason for Erasmus' anonymity is not far to seek. He was simply too compromised by the charges, however unfounded, that he was a partisan of Luther. If he hoped to have the plan even considered at Worms he had to distance himself from it. And Faber was a splendid alter ego.

Faber had come to the court in the Netherlands to seek the renewal of his appointment as an imperial councillor. Early in October he met Erasmus at Louvain. The two men were attracted to each other by the similarity of their views on a range of topics, not the least of which was educational reform. Faber had earlier proposed founding a new school at his cloister in Augsburg modelled on the Collegium Trilingue at Louvain. Despite the approval of Emperor Maximilian, he had run into the same kind of opposition as Erasmus had. The two men also found themselves in agreement on the necessity for finding a peaceful solution to the Lutheran problem. Thus Erasmus was pleased to write several letters of introduction for Faber to highly placed members of the imperial council and the circle of electoral princes – Jacob Villinger the imperial chief treasurer, Chancellor Gattinara, Bishop Erard de la Marck, and Elector Albert of Brandenburg (Epp 1149, 1150, 1151, 1152). He also wrote, in the same vein, to another important imperial councillor, his friend the Augsburg jurist Konrad Peutinger (Ep 1156). Superficially it was a letter of introduction for Faber. But it is likely that Faber and Peutinger already knew each other, both coming from Augsburg. The letter, more specifically, was intended to gain Peutinger's support for the proposal Erasmus had formed and discussed with Faber.

By this time the imperial election was over and the court had adjourned to Cologne, where Erasmus arrived shortly as well. He and Faber showed the draft of the proposal not only to Peutinger but to Electors Albert of Brandenburg and Frederick the Wise. Then the proposal was revised, put in final form, and printed. The printed version not only did not carry the name of Erasmus, it did not even carry that of Faber, though it had been presented to Peutinger as 'Faber's plan' (Ep 1156:108–9). Later Erasmus claimed for himself only that 'the thing was indeed shown me while the emperor was in Cologne, but in manuscript' (Ep 1199:39–40). But the *Consilium cuiusdam* was unmistakably his proposal. It betrays his authorship not only in its style but in its familiar Erasmian arguments.[58]

In keeping with its purpose, the *Consilium cuiusdam* is a sober and statesmanlike document. It is also a very circumspect one. For example, emphasis is placed throughout on the reputation of the pope, damaged as it is by the bull condemning Luther in terms so unlike the 'gentle character' of Pope Leo and exhibiting none of his 'sharp intelligence.' 'This creates a strong suspicion that certain parties are taking advantage of his naturally pleasant, easy-going temperament to forward their own private ambitions' (109).

As to Luther himself, Erasmus continues, there is much that is profitable in his writings and many men of unimpeachable orthodoxy admire them. He has never been refuted in open debate, though he has consistently sought such debate, and continues to do so. Rather he has simply been attacked, savagely and without provocation.

How to proceed? 'The truth is that investigating matters of faith is the particular function of the Roman pontiff, and what is his by right should not be taken from him' (111). Yet, in this case, we must look not only to what Luther deserves, but what is best for the peace of the church. Moreover, Luther is rapidly becoming a popular figure in Germany where 'many growl that the yoke of the Roman see can be borne no longer' (111). The princes are reminded of the Hussites and of 'how Bohemia remained stubborn for so many years, and came near to dragging the neighbouring regions onto its side' (111). Thus, 'for the public good' the pope 'ought to allow this question to be passed to others – men of outstanding knowledge, proven virtue, and unstained honour, whom no one could possibly suspect of wishing, whether through fear of punishment or hope of advancement, to flatter the pope or forget the truth of the Gospels, or of favouring the other party for some purely human motive' (111).

The proposal continues, 'These arbitrators should be chosen from their subjects by each of the three kings who are themselves furthest from suspicion – the emperor Charles, the king of England, and the king of Hungary. They should read Luther's books through and through with care, hear his side of the case, and pronounce their decision in his presence. And that decision will be final' (111). Far from lessening the pope's authority, such a responsible concession of his prerogative will bring him universal approval.

If, after the judgment of the arbitrators is rendered, Luther stands by the points that have been condemned by the arbitrators, no one any longer will support him. And, if he recants, the entire affair will be settled without further confusion to the Christian commonwealth. Finally, if this proposal fails, 'the next best course is evidently to pass the matter to the next general council' (112).

Unfortunately, by the time Luther was summoned to Worms in mid-April 1521, the situation had passed well beyond such a solution as Erasmus and Faber had proposed. Luther had become more violent in his criticism of Rome and of traditional theology. In June 1520 his inflammatory tract *To the Christian Nobility of the German Nation Concerning the Reform of the Christian Estate* appeared. This was followed in October by *On the Babylonian Captivity of the Church*, a thoroughgoing attack on the sacraments that 'surpassed everything which he had written so far against the Roman church' (Brecht 381–2). By the end of February 1521 Erasmus was aware of it and wrote, in despair, 'Luther destroys himself with his own weapons' (Ep 1186:26). A few weeks after *On the Babylonian Captivity of the Church*, there appeared Luther's *On Christian Liberty*. Erasmus wrote, 'He is proposing something more frightful every day' (Epp 1189:9–10, 1202:56–63, 172–5, 1203:9–14). Then on December 10 Luther publicly burned the bull *Exsurge Domine* and a copy of the canon law (Ep 1203:30).

By these acts Luther had assured that he would be condemned at the diet. Then he appeared at Worms in April 1521 and continued his defiance not only of the bull but also of the ban of the empire. The emperor had no choice but to condemn him, which condemnation he proclaimed on 25 May, the day following the official conclusion of the diet. This was the famous Edict of Worms. Elector Joachim of Brandenburg summarily declared it approved by the imperial estates without further discussion or changes. Luther had already left the meeting and been swept away to the security of his elector's castle of the Wartburg. No one knew where he was, although Erasmus – who was surprisingly well informed about these events – speculated that he was 'perhaps in safe keeping' (Ep 1203:14).

From this point Erasmus' alienation from Luther began. Over the past several months, while he had stalwartly defended Luther's right to be heard and lamented the extremism of his enemies, he had become increasingly alarmed at Luther's own extremism. He had repeatedly urged him to moderation – to no avail. In exasperation he had written to Nicolas Bérault in February, 'Oh, if that man had either left things alone, or made his attempt more cautiously or in moderation!' (Ep 1185:22–3). In the course of the following year, Erasmus' letters show a clear turning away from Luther. Referring to Luther's increasing crowd of enemies, he wrote, 'they have no ideas except to eat Luther alive, and it is not my business whether they prefer him boiled or roast' (Ep 1185:51–6). To Ludwig Baer in Basel he wrote, 'Luther has served us a pretty turn, most learned of men, by putting into the hands of certain raging madmen who detest the humanities just exactly the weapon they hoped for, with which they can let fly against the security of honourable men who were supporters in simple faith of the gospel teaching and the liberal arts' (Ep 1203:4–8). At the end of June he declared, 'Luther is finished among us here' (Ep 1216:81).

In the meantime, the German supporters of Luther, having failed in their efforts to enlist Erasmus in Luther's cause, tended to turn violently against him. Erasmus commented, '... for a whole year now not one of those who pass for Luther's supporters has written me a line, not one has come to see me or sent me greetings, although in the old days they almost did me to death with their polite attention ... They would have good reason to be angry with me, had I ever been in their camp or encouraged all this business. As it is, they are angry without a cause' (Ep 1225:303–10).

On the other hand, Erasmus' friends among the moderate and liberal Catholics were increasingly insistent that he come out forcefully and publicly against Luther. Even Pope Leo wrote to him, in January 1521, a friendly and supportive letter but clearly hinting that he must shortly take a more positive position in defence of the church against Luther, 'Never was the time more opportune or the cause more just for setting your erudition and your powers of mind against the impious, nor is anyone better suited than yourself – such is our high opinion of your learning – for this praiseworthy task' (Ep 1180:19–22). By mid-August Erasmus was resolved to 'try my hand at something which will be not so much an attack on Luther, who has had quite enough abuse thundered at him if abuse could get us anywhere, as an attempt to heal our present discords' (Ep 1224:330–4). A month later he had written his old friend Paolo Bombace in Rome asking him to secure a brief of permission from Pope Leo for him to read Luther's books preparatory to writing against him (Ep 1236:130–1).

IX

By this time also, Erasmus had resolved to leave Louvain. At the end of May he packed up his belongings and all his books, notes, and manuscripts and accepted the invitation of a friendly cleric, Pieter Wichman, to stay at his country house at Anderlecht outside Brussels. He had known for some time that he must go back to Basel: indeed, his friends there had been expecting him since Easter (Ep 1242 introduction). He had already sent Froben the copy for the third edition of the Greek New Testament and the completed manuscript for a large new collection of his letters, the *Epistolae D. Erasmi Roterodami ad diversos* (Epp 1174, 1206). These and other projects urgently demanded his presence at the Froben press. But there were still a few things to be done. He was revising his massive, multi-volume edition of St Augustine (Epp 1174:19–21, 1204) and continuing to work at the paraphrases of the New Testament books (Epp 1171, 1206). And he was reluctant to leave the Netherlands as long as the imperial court continued to reside there. For several weeks in July and August Erasmus was in Bruges to attend on the court as well as to meet with several of his old English friends – More, Mountjoy, Tunstall – who had accompanied Cardinal Wolsey to a diplomatic meeting with the emperor. This meeting had to do with a projected alliance between Henry VIII and the emperor in the face of the war which had already broken out between Charles V and Francis I. It was clear, under the circumstances, that Charles and the court would shortly leave for Spain.

Erasmus made his own plans to depart the Low Countries as well. The atmosphere in Louvain had been hopelessly poisoned by the rancorous controversies with the theologians there. Erasmus had written an open letter to the theological faculty, a final effort soberly and reasonably to assert that he was in no way associated with Luther and begging them to moderate their attacks on him (Ep 1217). But it was to no purpose. With the Louvain theologians, on the one hand, accusing him of being 'Luther's man' and Luther's German supporters, on the other, abusing him as 'an opponent of his faction,' he wrote in despair, 'If only the sacrifice of my life, and not merely of my reputation, would enable me to convert this most perilous storm into a calm! Personally, I see no way out, unless Christ himself, like some god from the machine, gives this lamentable play a happy ending' (Ep 1225:338–44). On 28 October he set out for Basel, reaching that city on 15 November, travelling for safety's sake with a troop of disbanded soldiers.

He had left Louvain forever: but not the controversies that had boiled up there. A few of them had been resolved, notably those with Dorp and Lefèvre. A few were in abeyance, the controversies with Briart and Lee, for example. But the largest number of them continued to simmer and to produce yet more controversies.[59] One of these was the so-called *Manifesta mendacia*. This work was written in response to a book published in March 1525 in Antwerp, attacking Erasmus viciously for his views on confession, fasting, and a number of other matters and accusing him, once more, of being in league with Luther. It was published under the pseudonym Godefridus Reuysius Taxander. But Erasmus immediately recognized it as the work of a group of Dominicans (Ep 1603:35), led by his old enemy from Louvain, Vincentius Theoderici. As he observed, 'no one could have written such a tasteless and unlearned book except Vincentius.' 'My God, what a mass of manifest lies it is!' (Ep 1582:3–4, 7–8). This phrase he adopted as the title of his apologia against Theoderici's work, *Manifesta mendacia.*

Theoderici had been constrained to publish under a pseudonym because he had been forbidden by his vicar to publish it under his own name (Ep 1603:38–40). It seems to have been an open secret that the work was indeed his. Erasmus assumed as much when, shortly after he had gotten a copy of Theoderici's book, he wrote to the theological faculty of Louvain begging them 'to make an end to seditious clamourings' and 'restore both myself to your good graces and religious studies to Christian accord' (Ep 1582:116–7). This appeal, he knew, would have little or no effect and he had already begun to prepare his own written response to Theoderici. The apologia was finished and readied for publication, complete with rebuttal citations and cross-references to Theoderici's text. But it was never published. The manuscript, in Erasmus' own hand, was part of a bundle of Erasmian materials preserved in the Royal Library at Copenhagen that only came to light in 1966.[60] Further, the piece was misidentified, first assumed to be a polemic against his Spanish critic Diego López Zúñiga,[61] then against Latomus.[62] It was only within the past year that the work was properly ascribed by Rummel, who edited and translated it for this volume.[63]

But why did Erasmus decide not to publish it? Rummel has suggested that he felt under some obligation to keep the peace with the Louvain theologians since he had solicited both from the pope and the emperor directives imposing silence on further controversy. On the other hand, these interventions had been almost totally ineffective in silencing the theologians at Louvain.[64] As Rummel has suggested elsewhere (n59 above), Erasmus may have concluded that a judicious silence was, after all, his best strategy in this case (Ep 2956:32).

Finally, the very nature of the controversy itself may have prompted Erasmus to suppress his apologia. The book Theoderici and his co-conspirators had written was a sorry and nondescript piece of work. It was so full of grammatical errors and solecisms that Erasmus said he would not even try to pursue them. The quality of the diction would 'make [the authors] the laughing stock of schoolboys' (131). The book is also poorly organized and repetitious. Much of it is directed against one or another place in Erasmus' writings where he is alleged to be in error on confession. While this is the dominant subject of the first part of the book, it is dealt with in no less than six other places. Among the charges are the most outrageous accusations – that Erasmus casts doubt on the divine origin of confession, that he seeks to abolish it altogether and advocates the practice of laymen confessing to one another. There are several passages accusing Erasmus of advocating the abolition of fasting, most of them deriving from misreading the *Epistola de esu carnium*, a reform proposal that he had addressed to the bishop of Basel, Christoph von Utenheim, in 1522. Erasmus is falsely accused of advocating clerical marriage, of attacking papal infallibility and the powers of the pope, and of attacking the veneration of saints and relics and the excesses of feast days. Most of these charges had also been made against Luther and the similarity of views between Luther and Erasmus is constantly stressed. Even the fact that in 1524 Erasmus had finally written a book against Luther, *De libero arbitrio*, is turned right around and he is charged with having written it under false pretences and with continuing to be secretly on Luther's side. In his response (117), Erasmus writes, 'Everywhere he calls Luther my disciple, although no one has so far been able to point out in my books a proposition that is among the condemned Lutheran positions.'

Erasmus' apologia, the *Manifesta mendacia*, is itself not much of an improvement on the work of Theoderici. It is, of course, more correctly and elegantly written. But in terms of organization it simply follows Theoderici's serpentine meanderings.

In only a few places does Erasmus bother to create a reasoned and substantial argument in rebuttal. For example, against the charge that he denied the divine origin of confession, he points out that what he is actually talking about is not confession in general but the fact that the present form of confession does not go back to Christ in its foundation. This does not cast doubt on confession itself: 'and,' he writes, 'I believe that [the practice of confession] must be observed no less than if Christ had handed it down to us.' (116). On a related matter, he responds to the charge that he made confession 'a matter of habit rather than a remedy' (120). What he had advocated (and does advocate) is that people not go back time and again to repeat the same sins in confession. If one confesses his sin once to a priest and in good faith, then 'instead of growing old in perpetual sorrow [he] takes courage, and with gladness and joy zealously embarks on a better life' (120). If he happens to relapse, let him confess to a priest only the sins he has committed since the last confession. 'Otherwise confession becomes a matter of habit rather than a remedy' (120–1). Men torment themselves in the enumeration of their sins, lest they omit or overlook one. Yet, while they are occupied in this way, they neglect the main point of confession itself.

On the touchy matter of clerical celibacy and a married priesthood Erasmus flatly states that Taxander '... is lying when he says that I prefer marriage to celibacy in my declamation about marriage. I prefer a chaste marriage to an impure celibacy, and I compare virginity with the life of the angels, whereas marriage is a feature of human life' (129). He goes on to argue that it is better to permit marriage to those clergy who cannot control themselves than to have priests who are more libidinous than if they had legitimate wives. He has never, he claimed, advocated wholesale marriage of the clergy. What he is talking about is impure priests: 'My comparison is between the fornicating and the married priest, not between the chaste priest and the married man' (129–30).

But in the great majority of instances in *Manifesta mendacia*, Erasmus simply cites the charge Taxander has made and points out where in this book or that – his *Exomologesis: De modo bene confitendi, Spongia, Institutio principis christiani, Colloquia, Methodus, De orando Deum, Annotationes, Paraphrases* – he has not said what he is charged with saying. More often still, he accuses his opponent of lying – purposefully, blatantly, impudently.

The *Manifesta mendacia*, like many of Erasmus' controversial writings, is a hastily written, impatient, exasperated book. He had dealt with many of these charges literally dozens of times. They simply would not go away. It is in this sense that the controversies begun during the years at Louvain continued to vex him and continued to demand responses throughout the rest of his life.

JKS

Page from the autograph manuscript of the *Manifesta mendacia*
Reproduced courtesy Royal Library, Copenhagen
Erasmus made a mistake in the numbering of the paragraphs,
jumping from 35 to 46. See page 125.

THE LETTER TO THE THEOLOGIAN
MAARTEN VAN DORP
WHICH WAS THEN APPENDED TO THE *MORIA*

Ad Martinum Dorpium theologum Epistola
quae fuit hactenus adiecta Moriae

translated by

R.A.B. MYNORS and D.F.S. THOMSON

annotated by

JAMES K. McCONICA

edited by

J.K. SOWARDS

This letter to Maarten van Dorp, a young friend of Erasmus and an academic at Louvain, is the earliest of Erasmus' long list of apologiae or 'defences.' Though it was written in letter form it was clearly an apologia. Thomas More immediately designated it as such (Ep 388) and Erasmus himself included it among his apologiae in both catalogues of his works, of 1524 and 1530.[1] This was not, of course, an unusual practice for Erasmus. His treatises *Encomium matrimonii* and *Declamatio de morte*, for example, both first appeared as letters.[2] In the case of the letter to Dorp, moreover, the letter form was chosen because it was in response to a letter Dorp had written him (Ep 304). And further, Erasmus clearly wanted to avoid the formal structure of the classical apologia in favour of the more informal epistle in order to preserve the somewhat avuncular tone of his reply to Dorp: he points out, for example, 'I am old enough to be your father' (23) and throughout the letter he protests his friendship for Dorp and his admiration for his gifts. Nevertheless, both Dorp's letter and Erasmus' reply were serious works dealing with serious matters. And both were carefully crafted.

Dorp's exordium is a model of humanistic flattery: Erasmus' name is 'synonymous with scholarship and high standards' (Ep 304:4–5) and protestations of friendship: 'Among all your friends whom your universal learning and your friendly sincerity have secured for you in such numbers in almost the whole of Christendom there is [none] who feels a more sincere affection for you than myself' (Ep 304:5–8).

Nevertheless, he continues, he must inform his friend that *The Praise of Folly* has aroused a great deal of hostility, especially among the theological faculty of Louvain, who regard it as an attack upon themselves and a mockery of their profession. Even he, Dorp protests, is offended by *Folly*'s ascribing foolishness to Christ himself and by *Folly*'s claim that life in heaven is 'nothing but a form of lunacy' (Ep 304:34) – surely these things can lead to the undoing of the weaker brethren among us. He lamely suggests 'that the easiest way to put everything right will be to balance your *Folly* by writing and publishing a Praise of Wisdom' (Ep 304:82–3).

Dorp forges on. Not only is there the matter of *The Praise of Folly* but he has heard that Erasmus intends to edit the letters of St Jerome and to publish a revised and elaborately annotated version of the New Testament. The St Jerome he praises, 'a task worthy of you' (Ep 304:93); but the New Testament project is another matter altogether, especially since Erasmus intends to correct the Latin Vulgate by resort to the Greek texts. How can one assert that the revered Vulgate has any 'admixture of falsehood or mistake' (Ep 304:104)? The whole church 'which has always used this edition and still both approves and uses it' (Ep 304:109–10) could not have been wrong 'for all these centuries,' nor 'all those holy Fathers' and 'those saintly men who relied on this version when deciding the most difficult questions in general councils, defending and expounding the faith, and publishing canons to which even kings submitted their civil power' (Ep 304:112–15). Moreover, how can one trust the Greek texts since the Greeks themselves have fallen into heresy? This will serve only to arouse doubts about the integrity of Scripture which will lead to doubts about religion, and the church itself.

In his conclusion Dorp exhorts Erasmus 'in the name of our mutual friendship' (Ep 304:158), at least to proceed cautiously with this dangerous project, if proceed he must 'to emend only those passages in the New Testament where you can retain the sense and substitute something that gives the meaning more fully; or if your note says that the sense simply must be changed, to answer these arguments in your preface' (Ep 304:159–63). He finally reminds Erasmus of a few mutual friends, the publication of the *Disticha Catonis*, which Erasmus had left in Dorp's hands,[3] and urges him to find some work to dedicate to Abbot Meynard Man, Dorp's patron. And, at last, 'Farewell, very learned and to me very dear Erasmus' (Ep 304:184).

Erasmus was convinced, quite correctly, that Dorp was speaking less for himself than for 'those two or three gods among the theologians' who 'are not propitious towards me' (Ep 337:365–6). It was thus his primary intention, in his reply, to address them and their objections and arguments, rather than Dorp's own. This subterfuge becomes the main feature of the literary artistry of his letter: the substance of his counter-arguments is what makes of the letter a true apologia.

Erasmus' letter, like Dorp's, is full of protestations of friendship: 'This letter of yours, my dear Dorp, gave me no offence – far from it. It has made you much more dear to me, though you were dear enough before' (7).

But it also displays a subtle, patronizing tone. He wonders, for example, 'whether these thoughts are your own or were slipped into your head by others, who put you up to write that letter that they might use you as a stalking-horse for their own designs' (7).

In regard to the satire in *The Praise of Folly*, he writes, '... if you ever have the leisure, do look rather more carefully into the ridiculous jests that Folly makes; and you will find them a good deal closer to the teachings of the evangelists and apostles than some men's disputations which their authors think so splendid, so worthy of their professorial eminence' (12).

With regard to Dorp's reluctance to follow Erasmus' advice and learn Greek, he writes, '... I fear that when you are older and have learned from experience, you will approve my advice and regret your decision and, as so often happens, you will not understand your mistake until it is too late to remedy it' (23).

On the point that Folly scandalized pious ears by referring to heaven as a form of lunacy, he writes, 'I ask you, my worthy Dorp, who taught an honest man like you this kind of innuendo, or (which I think more likely) what clever man took advantage of your simple heart to traduce me like this?' (18)

And, with regard to Dorp's argument that the Greek texts are suspect because of the heresy of the Greek church, Erasmus responds, 'I can hardly persuade myself to believe that you meant this seriously' (26).

On the other hand, Erasmus had no trouble believing that those who had prompted Dorp's letter meant their criticisms seriously. And he took them seriously. The bulk of his reply to Dorp is directed to these shadowy criticisms.

He identifies three topics in Dorp's letter: 'You say you regret the somewhat unfortunate publication of my *Folly*, you heartily approve my zeal in restoring the text of Jerome, and you discourage me from publishing the New Testament' (7). He proceeds to respond to them.

The greater part of Erasmus' reply is taken up in the defence of *The Praise of Folly*. His arguments, many of them repeated from earlier defences of the book, are elaborate and fully drawn. Indeed this letter is his longest and most comprehensive defence of the *Moria*. He himself somewhat regrets publishing the book. Yet, for all its limitations, it can be defended. He criticizes those who deserve criticism but in a general way and never hurtfully, never attacking individuals by name. Moreover, he writes, 'My purpose was guidance and not satire, to help, not to hurt; to show men how to become better and not to stand in their way' (9). It is in no way different from his other books, even the sober and improving *Enchiridion*. It is certainly not meant as an attack on the Louvain theologians, nor, for that matter, on theologians generally, only on those among them who are ignorant, poorly trained, and puffed up by their positions. It is an attack upon the quibbling sophistries of the scholastics, 'this bold irreverent tribe of modern theologians' 'so much adulterated with Aristotle' (17–18), not upon the older, sounder patristic theologians.

As for the boldness of Folly in claiming as fools the apostles, even Christ himself, and in claiming that good Christians become fools for Christ both in this life and the next, Erasmus carefully explains not only that this is the whole conceit of *The Praise of Folly* but that, just as the Scriptures prescribe, this is the folly that overcomes the wisdom of the world.

Since Dorp approves his project of editing St Jerome, Erasmus devotes little space to it, although, as he observes, 'those friends of yours who took

so much offence at my *Folly* will not approve my edition of Jerome either'
(24). For he is a true ancient theologian and they modern theologians who
hate the humanities and fear the study of Greek.

This provides the lead-in to the third and final part of the letter, his
defence of his proposed New Testament edition. He begins with Dorp's
claim that there are no errors in the Vulgate. Of course there are – owing
to a translator's clumsiness or inattention, a scribe's ignorance. And when
the text goes astray because of such lapses, where are we to go if not to the
original Greek? The argument that the Greek texts cannot be trusted because
the Greeks have separated themselves from Rome is manifestly absurd. The
Greek heresy has nothing to do with the scriptural texts and commentaries:
it is a matter not of scholarship but of theology. As to the authority of the
Vulgate, it is not canonical, simply customary. And even if it were approved
by canon or council, did they approve all the mistakes as well? And what
about discrepancies even between copies of the Vulgate?

Erasmus turns next to the charge 'that everybody will forthwith
abandon Christ if the news happens to get out that some passage has been
found in Scripture which an ignorant or sleepy scribe has miscopied or
some unknown translator has rendered inadequately' (28). The many
eminent theologians who have already approved his project think otherwise,
as, he is confident, will the pope when the book is published. 'I have no
doubt that you too will be delighted with the book when it is published,
although you now dissuade me from publishing it, once you have even a
brief taste of the studies without which no man can form a right judgment
on these questions' (29).

In conclusion he urges Dorp to present Erasmus' case to his theologian
friends as frankly as he has presented theirs to Erasmus. 'Make my peace
with them as far as you can' (30). He asks to be remembered to mutual
friends and assures Dorp he will indeed mention his Abbot Meynard in
some of his writings. 'Farewell, Dorp, dearest of men' (30).

Erasmus had written Dorp hurriedly from Antwerp, for he was on his
way to Basel and did not intend to stop at Louvain. The letter he sent was
probably briefer and less expansive than the final version[4] which he
published some three months later in Basel with *Damiani Senensis elegeia*.[5]
In contrast, Dorp apparently distributed his letter to Erasmus widely.
Erasmus himself did not get his copy of it and only learned of it when a
friend in Antwerp showed him a copy. It was on this basis that he wrote his
own reply.[6] As soon as the Basel version of the letter was available, Dorp
had both it and his original letter printed in a new edition of Erasmus'
Enarratio in primum psalmum by Dirk Martens in Louvain, October 1515.[7]
Both letters were printed together again in Bade's edition of the *Moria*, Paris

24 June 1524, and in the most important editions of the *Moria* during the rest of Erasmus' life.[8] Erasmus' letter was printed in the 1540 *Opera omnia* as one of his apologiae.

JKS

THE LETTER TO THE
THEOLOGIAN MAARTEN VAN DORP
WHICH WAS THEN APPENDED TO THE *MORIA*[9]

ERASMUS OF ROTTERDAM TO MAARTEN VAN DORP,
THE DISTINGUISHED THEOLOGIAN[10]

Your letter never reached me, but a copy of it – secured I know not how –
was shown me by a friend in Antwerp. You say you regret the somewhat
unfortunate publication of my *Folly*, you heartily approve my zeal in
restoring the text of Jerome, and you discourage me from publishing the
New Testament. This letter of yours, my dear Dorp, gave me no offence –
far from it. It has made you much more dear to me, though you were dear
enough before; your advice is so sincere, your counsel so friendly, your
rebuke so affectionate. This is, to be sure, the mark of Christian charity that,
even when it gives rein to its indignation, it retains its natural sweetness
none the less. Every day I receive many letters from learned men which set
me up as the glory of Germany and call me its sun and moon[11] and
suchlike grand descriptions as are more onerous than honorific. Upon my
life, I swear that none ever gave me so much pleasure as my dear Dorp's
letter, written to reproach me. How right St Paul[12] was! Charity is never
wrong; if she flatters, she flatters in order to do good, and if she is
indignant, it is with the same end in view. I wish I could reply at leisure to
your letter, and give satisfaction to so dear a friend. For I am truly anxious
that whatever I do should be done with your approval, for I have so high
an opinion of your almost divine intelligence, your exceptional knowledge,
and your keen judgment, that I should value Dorp's single vote in my
favour more than a thousand votes of other men. But I still feel the upset
of my sea-voyage and the weariness of the riding that followed, and am,
besides that, very busy packing; and so I thought it better to write what I
could than to leave a friend thinking as you do, whether these thoughts are
your own or were slipped into your head by others, who put you up to
write that letter that they might use you as a stalking-horse for their own
designs.

First then, to be perfectly frank, I am almost sorry myself that I
published my *Folly*. That small book has earned me not a little reputation,
or notoriety if you prefer; but I have no use for reputation coupled with ill
will. Although, in heaven's name, what is all this that men call reputation,
except a perfectly empty name left over from paganism? Not a few things

of the kind have survived entrenched among Christians, when for instance they use 'immortality' for leaving a name to posterity, or call a man interested in any form of literature a 'virtuoso.' In all the books I have published my sole object has always been to do something useful by my exertions or, if that should not be possible, at least to do no harm. We see even great writers misusing their gifts to discharge their own personal feelings – one singing of his foolish loves, another flattering those he has set his cap at, another using his pen as a weapon to avenge some injury, another blowing his own trumpet[13] and in the art of singing his own praises outdoing any Thraso or Pyrgopolinices.[14] So be it; for myself, in spite of my small wit and most exiguous learning, I have always had one end in view, to do good if I can; but if not, to hurt no one. Homer purged his dislike of Thersites[15] by giving an unpleasant picture of him in his poem; Plato criticized many men by name in his dialogues; did Aristotle spare anyone who spared neither Plato nor Socrates? Demosthenes had his Aeschines[16] as a target for vituperation, Cicero his Piso and Vatinius and Sallust[17] and Anthony. How many men Seneca cites by name as objects of his mockery or his censure! Among the moderns, Petrarch[18] used his pen as an offensive weapon against a certain physician; so did Lorenzo[19] against Poggio and Poliziano[20] against Scala. Who can you show me in the whole range of authors so modest that he never wrote with acrimony of anyone? Jerome himself, pious and serious as he was, sometimes cannot refrain from an outburst of indignation against Vigilantius,[21] from levelling insults against Jovinian[22] and bitter invective against Rufinus.[23] It is a long-standing habit of learned men to confide their griefs or their joys to paper as though to a bosom friend,[24] and to pour out all their emotions into that sympathetic ear. Indeed, you will find that some men have taken to authorship with no other purpose in mind than to stuff their books full of their own current feelings and in this way to transmit them to posterity.

But I, who in all the volumes I have published have spoken very kindly of so many men, whose fair name have I ever blackened? On whose reputation have I cast the smallest slur? What people, class, or individual have I criticized by name? If you only knew, my dear Dorp, how often I have been provoked to do so by falsehoods no man could endure! But I have always fought down my resentment, moved more by the thought of what posterity will make of me than by the wish to treat their malignity as it deserves. If the facts had been as well known to others as they were to me, I should have been thought not satirical but fair-minded and even humble and moderate. No, I said to myself, my private feelings are no other man's concern. How can these affairs of mine be within the knowledge either of people at a distance or of posterity? I will maintain my own standard and not sink to theirs. Besides which, no man is so much my enemy that I would not rather, if I could, be on friendly terms with him again. Why should I bar the way to this, why should I now use language of an enemy which I may wish in vain that I had never used when he has become my friend? Why should I award a black mark to a man from whose record it can never be erased, however much he may deserve that it should be? If I must make a mistake, let me praise those who have done little to earn it rather than criticize those who deserve criticism; for if you praise the undeserving, this is ascribed to your open and generous character, while if you paint in his true colours a man who richly deserves to be exposed, this is sometimes thought to be due not to his deserts but to your vicious disposition. I need not mention in passing that the reciprocal exchange of injuries is not seldom the source of some dangerous conflagration, no less surely than reprisals for wrongs suffered on either side sometimes give rise to some enormous war; or that, just as it is unworthy of a Christian to return evil for evil, so it is unworthy of a generous heart to void its resentment in slander as women do.

Reasons like these have convinced me that whatever I write should hurt no one and draw no blood, and that I should never deface it by mentioning any wrongdoer by name. Nor was the end I had in view in my *Folly* different in any way from the purpose of my other works, though the means differed. In the *Enchiridion*[25] I laid down quite simply the pattern of a Christian life. In my book on the education of a prince[26] I openly expound the subjects in which a prince should be brought up. In my *Panegyricus*,[27] though under cover of praising a prince, I pursue indirectly the same subject that I pursued openly in the earlier work. And the *Folly* is concerned in a playful spirit with the same subject as the *Enchiridion*. My purpose was guidance and not satire; to help, not to hurt; to show men how to become better and not to stand in their way. Plato,[28] serious sage that he was, approves the habit of taking wine with a man at drinking-parties on a generous scale, because he thinks some faults can be dissolved under the cheerful influence of wine which severity could not correct. Horace[29] too thinks good advice even when given in jest no less effective than when serious. 'To tell truth with a smile,' he asks, 'does aught forbid?' And long ago some very wise men perceived this, and thought fit to set out the principles of a good life in fables which are humorous and at first sight childish, because truth by itself is a trifle astringent, and when thus made palatable finds an easier entrance into the minds of mortal men. This surely is the honey which physicians in Lucretius,[30] when they have to give medicine to children, smear on the cup of wormwood. And the purpose for which those princes of old brought fools into their courts was simply this, that their freedom of speech might point out some lighter faults and put them right without offending anyone. Perhaps it may seem inappropriate to mention Christ in such a context. But if it is ever permissible to compare things heavenly and earthly, surely his parables have something in common with the fables of antiquity? The gospel truth slips into our minds more agreeably, and takes root there more decisively, when it has charms of this kind to commend it than if it were produced naked – a theme pursued at length by St Augustine in his *De doctrina christiana*.[31] I saw how the common throng of mortals was corrupted by the most foolish opinions, and that too in every department of life, and it was easier to pray than to hope for a cure. And so I thought I had found a way to insinuate myself in this fashion into minds which are hard to please, and not only cure them but amuse them too. I had often observed that this cheerful and humorous style of putting people right is with many of them most successful.

If you reply that my assumed character is too trivial to provide an excuse for the discussion of serious subjects, this is a criticism I shall perhaps admit. Ill-judged I do not much object to its being called; ill-natured I do object to. Though the first of these charges I could successfully rebut, if in no other way, at least by the precedents of all the eminent authors whom I have listed in my modest preface. What was I to do? I was staying at the time with More[32] on returning from Italy, and was detained indoors for several days by pain in the kidneys. My books had not yet arrived, and if they had, my illness prevented anything more ambitious in the way of serious study. I began to amuse my idle moments with an encomium on Folly, with no thought of publishing it, but to take my mind off my physical discomfort. I showed a specimen of what I had begun to several ordinary friends, in order to enjoy the joke all the more by sharing it. They were highly delighted, and urged me to continue. I did as they said, and spent a week on it more or less which, considering how trivial the subject was, already seemed to me too much. After that the same people who had encouraged me to write it carried it off to France where it was printed, but from an imperfect as well as corrupt copy. What a poor reception it met with is shown, if by nothing else, by the fact that over seven editions were printed in a few months, and those too in different places. I wondered very much myself what anyone could see in it. So if all this, my dear Dorp, is ill-judged, your culprit owns up, or at least puts up no defence. Within these limits and in an idle moment and to please my friends I judged ill, and only once in my whole life. Who can be wise all the time?[33] You yourself admit that my other things are of a kind that all religious and educated people highly approve of. Who are these stern critics, these grave and reverend Areopagites, who will not forgive a man for doing something ill-judged even once? What peevish pedantry is this, to take offence at one single humorous piece and instantly deprive the author of the credit won by nightly toil on his earlier works? What ill-judged things far worse than this I could produce by other men, even by eminent theologians, who think up the most frigid and contentious questions and do battle among themselves over the most worthless trifles as though they fought for hearth and altar! And they act their absurd parts, more farcical than the original Atellanes,[34] without a mask. I was at least more modest, for when I wanted to show how ill-judged I could be, I wore the mask of Folly and, like Socrates in Plato,[35] who covers his face before reciting an encomium on love, I myself acted my part in disguise.

You say[36] that the self-same people who disapprove of my subject think well of the wit, the wide reading, and style, but are offended by the freedom of my satire. These critics actually think more highly of me than I could wish. Not that I care a whit for their kind words, especially as I believe them to have no wit, wide reading, or style themselves; and if they were well supplied with these, believe me, my dear Dorp, they would not be so ready to take offence at humour which aspires to be useful rather than either witty or well read. I ask you: in the name of all the Muses, what can they have in the way of eyes and ears and taste who take offence at the satire in that small book? To begin with, what satire can there be in something which criticizes no one by name except myself? Why do they not remember what Jerome[37] so often maintains, that the discussion of faults in general carries no criticism of any individual in particular? If anyone does take offence, he has no cause of action against the author; instead he could bring an action for slander against himself as his own betrayer, for having made it plain that that criticism applies to him in particular, which was levelled against everyone, that is to say, it was levelled against no one except such as deliberately made the cap fit. Do you not see how all through the work I have refrained from mentioning people's names so carefully that I have been reluctant even to name a whole country in any critical spirit? For where I list the form of self-love[38] peculiar to each nation, I call the Spaniards proud of their military prowess, the Italians of their literary culture, the English of their good dinners and good looks, and allot to each of the rest in the same way characteristics of such a kind as anyone, hearing them laid at his door, might not be reluctant to accept them, or at least would greet them with a laugh. Besides which, though the subject I had chosen takes me through every class of men and I spend my time criticizing the faults of individuals, where have I ever said anything scurrilous or bitter? Do I ever uncover a sink of iniquity or stir the mud of Camarina[39] that lurks, as we know, beneath the life of man? Everyone knows how much may be said against evil popes, selfish bishops and priests, vicious princes, and, in a word, against any rank of society, if, like Juvenal, I had not been ashamed to record in writing what many men practise without shame. I have merely surveyed the humorous and comic, rather than the scurrilous aspect of things, but have done this in such a way as sometimes to touch on major topics, and point out things in passing which it is very important they should know.

I know you have no time to spare for the descent into these details, but yet if you ever have the leisure, do look rather more carefully into the ridiculous jests that Folly makes; and you will find them a good deal closer to the teaching of the evangelists and apostles than some men's disputations which their authors think so splendid, so worthy of their professorial eminence. You yourself in your letter[40] do not deny that much of what is there reported is the truth; only you think it inexpedient to 'let rough truths grate on tender ears.'[41] If you think one should on no account speak one's mind and never tell the truth except when it does not hurt, why do physicians use bitter drugs, and reckon their *hiera picra*[42] among their most highly recommended remedies? If they do so when treating the ailments of the body, how much more reasonable for me to do the same when seeking to cure distempers of the mind? 'Rebuke, reprove, exhort,' says St Paul,[43] 'in season, out of season.' The apostle thinks faults should be attacked in every possible way; and do you think no sore place should be touched, even when this is so gently done that no one could even feel hurt unless he deliberately hurts himself? Why, if there does exist a way of curing men's faults without giving offence to anyone, that is, if I mistake not, the most appropriate way of all: to name no one by name, to refrain from things which good people cannot bear even to hear mentioned (for as some things in tragedy[44] are too terrible to be displayed before the spectators and it is enough to tell the story, so in human behaviour some things are too disgusting to be described without embarrassment), and to recount what can be described in a lively and humorous fashion through the mouth of some ridiculous character, so that any grounds for offence are excluded by the light-hearted treatment. We all know what an effect a well-judged and well-timed pleasantry sometimes has even on the grimmest of tyrants. Could any supplication or any serious argument have mollified the heart of the king[45] in the story so easily as the soldier's jest? 'Not at all,' says he; 'if the flagon had not gone dry on us, we should have said far worse things about you.' The king laughed, and forgave them. There was good reason for the careful discussions[46] on wit and humour in those two great masters of rhetoric, Cicero and Quintilian. Such is the power of wit and liveliness that we can take pleasure in a witty remark even when it is aimed at us, as is reported of Julius Caesar.[47] And so, if you admit that what I said is true, and if it is humorous rather than indecent, what better means can be devised for curing the defects that are common to all men? For a start, pleasure alone is enough to attract the reader and hold his attention. For in every other department men's objectives differ; but pleasure attracts all alike, except those who are too stupid to feel any sense of pleasure from what they read.

Further, those who take offence where no names are mentioned seem to me to be swayed by the same sort of emotions as women who, if they hear anything said against loose members of their sex, are as indignant as if the criticism applied to them all individually; and conversely, if anyone praises virtuous women, they are as pleased with themselves as if what applies to two or three stood to the credit of the sex as a whole. Men should be above these ill-judged reactions, scholars still more, theologians most of all. If I find some accusation here of which I am not guilty, I take no offence, but think myself lucky to be free from failings which I see many people suffer from. If it touched on some sore place, and I see myself in the mirror, here too there is no call for me to be offended. If I have any sense, I shall conceal my feelings and not come forward to give myself away. If I am a virtuous man, I shall take the hint, and see to it that in the future no fault can be laid by name at my door like the one I see before me pilloried anonymously. Can we not allow this book at least the freedom conceded to those popular comedies even by the uneducated? Think of all the jibes discharged with such freedom against monarchs, priests, monks, wives, husbands, everybody![48] And yet, because nobody is attacked by name, everybody laughs; everyone either openly confesses his own fault or carefully covers it up. The most savage tyrants tolerate their zanies and court fools, though they are often criticized by them in public. The emperor Vespasian[49] took no steps against the person who said he had a face like a man straining at stool. Who then are these friends of yours whose ears are so delicate that they cannot endure to hear Folly herself cracking jests against the way men live in general without giving anyone a black mark by name? The Old Comedy[50] would never have been driven off the stage if it had refrained from mentioning leading citizens by name.

But you, my excellent Dorp, almost write as though my *Folly* had made the whole theology faculty my enemies. 'Why need you make such a bitter attack,' you say, 'on the faculty of theology?' and you lament the position I find myself in.[51] 'In the old days,' you say,[52] 'what you write was read with enthusiasm by everybody and they all longed to see you here in person. Now your Folly, like Davus,[53] has upset everything.' I know you write nothing merely to find fault, and I shall not beat about the bush with you. I ask you, do you call it an attack on the faculty of theology if foolish and badly behaved theologians quite unworthy of the name come in for some criticism? If you think those ought to be the rules of the game, a man would make enemies of the whole human race who said anything against criminals. Was there ever a king so brazen as not to admit that there are a few wicked kings unworthy of a throne? Is any bishop too proud to admit the same about his own order? Is the faculty of theology the only one out of so many which offers us no stupid, uneducated, quarrelsome person, nothing but Paul and Basil and Jerome over again? Quite the contrary: the more distinguished a profession is, the fewer men in it who are good enough. You will find more good ship's captains than good princes, more good physicians than good bishops. In any case this casts no aspersions on the faculty; it tends to the credit of the few who in a most noble faculty have behaved nobly. Tell me, why are theologians more offended (if some have really taken offence) than kings, primates, magistrates, bishops, cardinals, popes? Or than merchants, husbands, wives, lawyers, poets – for no kind of mortal man has been spared by Folly, except that they are not so stupid as to think everything a direct attack on themselves which is said in general about bad men? Saint Jerome wrote to Eustochium[54] on the subject of virginity, and in the process painted such a picture of the behaviour of lascivious women as Apelles himself could not have made more vivid. Was Eustochium hurt? Was she indignant with Jerome for casting aspersions on the good estate of virginity? Not in the slightest. And why so? Because, being a sensible woman, she did not think that, if any criticism was made of the bad members of her sex, it applied to her; on the contrary, she was glad to see virtuous women reminded that they must not sink to that level and equally glad to see bad women told to be different in future. He wrote to Nepotianus[55] about the lives led by the clergy and to Rusticus[56] on the monastic life, painting the faults of both classes in lively colours and taking them to task brilliantly. His correspondents took no offence, because they knew that none of it applied to them. Why was there no estrangement between me and William Mountjoy, who is by no means least among noblemen at court, when Folly made all those humorous comments on eminent courtiers? Because, being himself a most excellent and most sensible man, he supposed (what is in fact true) that attacks on wicked and foolish grandees are nothing to do with him. Think of all the jests Folly aimed at wicked and worldly bishops! Why did the archbishop of Canterbury take no offence at all this? Because, being abundantly endowed with every virtue, he knows that none of this is meant for him.

Why need I go on to recount to you by name the eminent princes, the other bishops and abbots and cardinals and famous scholars, none of whom

I have yet found estranged from me by one hair's breadth as a result of my
Folly? Nor can I bring myself to believe that any theologians were irritated
by it, except a few maybe who either do not understand it, or are jealous of
it, or are so cantankerous by nature that they approve of nothing at all.
Mixed in with that class of men, as everyone would agree, are certain
persons so ill endowed with talents and with judgment that they have never
been fit for learning any subject, let alone theology. They get by heart a few
rules from Alexander Gallus,[57] and strike up an acquaintance with a little
idiotic formal logic, and then get hold of ten propositions out of Aristotle,
and even those they do not understand; after that they learn the same
number of *quaestiones* from Scotus or Ockham, intending to resort for
anything else to the *Catholicon*,[58] the *Mammotrectus*,[59] and similar wordbooks,
as though they were a sort of horn of plenty. Whereupon it is astonishing
the airs they give themselves, for nothing is so arrogant as ignorance. These
are the men who condemn St Jerome as a schoolmaster, because he is over
their heads; who poke fun at Greek and Hebrew and even Latin, and,
though as stupid as pigs and not equipped even with the common feelings
of humanity, they suppose themselves to hold the citadel of all wisdom.
They sit in judgment, they issue condemnations and pronouncements, they
know no hesitations, are never at a loss – there is nothing they do not
know. And yet these men, often only two or three of them, often rouse the
greatest commotions. Nothing is so brazen, so pig-headed, as ignorance.
These are the men who conspire with such zeal against the humanities.
Their aim is to count for something in the councils of the theologians, and
they fear that if there is a renaissance of the humanities, and if the world
sees the error of its ways, it may become clear that they know nothing,
although in the old days they were commonly supposed to know
everything. These are the men who raise all this clamour and tumult; it is
they who run this conspiracy against the devotees of liberal subjects. They
do not like my *Folly*, because they have no understanding either in Greek
or Latin. If these gentry – not theologians, but men dressed up to look like
them – receive one or two shrewd hits, what has this to do with the
infinitely respectable body of theologians who are real scholars? If it is zeal
for religion that animates them, why do they object to my *Folly* in
particular? See what filthy, pestilent, godless stuff was written by Poggio![60]
Yet he is a Christian author; he is in everybody's pocket and has been
translated into almost every language. See how Pontanus[61] pursues the
clergy with slander and abuse! But he is read as a wit and a merry fellow.
See how much filth there is in Juvenal! But some think that even preachers
may find him useful. Look at the malice against the Christians shown by
Cornelius Tacitus,[62] the hostility of Suetonius,[63] the impious mockery

reserved for the immortality of souls by Pliny and Lucian.[64] But these authors are read by everybody as part of their education, and rightly so. Only Folly, because she discharged a few shafts of wit, not against scholarly theologians who deserve the name, but against the frivolous quibbling of ignorant dolts, and the absurd title of *magister noster*,[65] they find quite intolerable.

And it is two or three worthless fellows dressed up to look like theologians who are trying to arouse feeling against me like this, as though I had attacked and antagonized the whole faculty. For my part I have such high regard for theological learning that it is the only learning to which I normally allow the name. For that faculty I have such respect and veneration that it is the only one in which I have entered my name and sought to be enrolled,[66] though I am ashamed to claim so distinguished a title for myself, knowing as I do the gifts both of scholarship and of life required by one who would call himself a theologian. The man who claims to be a theologian somehow claims something more than ordinary men. This is the proper dignity for bishops, not for men like me. Enough for me to have learned with Socrates that I know nothing at all[67] and, where I can, to lend a helping hand to the studies of other people. For my part I do not know where they lurk, those two or three gods among the theologians who you say in your letter[68] are not propitious towards me. Personally I have been in many places since I published my *Folly*, and have lived in so many universities and great cities; and never have I felt that any theologian was annoyed at me, except one or two of the class that are enemies of all sound learning, and even they have never said a word of protest to me. What they may murmur behind my back I pay little attention to, relying on the verdict of so many men of good will. If I were not afraid, my dear Dorp, that someone might think I was boasting rather than speaking the truth, how many theologians I could list for you, renowned for holiness of life, eminent for scholarship, and of the highest station, some of them even bishops, who have never given me such a warm welcome as since the publication of my *Folly*, and who think more highly of that small book than I do myself. I could give you them one by one here and now, by name and title, did I not fear that for Folly's sake even such eminent persons might incur the displeasure of your three theologians. One of them[69] at any rate I suppose to be the author of all this commotion in your midst, for I can guess pretty well what has happened. And if I were prepared to paint him in his true colours, no one would be surprised that such a man should disapprove of my *Folly*; in fact I would not approve it myself unless such people did disapprove. Not that I really like it; but it is a good reason for misliking it much less, that it is not liked by these great wits. The judgment of wise and

learned theologians carries more weight with me; and they are so far from
accusing me of bitterness that they even praise my moderation and fairness
of mind for dealing with a naturally licentious subject without licence and,
given a humorous theme, for having poked fun without hurting. For to
answer only the theologians who are, I hear, the only men to have taken
offence, everyone knows how much is said even in public against
theologians who are immoral. Folly touches on nothing of the kind. She
confines her jests to their useless discussions on minute points, and even
these she does not disapprove of indiscriminately: she condemns the men
who see in them alone the stem and stern,[70] as they say, of theological
science, and who are so fully occupied with battles of words, as St Paul[71]
called them, that they have no time to read what was written by evangelists,
prophets, and apostles.

I only wish, my dear Dorp, that fewer of them were exposed to this
charge. I could produce for you men over eighty who have devoted their
long lives to nonsense of this kind, and have never read the Gospels right
through; I detected this, and at length they had to confess it themselves.
Even under the mask of Folly I did not dare say what I have often heard
deplored by many men who are themselves theologians, real theologians I
mean, upright serious scholarly men who have drunk deep of Christ's
teaching from the true springs. Whenever they are in company where it is
permissible to say freely what they think, they regret the arrival in the
world of this newer kind of theology and long for the return of the old sort.
Never was anything so sacred, so noble, giving so much the true flavour
and image of Christ's heavenly teaching. But the modern kind (to say
nothing of the portentous filth of its barbarous and artificial style, its
ignorance of all sound learning, and its lack of any knowledge of the
tongues) is so much adulterated with Aristotle, with trivial human fantasies,
and even with the laws of the Gentiles, that I doubt whether any trace
remains, genuine and unmixed, of Christ. What happens is that it diverts
its attention over much to consider the traditions of men, and is less faithful
to its pattern. Hence the more intelligent theologians are often obliged to
express before the public something different from what they feel in their
own hearts or say when among friends. And sometimes they are perplexed
about an answer to any earnest enquirer, for they see that what Christ
taught and what mere human traditions ordain are not the same. What can
Christ have in common with Aristotle? What have these quibbling
sophistries to do with the mysteries of eternal wisdom? What is the purpose
of these labyrinthine *quaestiones*, of which so many are pointless, so many
really harmful, if for no other reason, as a source of strife and contention?
But, you will say, there are things we must enquire into; on some points we

must even have a decision. I do not dissent. But on the other hand there are a great many better let go than pursued (and it is part of knowledge to recognize that certain things are not for our knowing), a great many things on which to doubt is a more healthy state than to lay down the law. Finally, if laws must be laid down, let it be done reverently and not in arrogance and in accordance with Scripture, not with the so-called reasoning thought up by ordinary men. As it is, of these petty arguments there is no end; yet even in them what disagreements arise between parties and factions! And every day one pronouncement gives rise to another. In short, things have come to such a pass that the sum of the matter depends not so much upon what Christ laid down as upon the definitions of professors and the power of bishops, capable or otherwise; and in all this everything is now so much involved that there is no hope even of recalling the word to the old true Christianity.

All this, and a great deal else, is perceived and regretted by men of great piety and at the same time great learning, and they regard as the principal cause of it all this bold irreverent tribe of modern theologians. If only it were possible, my dear Dorp, for you to look silently into my thoughts – you would understand how much I deliberately leave unsaid at this point. But all this my *Folly* left untouched, or at least touched on very lightly, in order to hurt no one's feelings. And I took care to observe the same restraint throughout, to write nothing improper or corrupting or revolutionary, nothing that might seem to involve criticisms of any class of person. If anything is said there about the cult of the saints, you will always find something added to make it quite clear that criticism is confined to the superstition of those who do not venerate saints in the way they should. If any reflection is cast on princes or bishops or monks, I always go on to explain that no insult is intended to persons of that class, only to its corrupt and unworthy members, for I would not hurt a good man while pursuing the faults of bad ones. In so doing, furthermore, I have done what I could by suppressing names to give no offence even to bad men. Lastly, by conducting all the action in terms of wit and humour through an imaginary comic character, I have tried to arrange that even peevish folk who are hard to please may take it in good part.

One passage, you say, is criticized as not oversatirical but impious. How can the ears of a good Christian, you ask,[72] endure to hear me call the felicity of the future life a form of lunacy? I ask you, my worthy Dorp, who taught an honest man like you this kind of innuendo, or (which I think more likely) what clever man took advantage of your simple heart to traduce me like this? This is just how those pestilent experts in calumny take a couple of words out of their context, sometimes a little altered in the process, leaving out everything that softens and explains what sounds harsh otherwise. Quintilian[73] picks up this trick in his *Institutio* and shows us how to play it: we recount our own story in the most flattering light, with supporting evidence and anything else that can mitigate or extenuate or help our case in any way; at the same time we recite our opponent's case, shorn of all this assistance in the most invidious language it allows of. This art they have learned, not from the teaching of Quintilian, but from their own malevolence; and its outcome often is that things which would have been most acceptable if reported as they were written, give great offence when recounted differently. Pray reread the passage, and observe with care the stages, the gradual process of the argument, which led me to describe that felicity as a species of lunacy, and then observe the language in which I unfold all this. So far from giving offence to really pious ears, you will find plenty there which might actually delight them. It is in the way you read it that a slight cause of offence arises, and not in what I wrote.

For, since the purpose of my *Folly* is to embrace the whole world of things under the name of foolishness and to show that the whole sum of human felicity depends on Folly, she ranged over the entire human race as high as kings and supreme pontiffs; thence she arrived at the apostles themselves and even Christ, all of whom we find credited in the Scriptures with some kind of foolishness. Nor is there any risk that someone at this point may suppose that the apostles or Christ were foolish in the ordinary sense, but that in them too there was an element of weakness, something attributable to our natural affections, which when compared with that pure and eternal wisdom, might seem less than wise. But this same folly of theirs overcomes all the wisdom of the world; just as the prophet[74] compares all the righteousness of mortals to rags defiled with a woman's monthly discharge, not that the righteousness of good men is something foul, but because the things that are most pure among men are somehow impure when set against the inexpressible purity of God. Now I have set forth a kind of wise folly, and in the same way I produce a lunacy which is a sane and intelligent stupidity. And to soften what followed about the fruition of the saints, I begin by recalling the three kinds of madness in Plato,[75] of which the most blessed is the madness of lovers, which is nothing but a kind of ecstasy. But the ecstasy of godly men is nothing else than a foretaste of future blessedness, by which we are totally absorbed into God and shall live in future more in him than in ourselves. But this is what Plato calls madness, when a man, being rapt out of himself, exists in the object of his love and has the enjoyment of it. Do you not see how carefully I distinguish a little further on between the kinds of folly and insanity, so that no ingenuous reader could be misled by the words I used?

But I have no quarrel with the meaning, you say; it is the words themselves that revolt pious ears. But why are not those same ears offended when they hear Paul[76] speak of the foolishness of God and the folly of the cross? Why do they not pick a quarrel with St Thomas[77] for using about Peter's ecstasy words like 'In his pious delusion he begins to speak of tabernacles.' That sacred and blessed rapture he describes as delusions! And yet all this chanted in church. Why did they not bring me to court long ago for describing Christ in a certain prayer[78] as a magician and enchanter? St Jerome[79] calls Christ a Samaritan, although he was a Jew. Paul[80] even calls him sin, as though that were more than to say a sinner; he calls him an accursed thing. What outrageous impiety, if one chose a malevolent interpretation! And what a pious tribute, if one accepts it as Paul meant it! In the same way, if one were to call Christ a robber, an adulterer, a drunkard, a heretic, would not all men of good will put their fingers in their ears? But suppose one expressed this in appropriate language; suppose one worked up to it, as though one were leading the reader by the hand up to this point gradually, until he saw how in his triumph through the cross he robbed hell of its plunder which he restored to the Father; how he joined himself with the synagogue of Moses, like the wife of Uriah, that from it might be born the people of peace; how he was intoxicated with the new wine of charity when he gave himself for us; how he brought in a new kind of teaching, very different from all the current convictions of wise and foolish alike. Who could be offended then, especially as now and again we find some of these words used in Scripture in a good sense? I myself in my *Chiliades*[81] (it occurs to me in passing) have called the apostles Silenus figures and even Christ himself a sort of Silenus. Give me a prejudiced interpreter to put a brief and invidious explanation on this, and what could sound more intolerable? Let a pious and fair-minded man read what I wrote, and he will find the allegory acceptable.

It surprises me greatly that those friends of yours have never noticed another thing – how cautiously I put these things forward, and the care I take to soften them by adaptation. What I say is this: 'But now[82] that I have donned the lion's skin, let me tell you another thing. The happiness which Christians seek with so many labours is nothing other than a certain kind of madness and folly. Do not be put off by the words, but consider the reality.' Do you see? To begin with, the fact that Folly holds forth on such a solemn subject is softened by a proverb,[83] where I speak of her having donned the lion's skin. Nor do I speak just of folly or madness, but 'a kind of folly and madness,' so that you have to understand a pious folly and a blessed madness, in accordance with a distinction which I go on to make. Not content with that, I say 'a certain kind' to make it clear that this is meant figuratively and is not literal. Still not content, I urge people not to take offence at the mere sound of my words, and tell them to watch more what is said than how I say it; and this I do right at the very beginning. Then in the actual treatment of the question, is there anything not said in a pious and thoughtful fashion – more reverently in fact than really suits Folly? But on that point I thought it better to forget consistency for a moment than not to do justice to the importance of the theme; better to lose sight of the rules of composition than to offend against piety. And finally, when my demonstration is finished, that no one may be upset by my having allowed a comic character like Folly to speak on such a sacred subject, I meet this objection too by saying: 'But I[84] have been long forgetting who I am, and I have overshot the mark. If anything I have said seems rather impudent or garrulous, you must remember it is Folly and a woman who has been speaking.'

You see that I have never failed to cut short all excuse for the slightest offence. But this means nothing to men whose ears are closed to all but propositions and conclusions and corollaries. Should I mention that I provided my book with a preface in which I try to stop malicious criticism at the outset? Nor have I the slightest doubt that it is found satisfactory by all fair-minded readers. But what can you do for men who are too obstinate to accept satisfaction or too stupid to know when they are satisfied? Simonides[85] said that the Thessalians were too slow-witted to be deceived by him; and you can find some people like them too stupid to be placated. Nor is it surprising that a man should find matter for complaint who looks for nothing else. Anyone who reads St Jerome in that spirit will find a hundred places open to objection, and your friend will find no lack, in that most Christian of all the Fathers, of grounds for labelling him a heretic; to say nothing for the moment of Cyprian and Lactantius and others like them. Finally, who ever heard of a humorous subject being submitted for examination by theologians? If this is a good idea, why not by the same token apply these principles of examination to any frivolous stuff written by our modern poets? What a lot of impropriety they will find there, of things that reek of ancient paganism! But since no one regards these as serious works, none of the theologians supposes them to be any business of his.

Not that I would ask to be allowed to shelter behind the example set by such men as these. I should not like to have written even in jest anything that in any way could weaken a Christian's piety; but I must be allowed a reader who understands what I have written and a fair and upright critic; one who is keen to learn the truth and not interested in making mischief. But suppose a man were to take into account the people you speak of, who in the first place have no brains and even less judgment; second, have never been in touch with liberal studies but are infected rather than educated by that mean and muddled schooling of theirs; and lastly, hate everyone who knows what they themselves do not know, bringing with them no object except to distort whatever it may be that perhaps they have half understood – such a man, if he wished to be free from calumny, would never put pen to paper. Need I add that some of them are led to make mischief by a desire for glory? Nothing is so vainglorious as ignorance combined with a delusion of knowledge. And so, if they have this thirst for fame and cannot satisfy it by honourable means, they would rather imitate that Ephesian youth[86] who made himself notorious by setting fire to the most famous temple in the whole world rather than live obscure. And since they themselves cannot produce anything worth reading, they devote themselves to picking to pieces the works of famous men.

Other men's works, I mean, not my own, for I am nobody. My *Folly* I myself think not worth a straw, so let no one suppose me concerned about that. Is it surprising if men of the sort I have described choose out a few statements from a long work and make some of them out to be scandalous, some irreverent, some wrongly expressed, some impious and smacking of heresy, not because they find these faults there, but because they bring them in themselves? How much more conducive to peace and suitable to a Christian's fairness of mind to be well disposed to scholars and promote their work; and then, if anything ill thought out should escape them, either to overlook it or to give it a friendly interpretation, instead of looking for holes to pick in a hostile spirit and behaving like an informer rather than a theologian. How much more promising to work together in order either to instruct or to be instructed and, to use Jerome's words, to take our exercise in the field of the Scriptures without hurting one another![87] But it is astonishing how those men know no middle course! Some authors they read in a spirit of being ready to defend the most blatant errors on any pretext however frivolous, and towards some they are so unjust that nothing is too carefully phrased for them to pick holes in it somehow. How much better it would have been, if instead of rending others in pieces and being rent in turn, wasting their own time and other people's, they had learned Greek, or Hebrew, or Latin at least! A knowledge of these is so important for our understanding of Scripture that it really seems to me monstrous impudence for one who knows none of them to expect to be called a theologian.

And so, my excellent Maarten, devoted as I am to your welfare, I shall not cease to urge you, as I have often done before, to add to your equipment at least a knowledge of Greek. You are exceptionally gifted. You can write – solid, vigorous, easy, abundant stuff, evidence of a spirit as productive as it is wholesome. Your energy is not merely untouched by years but still fresh and green, and you have successfully completed the conventional course of study. Take my word for it, if you crown such a promising start with a knowledge of Greek, I dare promise myself and everyone else that you will do great things, such as none of our modern theologians has ever done before. If your view is that for love of true religion we should despise all human learning, and if you think that the shortest way to such wisdom is to be somehow transfigured through Christ, and that everything else worth knowing is perceived more fully by the light of faith than in the books of men, I shall subscribe without difficulty to your opinion. But if, in the present state of human affairs, you promise yourself a true understanding of the science of theology without a knowledge of the tongues, particularly of the language in which most of Scripture has been handed down, you are wholly at sea.[88]

And I only wish I were as able to persuade you of this as I am desirous to do; for my desire is in proportion to my fondness for you and my interest in your work, and the fondness is very great and the interest very sincere. If I cannot convince you, do at least listen to the prayers of a friend to the extent of making the experiment. There is no forfeit I will not gladly pay if you do not admit that my advice was friendly and reliable. If my affection for you carries any weight, if there is anything in our being fellow-countrymen, if you attach any weight I will not say to my learning but to my prolonged labours in the humanities, if my age has any influence with you (for as far as years go, I am old enough to be your father), let me persuade you to agree to this out of affection or respect, if not for my arguments. You habitually call me eloquent; I shall never agree with you, unless on this point I can win you over. If I do succeed, the result will be great satisfaction for us both, for me in having given you this advice and for you in having taken it; and you, who are now the dearest of all my friends, will on this account be not a little dearer to me, because I shall have made you dearer to yourself. Otherwise I fear that when you are older and have learned from experience, you will approve my advice and regret your decision and, as so often happens, will not understand your mistake until it is too late to remedy it. I could recount a long list to you by name of men who in their old age became children again to learn Greek, because they understood at last that without Greek liberal studies are lame and blind.

But on this topic I have already said too much. To return to your letter. Thinking that the one way to reduce my unpopularity with the theologians and recover the good standing I once enjoyed would be to compose an encomium on Wisdom as a sort of recantation of my *Praise of*

Folly, you beg and beseech[89] me urgently to do so. For my part, my dear
Dorp, as a man who despises no one except myself and who would be glad,
if it were possible, to live at peace with the whole human race, I would not
refuse to undergo this labour, did I not foresee that any small share of ill
will I may have incurred from a few prejudiced and ignorant critics, so far
from being extinguished, would be made much worse. And so I think it
better to let sleeping dogs lie[90] and leave this Camarina alone.[91] This hydra,
if I mistake not, will be better left to weaken with time.

I now come to the second part of your letter.[92] My work on the
restoration of Jerome meets with your high approval, and you encourage
me to take up other labours of the same sort. You spur a willing horse;[93]
though what I need is not so much people to spur me on to this task as
helpers, such is its difficulty. But I hope you will never again believe
anything I say if you do not find me speaking the truth in this: those
friends of yours who take so much offence at my *Folly* will not approve my
edition of Jerome either. Nor are they much better disposed towards Basil,
Chrysostom, and Nazianzen than they are to me, except that their assaults
on me are more outspoken; though sometimes in moments of irritation they
are not afraid to say some very foolish and improper things about those
great luminaries. They are afraid of the humanities; they fear for their own
dictatorship. I can show you that I am not making this up. When I had
begun work and the news had already got around, up came certain
reputedly influential men and distinguished theologians, by their own
valuation, and adjured the printer by all that is holy not to allow any
admixture of Greek or Hebrew; these two languages, they said, are fraught
with peril and there is no good to be got out of them; they were designed
solely to satisfy idle curiosity. Even before that, when I was in England, I
happened to find myself drinking wine with a certain Franciscan,[94] a Scotist
of the first rank, who in public estimation is a very clever man and on his
own knows all there is to know. When I had explained to this man what I
was trying to do in Jerome, he expressed astonishment that there should be
anything in his works that theologians did not understand – and he such
an ignorant man that I should be surprised if there are three lines in all the
works of Jerome which he rightly understands. He added kindly that, if I
had any problems in Jerome's prefaces, they had all been clearly expounded
by LeBreton.[95]

I ask you, my dear Dorp, what can you do for these theologians of
yours, what can you ask for them in your prayers, except perhaps find a
reliable physician to cure their brains? And yet it is sometimes men of this
sort who talk loudest in any gathering of theologians, and these are the men
who issue pronouncements about the Christian faith.[96] They are terrified, as

though it were something perilous and pestilential, of the very thing that St Jerome, and Origen too even in his old age, tried so hard to secure for themselves, in order that they might truly be theologians. Moreover Augustine,[97] when he was already a bishop and an old man, deplores in his *Confessions* that in his youth he had been disgusted by the study which might have been of such value to him in his exposition of Scripture. If there is any peril here, I shall not take fright at a risk which men of such wisdom have been willing to run. If this is idle curiosity, I have no wish to be holier than Jerome – and how well these men served Jerome in calling what he did idle curiosity is a question they should ponder in their own hearts. There exists a very ancient decree of a pontifical synod[98] providing for the appointment of professors to give public instruction in several tongues, while for the learning by heart of sophistics and Aristotle's philosophy no such steps have ever been taken, except that a question is raised in the *Decreta*[99] whether it is permitted to study these subjects or no. And the study of them is disapproved of by many eminent authorities. So what the authority of popes has instructed us to do we neglect, and what has been called in question and even disapproved of is the only thing we accept. Why? Not but what they are as badly off in Aristotle as they are in Scripture. They are dogged everywhere by the nemesis that waits for those who despise Greek; here too they are subject to delusions, half asleep, bleareyed, blundering, producing more monstrosities. To these eminent divines we owe the loss of so many of the authors listed by Jerome in his catalogue;[100] so few survive because they wrote over the heads of our *magistri nostri*.[101] We owe it to them that we possess St Jerome so corrupt and mutilated that it costs others almost more labour to restore his text than it did him to write it.

Then again what you write in the third part[102] about the New Testament makes me wonder what has happened to you, or what has beguiled for the moment your very clear-sighted mind. You would rather I made no changes, unless the Greek gives the meaning more fully, and you say there are no faults in the version we commonly use. You think it wrong to weaken in any way the hold of something accepted by the agreement of so many centuries and so many synods. I ask you, if what you say is true, my most learned Dorp, why do Jerome and Augustine and Ambrose so often cite a different text from the one we use? Why does Jerome censure and correct many specific errors which we still find in our edition? What will you do when there is so much agreement, when the Greek copies are different and Jerome cites the same text as theirs, when very oldest Latin copies concur, and the sense itself runs much better? Do you intend to overlook all this and follow your own copy, though it was perhaps corrupted by a scribe? For no one asserts that there is any falsehood in Holy Scripture (which you also suggested), nor has the whole question on which Jerome came to grips with Augustine anything at all to do with the matter. But one thing the facts cry out, and it can be clear, as they say, even to a blind man,[103] that often through the translator's clumsiness or inattention the Greek has been wrongly rendered; often the true and genuine reading has been corrupted by ignorant scribes, which we see happen every day, or altered by scribes who are half-taught and half-asleep. Which man encourages falsehood more, he who corrects and restores these passages, or he who would rather see an error added than removed? For it is of the nature of textual corruption that one error should generate another. And the changes I make are usually such as affect the overtones rather than the sense itself; though often the overtones convey a great part of the meaning. But not seldom the text has gone astray entirely.[104] And whenever this happens, where, I ask you, do Augustine and Ambrose and Hilary and Jerome take refuge if not in the Greek original? This is approved also by decrees of the church; and yet you shuffle and try to reject it or rather to worm your way out of it by splitting hairs.

You say[105] that in their day the Greek copies were more correct than the Latin ones, but that now it is the opposite, and we cannot trust the texts of men who have separated from the Roman church. I can hardly persuade myself to believe that you meant this seriously. What? We are not to read the books of renegades from the Christian faith; and how pray do they think Aristotle such an authority, who was a pagan and never had any contact with the faith? The whole Jewish nation turned away from Christ; are we to give no weight to the Psalms and the Prophets, which were written in their language? Now make me a list of all the heads under which the Greeks differ from the orthodox Latins; you will find nothing that arises from the words of the New Testament or has anything to do with this question. The whole controversy relates to the word *hypostasis*, to the procession of the Holy Spirit, to the ceremonies of consecration, to the poverty of the priesthood, to the powers of the Roman pontiff. For none of these questions do they lean on falsified texts. But what will you say when you see their interpretation followed by Origen, Chrysostom, Basil, Jerome? Had somebody falsified the Greek texts as long ago as that? Who has ever detected falsification in the Greek texts even in one passage? And finally, what could be the motive, since they do not defend their particular tenets from this source? Besides which, that in every department of learning the Greek copies have always been more accurate than ours is admitted by no less than Cicero,[106] who is elsewhere so unfair to the Greeks. For the difference between the letters, the accents, and the actual difficulty of writing all mean that they are less easily corrupted and that any corruption is more easily mended.

Again, when you say[107] that one should not depart from a text that enjoys the approval of so many councils, you write like one of our ordinary divines, who habitually attribute anything that has slipped somehow into current usage to the authority of the church. Pray produce me one synod in which this version has been approved. How could it approve a text whose author is unknown? That it is not Jerome's is shown by Jerome's own prefaces. But suppose that some synod has approved it? Was it approved in such terms that it is absolutely forbidden to correct it by the Greek original? Were all the mistakes approved as well, which in various ways may have crept in? Was a decree drawn up by the fathers of the council in some such terms as this? 'This version is of unknown authorship, but none the less we approve it, nor do we wish it to be an objection that the Greek copies have something different, however accurate they may be, or if a different reading is found in Chrysostom or Basil or Athanasius or Jerome, even though it may better suit the meaning of the Gospel, notwithstanding our high approval of these same authorities in other respects. Moreover, whatsoever in future may in any way, whether by men with a little education and rather more self-confidence or by scribes unskilled, drunken, or half-asleep, be corrupted, distorted, added, or omitted, we in virtue of the same authority approve, nor are we willing that any man should have licence to alter what has once been written.' A very comical decree, you say. But it must have been something like this, if you are to frighten me from this kind of work by the authority of a synod.

Finally, what are we to say when we see that even copies of our Vulgate version do not agree? Surely these discrepancies were not approved by a synod, which of course foresaw each change that would be made? I only wish, my dear Dorp, that the Roman pontiffs had sufficient leisure to issue salutary constitutions on these points, which would take care for the restoration of the works of good authors and the preparation and substitution of corrected copies. Yet I would not give any seats on that commission to those most falsely so-called theologians whose one idea is that what they learned themselves should be the only thing of current value. And what have they learned that is not utter nonsense and utter confusion? If they once become dictators, farewell to all the best authors! The world will be compelled to accept their brainless rubbish as oracles; and so little sound learning is there in it, that I would rather be a humble cobbler than the best of their tribe, if they can acquire nothing in the way of a liberal education. These are the men who do not like to see a text corrected, for it may look as though there were something they did not know. It is they who try to stop me with the authority of imaginary synods; they who build up this great threat to the Christian faith; they who cry 'the church is in danger' (and no doubt support her with their own shoulders, which would be better employed in propping a dung-cart) and spread suchlike rumours among the ignorant and superstitious mob; for the said mob takes them for great divines, and they wish to lose none of this reputation. They are afraid that when they misquote Scripture, as they often do, the authority of the Greek or Hebrew text may be cast in their teeth, and it may soon become clear that what used to be quoted as an oracle is all a dream. St Augustine, that very great man and a bishop as well, had no objection to learning from a year-old child.[108] But the kind of people we are dealing with would rather produce utter confusion than risk appearing to be ignorant of any detail that forms part of perfect knowledge, though I see nothing here that much affects the genuineness of our Christian faith. If it were essential to the faith, that would be all the more reason for working hard at it.

Nor can there be any danger that everybody will forthwith abandon Christ if the news happens to get out that some passage has been found in Scripture which an ignorant or sleepy scribe has miscopied or some unknown translator has rendered inadequately. There are other reasons to fear this, of which I prudently say nothing here. How much more truly Christian it would be to have done with quarrelling and for each man cheerfully to offer what he can to the common stock and to accept with good will what is offered, so that at the same time you learn in humility what you do not know and teach others ungrudgingly what you do know! If some are so ignorant that they cannot rightly teach anything or so conceited that they are unwilling to learn, let us think no more of them (for they are very few) and concentrate on those who are intelligent or at any rate promising. I once showed my annotations, when they were still raw, still fire-new from the mint, as they say, to men of the highest integrity, eminent theologians and most scholarly bishops; and all admitted that those rudimentary pieces, such as they were, had shed a flood of light for them on the understanding of Holy Scripture.

Furthermore, you tell me,[109] but I knew already, that Lorenzo Valla had been active in this field before me, for I was the first to publish his annotations;[110] and Jacques Lefèvre's notes on the Pauline Epistles I have seen. I only wish they had finished off their work, so that my efforts might not have been needed. Personally I think Valla most praiseworthy, as a man more concerned with literature than with theology, for having shown enough energy in the study of Scripture to compare the Greek with the Latin, while there are not a few theologians who have never read the whole Testament right through; although in some places I differ from him, especially in those that relate to theological science. And Jacques Lefèvre[111] had his notes in hand already when I was getting this work under way, and it happened, a trifle unfortunately, that even in our most friendly conversations[112] neither of us thought of mentioning his plans, nor did I learn what he had been at until his work appeared in print. His attempt also I heartily approve, although from him too I dissent in some places, reluctantly, for I should be happy to agree with such a good friend in everything, were it not necessary to consider truth more than friendship,[113] especially where Scripture is concerned.

But it is not yet quite clear to me why you confront me with these two names. Is it to deter me from the project as though I were already anticipated? But it will be clear that even after such good men I had good reason to attack it. Or do you suggest that their efforts, like my own, were unpopular in theological circles? Personally I cannot see that Lorenzo added to his existing unpopularity; and Lefèvre I hear is universally approved. I might add that we do not attempt an exactly similar task. Lorenzo only annotated selected passages, and those, it is clear, in passing and with what they call a light touch.[114] Lefèvre published notes on the Pauline Epistles only, and translated them in his own way; then added notes in passing if there was any disagreement. But I have translated the whole New Testament after comparison with the Greek copies, and have added the Greek on the facing pages, so that anyone may easily compare it. I have appended separate annotations in which, partly by argument and partly by the authority of the early Fathers, I show that my emendations are not haphazard alterations, for fear that my changes might not carry conviction and in the hope of preserving the corrected text from further damage. I only wish I had been man enough to perform what I so laboriously undertook! As far as the business of the church is concerned, I shall have no hesitation in presenting my labours, such as they are, to any bishop, any cardinal, any Roman pontiff even, provided it is such a one as we have at the moment. In the end I have no doubt that you too will be delighted with the book when it is published, although you now dissuade me from publishing it, once you have had even a brief taste of the studies without which no man can form a right judgment on these questions.

Observe, my dear Dorp, how by one kind deed you have made two parties grateful to you: one is your theologian friends, on whose behalf you have so diligently accomplished your mission, and the other is me, for your friendly advice is fresh evidence of your affection for me. You in your turn will take in good part the equally outspoken return I have made you, and if you are wise you will adopt my advice (for I have no one's interests at heart but yours) rather than theirs, whose sole object in trying to bring over to their party a gifted nature like yours that was meant for great things is to strengthen their own forces by the acquisition of such a leader as you. Let them follow better courses if they can; if not, you at least must follow only the best. If you cannot make them better men, as I hope you will try to do, at least mind that they do not make you a worse one. What is more, you must present my case to them with the same frankness with which you have put theirs to me. Make my peace with them as far as you can, and make them see that I follow this course not in order to discredit those who know nothing of these languages, but for the general good, which will be available to anyone who cares to use it and will not be a burden on the man who prefers to do without; also that my attitude is that, if anyone arises who can or will teach us something better, I shall be the first to tear up and abandon what I have written and subscribe to his opinion.

Give my most cordial greetings to Jean Desmarez,[115] and show him our discussion on the *Folly* on account of the notes on it which my friend Listrius[116] dedicated to him. Commend me warmly to the learned de Neve[117] and to that very kind Nicolaas van Beveren,[118] the provost of St Peter's. Abbot Meynard,[119] whom you praise so highly (and, knowing your sincerity, I am sure he deserves it), I love and respect already for your sake, and shall not fail, when I have the opportunity, to mention him with honour in what I write. Farewell, Dorp, dearest of men.

Antwerp, 1515

APOLOGY OF DESIDERIUS ERASMUS OF ROTTERDAM, REFUTING RUMOURS AND SUSPICIONS WHICH VARIOUS CRITICS HAVE DRAWN FROM THE DRAMATIC DIALOGUE WRITTEN BY JACOBUS LATOMUS, AUTHORIZED TEACHER OF SACRED THEOLOGY

Desiderii Erasmi Roterodami Apologia
rejiciens quorundam suspiciones ac rumores,
natos ex dialogo figurato,
qui Jacobo Latomo sacrae theologiae licentiato inscribitur

translated and annotated by

MARTIN LOWRY

Erasmus' controversy with Latomus, like his earlier dispute with Lefèvre d'Etaples, stemmed from the triumphs of 1516. The scholars of Western Europe had been awaiting a New Testament printed in the original Greek for almost twenty years, and the relevant sections of the Alcalá Polyglot, though still unpublished, were already in print. When expectations had been raised for so long, it is not surprising that the *Novum instrumentum* was greeted with acclaim. On 27 August Erasmus wrote to Reuchlin, 'The New Testament has made me friends everywhere.' It was no idle boast. Over the next few months letters came from Henry Bullock of Cambridge, William Latimer of Oxford, Adrianus Barlandus of Louvain, and François Deloynes of Paris, all bearing witness to the enthusiasm with which the new text had been greeted in their universities.[1]

Fame naturally involved risk. Erasmus and Froben had worked rapidly, and from a narrow selection of manuscripts, none of them copied earlier than 1000 AD. Their text, and Erasmus' new translation, were vulnerable on many counts. On 31 October 1516, Thomas More warned that the English Franciscans had divided Erasmus' work systematically between them to comb it through for errors, and this spectre of an organized theological cabal would haunt Erasmus more and more over the following years. The professional jealousy of fellow-humanists like Lefèvre would soon surface. And even partisanship of admirers could be dangerous. On 24 March 1517 Peter Schade, who Latinized his name to 'Mosellanus,' wrote to Erasmus from Leipzig where he was struggling to establish Greek studies and needed all the influential support he could muster. Though no reply was dispatched at the time, this was one of the associations that would later provoke the controversy with Latomus.[2]

For some time these difficulties were either latent or distant. By mid-summer 1517 Erasmus had settled in Louvain, where the immediate prospects for humanist study were exciting enough to outweigh anxieties about 'the hatred and ill will' of a few prominent theologians, or the sense of grievance over Lefèvre's criticism. On 22 June Jérôme de Busleyden, a holder of many benefices and beneficiary of an archbishop's will, bequeathed funds for the establishment of a college within the university where the three biblical languages Latin, Greek, and Hebrew, would be taught side by side. Shortly afterwards he left for Spain in Duke Charles' retinue, and died at Bordeaux on 27 August. If it could be implemented, Jérôme's bequest would make Louvain the counterpart of Spain's Alcalá and England's Corpus Christi College, Oxford, where Cardinal Ximénes and Bishop Foxe of Winchester had recently established similar institutions for the humanistic study of the Bible. Erasmus' enthusiastic support for the scheme provided the local background for the coming controversy, and for Latomus' concentration on the issue of 'the three languages.'[3]

For the remainder of 1517 and most of the following year the plans moved ahead well. Erasmus was favourably surprised by the warmth of the theologians, who spoke of electing him to their faculty: and even before the first funds from the bequest had been received, he had seen and seized an excellent opportunity of putting them to use. A Spanish 'converso' Jew named Matthaeus Adrianus, who had sought refuge in Italy during the 1490s, taken a medical degree, then drifted northwards by way of Basel, appeared at Middelburg in 1515, with the reputation of being an excellent Hebrew scholar and a reckless spender. On 30 October Erasmus wrote urging Jérôme's brother and executor Gilles de Busleyden to hire him. The generous salary tempted Adrianus, and Hebrew lectures began on 2 February 1518. On 26 April Erasmus wrote to the distinguished Greek émigré Janus Lascaris, whom he had met in Venice ten years earlier, hoping either to interest him directly in the scheme or to find a suitable Greek lecturer on his recommendation. Ultimately the choice fell on Rutgerus Rescius, who had followed Aleandro's Greek courses in Paris earlier in the decade. By 1 September Adrianus Barlandus had been appointed to the less valuable Latin tutorship and the full range of courses could be launched. Even the difficulties had worked to the advantage of the new college, for negotiations between Busleyden's executors and the faculty of arts had failed to find suitable premises for the lectures, which had to be held in specially leased property, beyond the immediate control of the university authorities.[4]

But as in every academic feud, victory had been bought at the price of creating a disgruntled cadre of defeated colleagues. During the winter months these opponents came to associate the quickening events in the wider world with recent developments at Louvain, and presently returned to the attack with a sharpened sense of identity and anxiety. At the beginning of August, Mosellanus, still trying to secure full recognition of his Greek courses by the university authorities at Leipzig, published an oration which insisted that biblical texts could not be understood without a knowledge of the ancient languages, and drew heavily on the ideas expressed in Erasmus' prolegomena to the *Novum instrumentum*. In November a part of these introductory materials was reissued in an extended form as *Ratio seu methodus verae theologiae*.[5] It is not certain when copies of Mosellanus' oration first reached Louvain, but both works focused attention on the linguistic debate. Occasional references to 'Eleutherius' (Luther) were beginning to creep into Erasmus' correspondence from the middle of October, and early in 1519 two letters reached him from Leipzig, where preparations for the famous confrontation between Karlstadt and Eck were in full swing. The first, dated 5 January, came from Melanchthon and assured Erasmus that Luther 'desired his good opinion at all points.' The second, written only a day later, was a further request for support from Mosellanus. Brushing the theological debate aside as a rather contemptible sideshow, he described the contest between himself and the 'sophisters' as something like an open war, which Erasmus could settle in his favour with 'even one letter to show your feelings.'[6]

Though the atmosphere in Louvain never became as venomous as that in Leipzig, the publications combined with the rumours to raise it to a critical point. On 6 March 1519, Alaard of Amsterdam announced that he was about to open a course of lectures on Erasmus' *Methodus*, and was forbidden to do so on the ground that he was a private teacher only, not an officially recognized member of one of the university faculties. The dialogue *De trium linguarum et studii theologici ratione* seems to have been hurried through publication at Hillen's press in Antwerp during the two weeks after the ban on Alaard's lectures and partly to justify it. Erasmus had seen the work by 30 March, when he passed it to Maarten Lips with a brief note which called the dialogue 'a scholarly and elegant performance,' but perhaps the product of several authors rather than Jacobus Latomus alone.[7]

Though Latomus would later claim the work as his own, his previous career had been so quiet that he may well have seemed an unlikely opponent. Born Jacques Masson at Cambron, near Mons, he had studied at the Collège de Montaigu in Paris and was therefore a product of the rigorous scholastic discipline established by Standonck and despised by Erasmus, who had studied there in 1495–6. Latomus had received his MA in 1502, and been head of the hostel for poor students – the 'domus pauperum' – at Louvain ever since. He had shown no inclination to thrust himself into the public eye as a writer of polemics, and Erasmus seems to have regarded him as a friend – evidently one of the theologians whose surprising warmth he had noted in 1517. Latomus was not a likely opponent: and the dedication of his dialogue to Guillaume de Croy, the titular cardinal of Toledo who was completing his studies at Louvain under Vives, suggested a calculated and collective move by the theologians to swing influential opinion against the humanist methods of the Collegium Trilingue.[8]

The dialogue itself was a strange hybrid, whose two books puzzled Erasmus and are still less clear to the modern reader. Unlike Lefèvre, the author – or authors – named no names and cited no passages. The first book was an imaginary discussion between a devotee of the humanist approach called 'Peter,' a student of theology called 'John,' and a new student called

'Albert,' wavering over his choice of courses. The name of 'Peter,' and his enthusiastic report of the recent inauguration of Greek studies at Leipzig, made this a transparent allusion to Mosellanus, who was the real target of the first book. The tone is relaxed, at times even frivolous. When John argues that not all parts of Gratian's *Decretum* are true 'decrees,' or that the blood of Christ could not have dripped upwards to stain Pilate's notice, he does so with the bland excuse that if Peter calls theologians word-splitters, he must expect them to split words. It was an approach which Erasmus found offensive and difficult to handle.[9]

But in the second book Peter is discarded, Albert left as a poser of occasional questions, and even John reduced to a mouthpiece for the opinions of a respected elderly theologian who is neither named nor introduced as a direct speaker. The book is more a reported monologue than a dialogue. The aim shifts from demolishing Mosellanus' oration to reinforcing the established theological syllabus against possible undermining by Erasmus' *Methodus*. The change of tone and target, as well as the stress on the venerable quality of the theologian, led Henry de Vocht to suggest that the second book might have been composed earlier, and that the source of its ideas, if not the actual co-author, might have been Jan Briart of Ath, dean of the theology faculty and a veteran of the court of Margaret of York. It is an intriguing possibility, but since we are uncertain when Mosellanus' dialogue became known in Louvain and since evidence for Briart's hostility rests chiefly on Erasmus' suspicions, we should perhaps not treat it as anything more.[10]

But for all his public objections, in private correspondence Erasmus welcomed the obliqueness and anonymity of Latomus' dialogue, which may have played a part in preventing the controversy from running out of control. On 21 March Matthaeus Adrianus reaffirmed in a lecture the importance attached by the Collegium Trilingue to the ancient languages, and in the next few days probably played his part among the 'friends' who persuaded Erasmus to reply in print.[11] The *Apologia* may not have been 'thrown off in a couple of days,' as its author claimed, but it cannot have taken much longer since Erasmus had only heard of the attack when he returned from Mechelen some time after 21 March, and his reply was completed on the twenty-eighth.[12] Symptoms of hasty composition abound throughout the text: in the vague citations of chapters 7 and 49, the contorted language of 96, in the paraphrases or translated quotations of 42, where I suspect Erasmus was not only bluffing but cheating. His agreement that Latomus had written 'with very little venom,' and his dismissal of his own riposte as 'an answer that might be thought no answer at all,' both contrast strongly with the nagging resentment which he had shown against

Lefèvre during the previous year. 'My apologia has now been printed four times,' he had remarked with some satisfaction on 6 March 1518, wondering why Lefèvre would neither admit defeat nor carry the argument further. The *Apologia in Latomum* was printed once by Thibault in Antwerp shortly after its completion on 28 March, and once by Froben in May of the same year. Then it had to wait for the posthumous edition of Erasmus' complete works in 1542. The present translation is based on a collation of that text with LB IX 79–106. The author's laments in his introduction and final chapter about the time wasted on 'such dreary stuff' are consistent with his more private comments.[13]

But it would be a grave error to dismiss this whole affair as a controversy without significance or consequence. The gradual heightening of tension in Louvain reveals how sensitive a university could be in its reaction to the experience of other centres, and how easily different disputes could become linked to the same issue. The suspicion of the Collegium Trilingue, and the excitement over the confrontation between Luther, Eck, and Karlstadt, were distinct developments in separate cities: but they fed off each other. Erasmus, as we have noticed, completed his *Apologia* on 28 March 1518. His first personal letter from Luther carried the same date, and must have arrived while the debate in Louvain was still alive.[14] When Erasmus had lost interest in it, his friend Wilhelm Nesen returned to the fray with a blistering *Dialogus bilingium et trilinguium*, which he published in July. In 1520 Adrianus published the speech he had pronounced on 21 March of the previous year: but the printer was Johann Grunenberg of Wittenberg. Adrianus had left the Collegium Trilingue for the Lutheran centre in November 1519. Latomus took the matter seriously enough to compose an *Antapologia*: and in due course he proceeded from his attack on the three ancient languages to write in defence of the power of the pope and against the errors of Luther, ending his life in 1544 as a pillar of the established church.[15]

ML

APOLOGY OF DESIDERIUS ERASMUS,
REFUTING RUMOURS AND SUSPICIONS
WHICH VARIOUS CRITICS HAVE DRAWN
FROM THE DRAMATIC DIALOGUE
WRITTEN BY JACOBUS LATOMUS,
AUTHORIZED TEACHER OF SACRED THEOLOGY

BOOK 1

As my life in this world ebbs away, gentle reader, I had decided to put it
to more sparing and careful use. But now I am flung off course and driven
to the point where I have to find time to refute the slanders heaped on me
by some of my enemies. In fact I can understand Hercules' problem with
that hydra in the Lernaean swamp, with several other heads squirming up
whenever he cut one off.[1] In recent days one Jacobus Latomus, a theologian,
has brought out a dialogue on the three [scriptural] languages and on the
approach to theological studies. In this work he differs from me on a
number of points. But so ready is the human mind to believe the worst of
everyone that men are treating his book like a slanderous pamphlet which
the writer meant for me, while disguising his real target.

In fact Latomus has behaved like the gladiator with the net, telling his
opponent 'It's not you I'm after, it's the fish on your helmet.'[2] I must
confess that I was in two minds whether to turn my back on this kind of
gossip, which breaks out at random in human society and often dies away
of its own accord, or to spend a few hours dealing with the problem,
especially since it was clear that Latomus' book offered a chance for many
busybodies to pick quarrels, and was fouling the honest pursuit of learning.
The first idea appealed to me. But my friends approved the second, and I
am obeying them to the point of picking out and replying to the few
passages which seem most likely to breed suspicion. I shall not be using
fictitious characters for my task, nor shall I make a show of great names, as
Latomus did. Such dreary stuff as this seems to me unfit for dedication to
eminent patrons. This will be a straight talk to the honest reader. To lie, as
it were, in ambush, and wing your man so that he feels the wound but has
no chance to defend himself, is the sort of attack that only the blackest
criminal would use. Latomus' own character, or his profession as a
theologian, ought to have stopped him from laying himself open to this sort
of charge, especially as I have given him no reason to change the friendly

association which we formed some time ago. But I shall let the bare facts make the issue quite clear.[3]

1   Who could fail to see that even what he says in the introduction to his work does not fit me? He claims, for example, that some rely so heavily on particular learned disciplines that they despise others whose worth has been tried by tradition and proved by long experience, and that they do so without concealment, in books which are published and widely distributed. I confess that if there is any aim which I have set myself, it is to link linguistic skills, elegant expression, and a knowledge of ancient authors with the traditional methods of study. But I have always stopped short of despising any subject, whether traditional or otherwise. Sometimes I have dropped hints of what I wished to be changed or added in certain areas. But let them cite a single person whom my words have called from the subject which he had made his own. I shall show how I have urged those who were ready to give up to persevere instead.

2   His next point, a general attack on all who criticize the scholastic exercises followed in our universities and spurn those who teach them for their dreary, humdrum style of speaking, applies to me still less. I ask you, is a person criticizing academic exercises when he asks that they be conducted with restraint, and with a view to improving knowledge and behaviour rather than making money and showing off? Or is he despising established teachers when he declares that there is much in their work which is worth reading? Or does disagreeing with them here and there amount to rejection, when they disagree with one another and when those who lean particularly towards the modern authors allow themselves to differ both from still more recent and from earlier writers? Is it rejecting modern writers, to advise reading the ancients as well? Or are they asking me to urge readers to turn to Scotus and Holcot as models of literary elegance?[4]

3   What about this 'insult to worthy men' or this 'inevitable corruption of youth' which Latomus stresses?[5] Where in my writings do I demolish so much evil that I damage what good remains, or sweep away so much chaff that I take the grain with it? Perhaps they are calling 'good, healthy stuff,' the blemishes which I have tried to remove from some books. I suppose there are men who find it natural to career off madly to the opposite extreme when they are trying to come to the aid of some subject which has fallen out of fashion. If a person so hates all-out war that he utters fearful

warnings against any form of war, he is not going to lack arguments to use or the examples of great men to guide him.

4   I do not believe that anyone could be so suspicious-minded as to think that his next sally, about Bartolus and Baldus, has anything to do with me. Latomus calls them the greatest authorities of the law – I don't know whether he is serious. I only wish they lacked nothing except refinement of expression. But I cannot follow his train of reasoning.[6]

5   You cannot deny that I have always beckoned students of theology towards the sources provided by the Holy Scriptures, and to the early commentators. I did so because I could see that many passed over these early sources completely and sunk into an old age – more often a grave – of tedious little questions. But where do I call them from their volumes of Thomas Aquinas, Scotus, Bonaventure, or Alexander?[7] Is a person calling his readers away from these writers just because he happens to prefer the ancient authorities – authorities, I might say, whom the church puts forward as its greatest champions, who were gifted with the profoundest learning and the most exquisite style, and whose holy lives are wafted to us from the pages of their books?

6   Let them cite a single passage even in some comical work of mine where I have written that time spent on authors like Scotus is time wasted. All my efforts have been directed towards helping the schools in any way that I could, not disturbing them. Surely it is clear that people who make insinuations of this kind at my expense are trying to stir up the students, the lawyers, and the theologians against me?

7   I quite agree that in my *Ratio verae theologiae* I preferred the ancient authors to the moderns as one might prefer springs to reservoirs.[8] Latomus – or at least the character he puts forward as his mouthpiece – takes the opposite view and considers the more modern writers preferable to the ancients: that is to say, he thinks that they deserve our first attention. This is how I read his meaning. In fact this is one of those questions on which Paul thinks each individual should follow his own judgment. The result will be weighed up later.[9] My view is that Latomus is too good a man even to want to use arguments like these against a friend who has deserved no such treatment, and too sensible a man to want his intellectual development to start from this sort of beginning.

8   Up to this point I have discussed a few points in his prologue, or at least

those points which seem to have aroused the suspicions of a number of readers.

9   Now I shall run quickly through the remainder of the first dialogue as well. What one is to make of the real people behind the characters in the dialogue concerns me not at all. I can see no reason why an enthusiast for languages and rhetoric should be called Peter rather than Marcolophus, why an academic theologian should be called John rather than Bartholomew, or why someone who knows no theology at all should be called Albert rather than Hannibal. Nor is it my task to identify that eloquent Nestor, who holds pride of place in this dialogue and who is thought so important that everything he says is repeated like the response of an oracle. The passages where John is represented arguing with Peter read more like farce than serious discussion.[10]

10   But I must say that the form usually observed at the beginning of a comedy, as well as a dialogue, seems to have slipped from the author's mind, for he presents Peter, who is supposed to be devoted to rhetoric, speaking very poor Latin. 'From now on he is sure to be leaving all else aside and getting on with this alone,' writes Latomus for what should have been 'he is sure to be doing this.' Even those who are orators and nothing else are not so stupid as he makes Peter out to be. They would never lack an answer to this sort of quibbling.[11]

11   Latomus scores a cheap point off a citation which is made from the papal decrees but which is not in fact a decree, merely the opinion of a priest of particular influence – Augustine, to be sure. It's as though we were not allowed to cite an incident contained in the Life of a particular pope or emperor as if it came from the 'Lives of the Popes and Emperors': or as if the passage in the preface to the Life of Alexander which reads 'or in the circumstances which followed Alexander's death' could not properly be said to come from the 'Life' of Alexander. The whole work concerned carries the title 'Decrees of the Popes,' unless we prefer to call it *Decretum*, as some do. What is to stop us calling the opinion of Ambrose or Augustine or Jerome *decretum* when the opinions of the philosophers are called *dogmata* – that is, 'conclusions'?[12]

12   Peter in fact corrects his quotation rather neatly in the dialogue: 'I meant to say,' he adds, 'that this view of Augustine's has found its way into canon law and, as the crude expression has it, become sanctioned.' Now the opinion of Augustine carries a good deal of weight even with those who

feel that nothing is lacking in more recent writers. Augustine[13] is by no means on his own when he says that a knowledge of languages contributes greatly to the understanding of Holy Scripture, and he makes this point on several occasion. So why does this dialogue attach so little importance to this when it allows so much to some nameless old man?

13   It may be true, as Panormitanus claims, that this work has never been formally adopted by a pope or a general council. The fact remains that it has passed into widespread use in universities throughout the world. Some theologians attach such importance to it that when I was working on my edition of Jerome, they seriously advised me not to change or delete any passage of his works which had been cited by Gratian in his *Decretum*.[14] Yet it hardly shows the judgment we would expect of a theologian to say that Augustine wrote without error when he takes our side, but to hold that we should read him critically and take little notice of his opinion when he disagrees.

14   John is being entirely frivolous when he says 'According to the spirit of the decree on the training and hiring, at public expense, of teachers in the three scriptural languages, as passed at the Council of Vienne by Clement V, we ought to be hiring Goths, Vandals, even teachers from darkest Africa.' At that time discussion was turning towards races which ruled wide territories but were too far from understanding our literature to have any idea of Christian doctrine.[15] In fact both the Goths and the Vandals were already Christians like ourselves. But if the Goths, Vandals, and Danes had at that moment been strangers to the teaching of the Gospels perhaps it would not have been wholly ridiculous to learn their languages to see if verbal contact could lead them to Christ. That would have been our duty, if we really were as eager to spread the Christian faith as we like to make out. But let us grant that no exact provision is made in that decree for the Greek and Latin languages: if it is necessary to learn strange languages in order to spread Christ's teaching, it must be far more necessary to learn Greek, Latin, and Hebrew in order to understand that teaching. You cannot spread what you do not understand. What point was there in making special provision for Greek and Latin at a time when the knowledge of both was quite widespread? I am not in the least impressed by the amendment in which Greek was struck out and Arabic substituted. Nor shall I make an issue of Hebrew and Chaldaean being related languages, in both of which the books of the Old Testament survive, both therefore essential not only for preaching Christ among foreign nations, but for understanding the Scriptures ourselves. Perhaps the same point could be made about Arabic.

Finally, Pope Clement's decree does not contain the demand that our books should be translated into the languages of these other nations – that is a point that John is put forward to make on his own account. To conclude – what Peter has to say about learning languages during the course of this exchange may also apply to me. In more than one place I have urged aspirants to true learning towards the study of language and so far I feel neither shame nor regret for the advice I gave.

15 It is just possible that someone might think the silly little quip that follows – the one about the three languages sanctified by their inscription on the cross of Christ – was aimed in my direction. In my *Annotations on the New Testament* I did write that these three languages should be close to the hearts of all Christians because they were the only ones sanctified on the cross of Our Lord Jesus Christ.[16] I do not remember saying anything about his blood. And to tell the truth, I was ashamed of the joke that Latomus brings in at this point about the notice's being placed above the cross and therefore incapable of being sprinkled by the blood of Christ. As though something pinned at the top of the cross could not have been sprinkled by his blood! The Greek does not in any case say 'above the cross' but 'on the cross' – just as hairs are said to be 'on the head' or 'on top of it.'

16 I prefer not to mention those silly comedian's jokes of his about soldiers' lances and about *all* languages being sanctified on the cross. It's not even worth the trouble of refuting them. If we really think it is ridiculous to say that three languages were sanctified on the Lord's cross, then in my view we must start by laughing at a man who is by no means ridiculous and who made the point before I did. And we must laugh at the faith of Christians who revere this notice in the three languages wherever they see it depicted. If the wood of the cross is said to have been sanctified by the touch of that holy body, what is to prevent us from calling the notice, which formed part of the cross, every bit as sacred? It does not follow that any bit of wood must be thought sacred just because our Lord's cross was wooden. Nor can one apply the same argument to those pikes which tear the innards out of innocent men today, as to the languages which enshrine the mysteries of Holy Scripture. If my restraint as a Christian did not hold me back, I might at this point say how unseemly it is for a mere beginner in sacred theology to play stupid word-games of this kind in a book by which the beginner in genuine theological studies is shaped. In the meantime I sometimes wonder what happened to that mild old gentleman who could not bear people making fun of a man even if he made a serious mistake. When our present author draws no distinction between these three

languages and others, he differs greatly from St Hilary who thinks them the chosen and sacred medium for preaching God's word and the coming of his kingdom. He takes this view just because Pilate wrote 'Jesus Christ, King of the Jews' in these languages.[17]

17   Those who feel that the next point has some connection with me have more excuse for their opinion, even if it is mistaken. In my *Ratio verae theologiae*, I urged students of the subject to apply themselves to languages. To prevent anyone from withdrawing in a fit of despair, I add that in a few years it is possible to learn enough of the languages concerned to exercise one's own judgment, first and foremost because the language of the Scriptures is simple and straightforward as far as its vocabulary is concerned, second because we get a good deal of help from the hard work of other scholars. Finally I say that, given an adequate teacher and a mind that is eager to learn, two languages, Latin and Greek, can be learned more quickly than Latin alone. Latomus' Albert takes this point up to make some silly quip about having spent seven years studying Latin and now needing the same to learn Greek. It's as though it were not enough for a young man to learn the basic principles of Latin and Greek speech from the writers of those two languages before his eighteenth year: as though there were still not ample time for him to work clear through his theology afterwards; or as though St Augustine, and St Ambrose too, had not turned to theology far later in life than that.[18] Augustine, certainly, we credit with a perfect knowledge of theology. For the moment I shall pass over the fact that not all are born to be theologians anyway. Some are better suited to literary studies, some to other disciplines. I do not expect a knowledge of languages from all theologians, but at least from those who are capable of achieving it. Let the rest rely on other people's work, so far as I am concerned, so long as they do not make malicious attacks on those who are luckier than they are. Meanwhile, I'm not even letting it enter my head that some labour-saving devices only waste time, and that the worker who spends a few hours getting his tools ready often takes no longer to finish the job than the man who buckles down to it straight away, but without preparing them properly.

18   For Latomus takes it as read that in learning languages we shall know nothing of the material we are going to be discussing, granted that nothing worth knowing can be learned from Homer, Pindar, Theocritus, Hesiod, Euripides, Sophocles, Herodotus, Thucydides, Xenophon, Demosthenes, Plutarch, and Lucian. Well – will you learn nothing if your study of Greek involves the Greek texts of Aristotle and his commentators? Yet some of our

contemporaries guard his reputation as 'the most learned philosopher' so jealously and commend him so highly – as if anyone who denied him that title were stark mad – that one feels surprised that they stop short of calling him 'the holiest philosopher' as well. Do you learn nothing when you read the Gospels or the Acts of the Apostles? Were you to read them in Greek, wouldn't you learn something of substance along with the language? The same point could be made about Chrysostom, Basil, and the other Greek commentators.[19] If a doctor happens to read Hippocrates and Galen in Greek, will he learn nothing but the language?[20] And such are the changes in human fashions that a time may come when no one lectures publicly in the schools on Aristotle, Galen, or Hippocrates unless he uses the Greek text. If that should happen I don't suppose the students would come off any worse than they do now, when their teachers know neither Greek nor Latin and proclaim their views with greater obstinacy, the less judgment they show.

19   There are those who think that anything derived from Cicero or Theodorus Gaza cannot miss a trick. Now Gaza may have been a great man, but he seems a rather unsuitable person to pass judgment on St Jerome's language. I appear to have said something of the kind in my Life of Jerome. Albert in the dialogue – whoever he may be – was perhaps taking up this point. If that is so, he failed to notice that in the passage concerned I am not talking about correct linguistic usage but about the most fluent and effective style of diction, which is particularly difficult to judge. Anyone who cares to reread the passage will find that what I say is true. I am not rejecting Gaza's view just because Gaza as a Greek could not pronounce with any assurance about the phrasing of a language that was not his, but even more so because, being Greek-born, he took an unfairly critical view of Latin writers.[21] He was especially hard on Cicero, for instance, as Greeks have always tended to be. Now would I ever expect an aspiring theologian to absorb enough Greek to sit in judgment on the styles of Aeschines and Demosthenes, or Lysias and Isocrates? Not everyone who talks Latin automatically becomes 'an heir of Cicero' – only someone who can copy Cicero's expression. This line of reasoning demolishes the point that Latomus adds about Cicero and his faulty judgment of Greek style. Anyway, nobody could think this applies to me, for so far as I know I have not touched the subject in any of my work.

20   It is not my task to discuss whether lawyers, doctors, and mathematicians need to know Greek literature, and this is not the place to open the question. But it is beyond doubt that those involved in teaching

these subjects have hitherto made some horrible blunders and made them
largely through their ignorance of Greek writings. Let us grant that a man
who does not understand the meaning of the word 'therapy' or the title of
the book he is expounding may still know how to cure his patients. When
Galen's *Therapeutics* are widely referred to as his *Therapeutic*,[22] it may not
matter, but it is still bad taste and it undermines the confidence felt in a
teacher by his fellow scholars. Misuse of language does not stop being
horrible just because we're used to it. If you look at the facts, it is just as
ridiculous to say 'therapeutic' for 'therapeutics' as to say 'tablet' for 'table'
or 'caddie' for 'candle.'

21   If we find ugly words in papal letters or briefs we should tolerate them
rather than approve them. We must not attach such importance to their
presence that we rush out and hire someone to teach us the same awful
language. In fact, in the first book of the *Decretals*, in the section 'On
rescripts' and the chapter 'At audience,' specific warning was given that
letters in which an obvious vulgarism or faulty grammar could be found
must be considered suspicious, perhaps tampered with or forged.[23] A few
years ago a number of scholars used to receive a salary from the papal
treasury for removing vulgarisms from papal letters. But suppose we do
have to speak in vulgarisms just because papal briefs and rescripts contain
a number of words derived from common usage rather than classical Latin:
on that basis there would be a far stronger argument for learning the
languages of Greece and Rome, as papal letters are almost entirely in Latin
and contain a good deal of Greek as well.

22   It may be madness to argue that anything written in Latin or Greek is
automatically sacred. But it's a far more acute form of madness to declare
anything sacred just because it is barbarous and ungrammatical. Who would
deny that a good law can be written in barbarous language? After all, the
Gospels are widely read in French and German. But being barbarously
written does not make a law good, and it is hardly proper for a scholar to
speak ungrammatically among other scholars. Augustine excuses bad
grammar, but only among the lower classes who in his time talked Latin in
any sort of way. And he does not excuse it in all circumstances, but only
when an expression which is poor Latin happens to be clearer, or to be
without ambiguity. And that excuse was not extended to those who write
books, or address scholars. Jerome actually castigates the flaws in their
language in his discussion of the substance of the faith against Rufinus and
Jovinian. How can they be trusted to judge matters of importance, he asks,
when they are so slack and unthinking in their use of language?[24]

23   I cannot wholly disagree with the suggestion of John, when he taunts our idleness in failing to hire someone to remove whatever Greek words have found their way into civil law, medical texts, or theology, and write in the Latin terms instead. But back will come the nagging feeling that he himself introduced a moment ago: we are not allowed to change papal bulls in any way and they, too, contain a number of Greek words. I think we could say the same about the order of service for the mass, as they call it, in which quite a few Greek phrases are declaimed. Our mercenary little Greek will not dare to change them in case we criticize 'Kyrie eleison, Christe eleison.' Suppose the rest of the world simply refuses to take it on trust from our little Greek factotum, and prefers to use its own eyes rather than those of other people? Or suppose our man knows Greek but has not the faintest idea what the words are describing? It is a general rule that understanding a language depends on knowing the objects to which it refers. No one will translate medical texts correctly if he knows no medicine but only Latin and Greek. Nor is a mere knowledge of language enough to let you translate Ptolemy or Euclid correctly. Suppose there are some words our translator does not understand? Suppose some have different meanings, or cannot be rendered by a simple equivalent? Suppose there are some words our translator does not understand? Suppose some have a special connotation, which cannot be conveyed into another language? Suppose some readers – doctors in particular – have become accustomed to the Greek words all their lives and are not prepared, at an advanced age, to learn new terms? Suppose the Latin word proves to be more difficult than the Greek? That often happens with technical terms. Last of all, what is to happen if the Latin words which our hired translator has introduced become corrupted, and the little Greek is not at hand to advise? Suppose you are dealing with Greek words such as 'philosophia,' 'techne,' 'elephas,' 'rhinoceros,' 'platanus,' and three hundred thousand others of the same kind which many centuries of common usage have naturalized within our Latin vocabulary: if you are quite ignorant of Greek you cannot even understand their meaning completely. There is no need to labour this point by citing more evidence, when Latomus' little pamphlet provides more than enough examples. He really beats the academics at their own game when he offers us 'limping' for 'at leisure' and 'tiles' for 'skills,' besides quite a few others of the same kind. It's impossible to ignore them, unless perhaps we think the exact pronunciation or spelling of a single word is unimportant, though the whole sense of a passage often turns on the way one single syllable is written.[25]

24   I must confess that I read the remainder of the debate with some

amusement. Our author tries to outdo Socrates' dialectical method by showing that, to understand a craft, one does not have to understand the language in which it was first set out. We may all need shoes, but that does not mean that we must all learn to be cobblers. Well, I suppose no one forces anybody else to become a baker, a cobbler, or a blacksmith. But at least no one forces these craftsmen to leave their country, as certain parties have tried to drive the whole linguistic profession from the university here in Louvain.[26]

25   I do not fully understand what he means by his next point, which deals with mathematics, metaphysics, and music. Perhaps he feels that these are 'crafts' and as necessary to everyone as those of the baker and the tailor.

26   From these subjects we go rolling on to painting, construction, and gunnery. The train of reasoning assumes that knowing what words the German or Spanish inventor normally used to describe the tools of his trade in his own language is relevant to understanding the craft itself. Now let us suppose that the rules of gunnery had been laid down in Greek, that it had as many terms in that language mixed into its vocabulary as music and medicine have, that its importance was as great, and its practice as widespread as those of medicine or theology. Finally, let us assume that the books which deal with that craft contained as many corrupt passages, doubtful readings, gaps in the text, and incomprehensible sections as the books we have to consult. Were all this true, I have no doubt that specialists in gunnery would be taking to Greek under the approving eye of their greatest expert Johann Poppenruyter.[27] Yet we theologians not only refuse to take up Greek – we try to have it hissed out of the lecture-rooms. Meantime, I shall not try to pursue the kind of inappropriate comparison that Latomus' character John uses in his Socratic flights. The fact is that even a dumb person could learn painting or gunnery: that cannot be said of philosophy or theology. If we think that explaining the sacred texts is important to theology, if we judge it a sign of holiness to show wisdom in revealing the hidden mysteries of the Scriptures, which often lurk behind the formation of the very letters, then we must admit that no single subject is more dependent on languages than theology. What point is there in following the argument further? It may be possible to deny that, since the time of those careful early commentators, many passages have been restored to their true form through reference to the Greek, though right up to that moment the books in circulation contained corrupt passages. And someone may prove me wrong if I claim that many sections which until now have puzzled commentators of the highest repute, have now been fully explained,

and that light has been shed on many more which were once shrouded in obscurity. If such views can be sustained, I shall admit that aspiring theologians are right to shun the study of the Greek language.

27   As far as medicine is concerned, anyone who wishes should reckon with the contribution of Niccolò Leoniceno, Ambrogio Leoni, Guillaume Cop and Thomas Linacre, who are unquestioned leaders of this profession in our time.[28]

28   Now let us grant that Accursius shows a deeper knowledge of the law than Poliziano, who never lectured on the subject, or than Budé, who has chosen to wander through every problem that different writers and subjects could put in his way rather than devote his energies to one field.[29] What is to stop some expert in both the classical languages appearing and showing a legal sense that is sharper than those of Bartolus and Baldus? If you wish, I could produce one or two lawyers who would find it easy to point out the numerous passages in which those two leading champions of their profession went madly and hideously astray. Lastly, we ought at least to follow the example of politeness which the lawyers have set us. They may attach the greatest importance to their Bartolus, but they are still grateful to Poliziano for helping them to understand some points more accurately. They do not call Budé to account just because he pointed to certain passages which until his time had been misunderstood and misread by lecturers in the law.

29   If the courts are so degenerate that nothing except the outlandish is accepted there, then that is an indictment of contemporary taste, not a proof that Greek and Latin have no use. If the world comes to its senses again, these droves of procurators and advocates, who now find themselves in such demand that their pockets are lined with gold, may yet be wondering where to find their next meal. The same could well be true of doctors and theologians. In the times of Plato and Cicero no great account was taken of advocates. Now they rule the roost. Perhaps human affairs will take a turn that casts them into obscurity again. Yet I must say that there are some lawyers – and not the least prominent either – who make it their habit and their pride to link Greek and Latin literature with the normal pursuits of their profession.[30]

When our two-faced juggler of words winds up his next syllogism, surely any reader could see that he is being frivolous? 'Every person, without exception, is obliged to obey the law of Christ: no one can understand that law unless he understands Greek and Hebrew; therefore everyone in the world must learn Greek and Hebrew.' This is to assume that there is no difference between the understanding of Christian law which we might expect of an ordinary layman, and the knowledge we should demand of a theologian who must pore over the sacred texts. It is to assume that the principles sufficient for the salvation of a person's soul cannot be given to him by word of mouth. As I read through some of the discussions which Latomus puts into the mouths of Peter and John, I couldn't help being reminded of that quip from Demonax – 'One of them's milking a billy-goat, and the other's trying to catch it in a sieve.'[31]

30 When Lorenzo Valla expresses amazement that any theologian should lecture on, or undertake to discuss the Holy Scriptures without a knowledge of languages, he is not expressing an opinion about each and every theologian, but about the perfect theologian. He is not referring to every commentator, but to the kind of man who believes himself capable of unravelling every single problem.[32] Our more modern scholars do this without stumbling over a syllable: even those of the ancients who were expert linguists did not dare to promise such a thing. In their works they do not assert, so much as probe and discuss. They admit that they cannot find the solution which they seek. Their knowledge of language at least gives them the advantage of feeling uneasy and seeing the difficulties in a passage. I must say that I find a suspicion of arrogance in the very title 'theologian' – one who explains the divine – when those who expound the wisdom of this world have preferred to be called 'philosophers' – seekers of wisdom – rather than 'wise men.' No one who wishes to plead for Aquinas, Remigius, Nicholas of Lyra, or Hugh of St Victor, should make the mistake of confusing their situation with that of Chrysostom, as John does at this point in the dialogue. He should rather defend them against the charge of making dogmatic assertions on points which they did not understand and falling into obvious error because of their imperfect knowledge of Greek. If that is not possible, what point is there in splitting hairs about corrupt texts of Greek or Hebrew writings? No one discounts commentators because they lack the support of linguistic knowledge: but we discount those who remain committed to this narrow circle of recent authorities and treat their views like the responses of an oracle, in spite of the general agreement that they are adrift on many points. Who would deny that it is possible to make some correct comment on the Holy Scriptures, even if the writer knows no language except Gaelic? But this at least we owe to the ancient linguists, that their successors do not make nearly as many blunders as they would have done if they had been obliged to rely on their own wits. This is not the place to raise the question of St Matthew's

Gospel being written first in Hebrew: it seems more likely to me that it was written in Greek. But I realize that St Jerome says in a number of passages that he has seen such a [Hebrew] manuscript, though he never establishes the point by quoting references. There are many passages in Matthew where corroboration through reference to the original [Hebrew] would have been desirable. Jerome himself considers that there are some points in the Greek manuscript where words have been left out and others where they have been added. He makes frequent references to a 'Gospel of the Nazarenes' and his quotations are always quite different from those in our Gospel. Origen does the same. At one point Jerome writes that the Gospel which is entitled 'Of St Matthew' by the Nazarenes appears to be the archetype for these quotations. We shall discuss later what reply we can give to the information which Jerome provided in his list of ecclesiastical writers.

31   But suppose we grant that this Gospel was written in Hebrew, and further grant that it still existed in Chrysostom's time – surely that does not automatically put Chrysostom on the same level as Aquinas and Remigius? On this reckoning Chrysostom surely prevails, first because even if he did not draw his information from the spring itself, he definitely drew it from the nearest pool: second because he was assisted by the commentaries of Origen, who knew Hebrew, and by those of innumerable other Greeks. Lastly, to put them all on a level, it is quite clear that Remigius and the moderns went wrong in their handling of the language, and it is not clear that Chrysostom did anything of the kind. In fact we have been able to correct their mistakes from his work. By all means allow for the possibility that Chrysostom slipped up here and there in his commentaries: the error cannot be detected because the material needed to check it is not in existence. Besides it is quite possible that if he had known Hebrew and consulted the original, he would have given different and perhaps fuller explanations than some of those which he offers.[33]

32   I think we should be lenient to the Greek scholars who expounded the books of the Old Testament to us without a knowledge of Hebrew literature. They did the best they could. The most learned of them all did not feel satisfied with himself until he had turned, at an advanced age, to learning Hebrew and Chaldaean. And even those who did not have time to learn those languages had Jews present to advise them and referred to the books of men who knew Hebrew. At no point do they consider it unimportant whether a commentator knew his languages or not. Yet there are times when Latomus' John – whoever he is – pleads the cause of the Greek commentators and Hilary so eloquently that he leaves Jerome without

defence. Yet if they were correct in thinking that there was no point in looking beyond the Greek version of the Septuagint, then Jerome, whose influence in this field has been enormous, was in fact a fool.[34] He sweated and spent sleepless nights to give us an Old Testament based on the Hebrew sources. He was sure that they preserve the correct text. He openly attacked the version of the Septuagint, sometimes calling it a tissue of lies, pruning away many of its readings, adding many others, and changing the context of many more. Critics like Latomus are perhaps set on rejecting the example of Origen even though, setting aside some of his opinions, there is no authority whom I consider more weighty. And if Jerome was rash to disagree with the Septuagint in following the Hebrew texts, then why does the church of Rome adopt his view? I won't leave the way open to quibbling by saying that it always does so: but it certainly accepts those contained in a number of his books.[35]

33 Now if the Jews tampered with their own texts after the time of Christ, then Jerome was definitely unwise to use those texts as sources for his own corrections to the Old Testament. So what, one wonders, did the church have in mind when it attached such weight to the corrections which he carried out? Jerome may complain at times that some books have been corrupted by the shameless impiety of the Jews: but the damage was not so serious as to scare him off using old and carefully corrected manuscripts to emend passages which the Septuagint had rendered wrongly.

34 Latomus is incorrect in quoting Chrysostom's fifth homily on St Matthew as evidence of this 'Jewish impiety': Chrysostom is not denouncing the Hebrew texts, but some of the commentators – Symmachus, Theodotion and Aquila, as far as I remember. He prefers to follow the Septuagint in this instance.[36] Though those translators had not had the chance to know Christ, they seem at least to have given a straightforward version of what they could understand. On the other hand he is most suspicious of the three commentators who clung obstinately to their Jewish prejudices even after they had heard Christ's gospel preached. It was as though their hatred of the Christian faith and their attachment to Judaism made them want to keep some of the mysteries hidden from us, and positively try to render some passages incorrectly. At this point Chrysostom raises the issue of the Hebrew word 'aalma,' which the Septuagint rendered as 'virgin.' But others cited the more recent commentators who translated the word 'girl' rather than 'virgin.' What is at issue here is plainly not the accuracy of the Hebrew manuscripts but the faith of the commentators themselves. It is hardly

surprising to find Chrysostom preferring the Septuagint to commentators whom he suspects of impiety. I think he would have been just as ready to demote the Septuagint if he had been dealing with a scholar of sound beliefs and a good knowledge of scriptural language, who had given us an Old Testament that was based on a comparison of accurate manuscripts. And this is exactly what Jerome did for us Latins. If somebody wants to ban all correction from the Scriptures in case the church should appear to have made a single mistake, then I should like him to answer the following questions for me. Did the church have an edition of the New Testament before Jerome produced his corrected version? If there were no mistakes in the earlier edition, then why did Pope Damasus order a revised edition to be prepared? If there were such mistakes, then it follows that the church was using a version that could be improved. I would prefer not to speak of actual errors it may have contained. I feel it is enough to say that the church does not err on matters which are necessary to our salvation. But over a thousand years it has taken up a definite stand on many issues which used to be argued from various points of view as matters of dispute. We now have quite a few articles of faith which were unknown to our forebears: so what is to prevent advances being made on the knowledge of the early critics of biblical scholarship as well? The man who makes such advances does not follow any manuscripts which happen to come into his hands, nor does he stick to one only. He makes a selection. Nor does he rely only on the comparison of his manuscript authorities: he carries out careful research among the Greek and Latin commentators to find what the most reputable authorities have said about a passage, how they have explained it, what measure of agreement there is between them. And even then he does not deny any man's right to his own view unless the error is so obvious that it would be shameful to turn his back on it. Origen never dared to 'correct' the New Testament, nor did I remove a single letter from the accepted texts. He suggested and shared his conjectures. I suggested conjectures or relied on the most trustworthy authorities. But this is a matter which I shall discuss at greater length and at a more appropriate moment.

35   But even if we concede that the Greek and Hebrew manuscripts are as corrupt as our own, does that automatically deny us all hope of making good the damage which we find in our texts? Does it not often happen that, when several manuscripts are faulty but do not contain the same faults, the true, authentic reading can be found by comparing those faults to one another? There are mistakes in the books of Augustine, Cyprian,[37] Peter Lombard, Scotus, and Nicholas of Lyra: yet we use our judgment and hunt down the theological truths even from these flawed texts.

36   When Latomus cites that passage from the fourteenth chapter of the First Epistle of Paul to the Corinthians he is neither going against my method nor adding much to his own. In my note I do not condemn the reading contained in our manuscripts. I only try to reveal the doubt over that reading which was evidently felt by the very earliest commentators. I translate the words which appeared without variant in the Greek manuscripts which I saw and in accordance with Theophylactus' interpretation and the Greek scholia. But I mention in my notes that Ambrose had a different text, and from his Latin version I guess that his Greek text read 'he will not know' instead of 'let him not know.' Origen in his turn seems to have read 'is not known,' for his translator turns the passage, 'he who does not know this, is not known.' It may be: but on that occasion I had taken on the job of correcting Latin texts and translating the Greek but not correcting them – especially where they agreed and where their reading was supported by commentators.[38]

37   In the dialogue John finally admits that those who try to make the Scriptures as free from error as possible are doing a useful job. He accepts the advice of Jerome and Augustine, that our Latin texts be compared to the Greek and Hebrew books for correction: but he accepts it with the reservation that this work is in the hands of men, and therefore liable to error; it relies on conjectures, not rigorous proofs. I agree that emendation is a method for mere men – but they are remarkable men. I agree that it proceeds by conjecture – but that cannot be otherwise. And think, too, of the number of different factors that can be brought to bear – agreement among the Greek texts, the opinion of the early commentators, the oldest Latin manuscripts and the views of the leaders of our faith, even the sense of the passage itself and the way it fits into its context. Surely, when all these different elements combine, the conjecture becomes much more of a probability? Even if this rule is not foolproof we shall have to cling eagerly to it until our critics can give us a better one. Perhaps they are going to remind us of the ultimate safeguards of the final revelation: but if it comes to that and our own resources let us down, I feel quite confident that such a revelation will not be denied to us Christians.

38   As for Latomus saying that 'those who strive to do useful work in correcting Latin texts admit, etc' – I do not, indeed cannot, deny that these are my words. There are several passages in my *Annotations* where I prefer the accepted Latin reading to that which we find in the Greek manuscripts today. This does not make it any less true to say that there are numerous

places in our texts where the sense has either been restored, or explained, by reference to the Greek versions.

39   Readers clearly think that the next argument is pointed at me. In my *Ratio verae theologiae* I try to show that a knowledge of languages is valuable simply because there are some words whose precise meaning and connotation cannot be conveyed by a translator unless he embarks on a lengthy paraphrase. The point is too obvious to be denied. So John works his way round it with one of his usual plays on words. 'So,' he says, 'translators are making no progress and achieving nothing; they are hoodwinking us by trying to carry out a task which is impossible.' I suppose he is arguing that all the words of a foreign language have a special shade of meaning which can never be reproduced: or that it is quite useless for anyone to give us a general outline of the whole argument, to translate certain passages as best he can rather than as well as he would have liked, and then leave the searching critic to turn to the sources and work out the rest of the information for himself. Surely he cannot think that any translator would be conceited enough to promise that his work will be flawless? It is simply not true to say that someone is hoodwinking us when he is not even promising to carry out the impossible. Or were Jerome and Augustine wasting their time because they found some points of difficulty which they could not resolve?

40   I do not see what his next point has to do with me at all. I never wrote that a man who knows his languages has an immediate understanding of the mysteries of Holy Scripture. I only wrote that languages are a great help in reaching that knowledge to which, as I showed, many factors besides language must also contribute. Of course a linguist does not automatically acquire an intimate grasp of the divine mysteries: but it is equally true that, other things being equal, a man without knowledge of languages will be so much further from understanding those mysteries.

41   It is not my task to explain where Peter Lombard discovered the proposition that the divine essence neither comes into being nor brings anything else into being. If he was the first to see that point, it does not follow that he found it in the words of Holy Scripture. If nothing else, it could be that some angel or other revealed the matter to him, for not every mystery hangs on the meaning of a word. But at least it is certain that some do. The mistakes made by great theologians who either did not know their sources or failed to consult them are quite enough to prove that point.[39]

42   What follows next may be thought by some readers to apply to me, for in my *Ratio verae theologiae* I do argue that a great part of theological learning depends on the piety of the individual. Piety does not automatically make a man a theologian in the sense that we use that word: but one who does not love what he reads and says cannot truly be a theologian. As Plato says, 'A man who is on fire with the love of wisdom is neither totally without wisdom, nor completely in control of it.' Long before our time Augustine taught us to approach the study of sacred literature with a mind as pure and as free from vice as it could possibly be. Paul numbers that power of prophecy which enables us to expound the Scriptures and their mysteries as one of the gifts of the Holy Spirit.[40] Understanding the mystic texts with your mind is not enough: you must understand them with your soul as well. I cannot convince myself that the divine wisdom makes its way into a heart which is blotched with vices and foul lusts, especially when I read, 'Wisdom will not enter an evil soul, nor will it dwell in a body which is a slave to sin.'[41] Orators agree on the definition of one of their number as 'a good man, skilled in speaking.' So why should we be dissatisfied with 'A theologian is a pious man, skilled in speaking of the divine mysteries,' or 'Theology is piety linked to skill in speaking of the divine'? If we accept these definitions, then of course piety must form part of theology. According to Quintilian 'A man who is not ablaze himself will never set others afire, nor will one who does not feel grief himself succeed in arousing it in others.'[42] So a theologian who has not felt the touch of the spirit does not touch others with his words. He does not inspire others, unless he is himself inspired. To make my feelings perfectly clear, it does not seem to me to be the mark of a theologian to discuss the divine mysteries in an objective, unemotional way. But our verbal acrobat argues that theology is no more than an instrument or a vehicle to help a man on his way to some destination called 'piety.' Once he has reached it, he has no further need of the instrument.

43   The consequence of Latomus' view must be that knowledge of the Scriptures is useless to the unholy and unnecessary to the holy who, having reached their destined goal of piety, have no need of the means to proceed further. Yet theology is a necessity for the unholy as a cure for their unholiness, and a boon for the holy because it cherishes and increases their holiness until it reaches perfection. Meantime, each of them must forget what he has left behind and, like a determined runner, press forward to what lies ahead. On the path to God it is not safe to pause. So if we must always hasten, we must always need the Holy Scriptures to carry us along. Piety, or holiness, is that love which we feel for God for his own sake, and

for our neighbour for God's sake. Nothing is loved unless it is first known and nothing is known unless it is first loved. This means that love and knowledge are born from one another, nursed by one another, and grow beside one another. Paul, I am sure, does not call Christ 'the end of the law' in the sense that Latomus wants – that through him the law is to be annulled. He means that through Christ the law is brought to fulfilment. A boy who reaches manhood may no longer be a boy, but he does not cease to be a human being. Nor, when he says that love marks the end of the law, does Paul mean that love makes the law pointless.[43] He means that through the proclamation of love the law of Moses is brought to perfection while without love it remained cold, weak, and diluted. Even if holiness of mind is not actually a part of theology but merely something which helps us towards a knowledge of theology, it still seems to me a sensible proposition to argue that holiness accounts for a good part of theology. What one loves is easier to learn. The whole expression is rather similar to the turn of phrase which we use when we say that money is the ruin of men, because it leads them to ruin, or when we call a person a disgrace to his home, because he brings disgrace upon it.

The train of reasoning that leads us to conclude that the Holy Scriptures are as useless to the wicked as they are superfluous to the pious must therefore be declared absurd. So what view shall we take of the related proposition, that languages are unnecessary too?

So far, I have glanced at the arguments in the first dialogue which some think are directed at me. It's a short enough reply if you consider the full range of replies that could be made, but still far too long if you consider what a barren discussion it is. Already I regret having to write this work: already, excellent reader, I feel sorry for you – if anyone is going to read this miserable stuff. I would rather have spent ten times as much effort on something which brought pleasure to me in writing it for the one reason that it would have brought some profit to the reader. But one must bow to necessity. Not even the gods can fight against that, as the Greek proverb goes.[44]

BOOK 2

Well, since we have started, we shall do the same thing with the second of Latomus' dialogues as we did with the first. This time Latomus keeps the orator far away and brings forward a splendid old gentleman as his main speaker: so the discussion must, I think, be correspondingly more serious and restrained.[1]

44   I agree with the old gentleman's first point, that a naturally gifted youth should be treated with consideration: but I do not agree that he should be treated 'almost as if he were a man.'[2] He should be treated as a man. Sheep are driven, rather than led. Even youths are human beings, I think.

45   So Latomus and his speaker think that no one should be exposed to the rougher side of any opponent's tongue or pen? I only wish everyone approved that sentiment as much as I do. If they did, we should not have had to spend our days listening to offensive shouts being flung against individuals who are sometimes actually named, and sometimes left so transparently anonymous that the silence makes no difference anyway. We might have avoided all this endless snapping and snarling against men who deserved better treatment in study-groups here, in dinner-parties there, in secret little huddles everywhere, all of them dealing in the vilest kind of slander and falsehood. Nor would this infectious disease of slander have attacked so many who had come here to learn quite different subjects; and men who were really not born hooligans would not be applauding with such delight when they read compositions which are as pointless as they are damaging, as ill-conceived as they are poisonous. So far, I have written against only one man.[3] I was forced to do so, and I wrote less to attack him than to defend myself. Finally, I wrote nothing to destroy the bond of Christian fellowship which still exists between us. I do not think there is anything libellous in disagreeing with colleagues whom you are prepared to name. Were this not the case, then Latomus' old gentleman would be displeased with Aristotle: he names numerous opponents whose ideas he rejects, and even laughs at Plato's theory of forms. Plato would have disagreed too, for there is not a sophist whom he does not criticize in the most savage terms – and he names them.[4]

46   I think it is more honest, much further from the conduct of a street-corner clown, to name your opponent straight away rather than to slant the attack so that its target is as obvious as if his name had been declared. That way the critic slips aside, and the victim loses the chance of defending himself. Some may be in genuine doubt as to the author who was being criticized: so the suspicion spreads far and wide, the danger is greater, and the victim, who may be quite innocent, finds his reputation blackened by another person's mistakes. Making a stinging joke at the expense of some shameful lapse is not necessarily the sort of street-corner clown's jesting that I mean, so long as the person subjected to it is not one whose proven learning and uprightness alike deserve our respect. The general

advancement of scholarship sometimes demands that falsely inflated reputations be punctured, to prevent those authors being the only ones that pass from hand to hand and to stop their works being read without careful choice and consideration. Lastly, we often come across critics whose sheer persistence forces us to bring the names of famous men out into the open, however much we should have preferred to keep them quiet. For example, I did not bring out my text of the New Testament to point out the flaws in the previous edition but as an aid to learning. I knew there was going to be trouble, for there was no lack of protests before the work was even published: but when it appeared the general outcry was so dreadful that I was compelled to defend myself against this sort of slander in any way I could. So I pointed out the passages where Augustine, Aquinas, Hugh of St Victor, and Nicholas of Lyra had obviously gone wrong to prevent people saying that my work had been unnecessary, and so depriving me of my reward, and the reader of his instruction.

47   As far as the different academic subjects are concerned, no one has ever heard me claiming expertise in any single subject for myself, nor have I ever written or spoken disparagingly about a respectable field of study. All that I have done now and again is show where I disagree with the methods by which certain subjects have been taught.

48   It is worth noticing what a slippery customer Latomus' old gentleman proves himself to be. He does not condemn poetry outright: instead, he dodges the issue by suggesting that the greatest figures in the history of poetry should be kept out of the Christian commonwealth.

49   He takes a far more serious view than any other of the stories recorded by Homer and Lucian, which he calls unholy, obscene, full of vain superstition. Not that I think this has anything to do with me. I have set out in verse the kinds of things I should like to see children learn when they first start to read, and always take the greatest care that those of such a tender age should not take in anything improper along with their letters. There may be no lack of people who will suspect that this is a sidelong criticism that, in my little book *De pueris instituendis*, I throw in a suggestion that pupils should learn their stories from Homer, and their Greek style from Lucian.[5] Now, if Latomus' old man thinks their stories 'unholy' because they contain one or two less than godly things about the gods, then his argument is surely wrong: the fun they poke at the pagan gods whom we detest should make them all the more precious to us as Christians. All through his works Lucian so ridicules the gods that he earned the nickname

of 'the godless':[6] so there is no risk of a child's soaking up a cult for pagan
worship from his legends. If this is our concern we ought to be keeping
more of an eye on Aristotle, who makes quite frequent mention of the gods
and speaks of them seriously. Plato does so still more often, yet no one
forbids us to read him. Many historians write of the gods with respect
throughout their works and according to Latomus' argument they, too,
should be banned. In any case I cannot see why he calls such stories 'dirty'
for you will find nothing obscene in Homer nor even in Lucian, at least in
the dialogues which I have translated.[7] If Latomus wants to safeguard the
morals of the younger generation, he would do better to forbid the reading
of Catullus, Juvenal, Martial, or the *Carmina Priapeia*. People read Averroes,
who writes shocking blasphemies against Christ: they read Pliny, who
openly ridicules the very foundation of our faith, the immortality of souls;
they read Suetonius, in spite of his very low opinion of the Christian
church; they read Tacitus, who subjects our faith to a long chapter of abuse;
so why are Homer and Lucian the only authors named in this passage?[8]
And who on earth reads Homer and Lucian on the assumption that their
fables about the gods are true? Can we really think there is a danger of
boys reading the fables and being convinced that a lion and a fox actually
held a conversation? If one finds something titillating or improper in the
poets – and there are such passages even in the Scriptures – then my advice
is what it was before. A sensible teacher will either pass over the verses or
interpret them in a way that prevents the child's mind being tainted. I have
also shown how this can be achieved. Personally, I think there is more
danger in boys reading Poggio's *Facetiae* or Pontano's *Dialogues*, in which
Latomus' old gentleman seems to find little to criticize.[9] If we are so anxious
about their morals, then I think some confessors' manuals would make
more dangerous reading-matter for boys than Homer's legends. Plato does
not throw Homer out of his Republic – he shows him respectfully across the
frontier: and that was a state in which he wished wives to be held in
common, and where no human being has ever yet lived.[10] I, too, could have
wished that the poets had not included any lines that could damage
morality. But such is the way of the world: nothing is ever completely
perfect.[11] These insinuating popular songs, which people bring out year
after year in some new form, do far more damage to boys' minds and the
damage is far greater because absolutely everybody learns them. Latomus'
old gentleman would do better to vent his rage on them.

50   And now for another trick ... shall we call it 'poetic,' I wonder, or use
some other term? With tears in his eyes, our sage records his fearful
discovery – a number of well-born young men have carried their admiration

of pagan antiquity to such extremes that their faith in Christ has lapsed! Could anyone fail to realize that this is pure fiction? You may perhaps find some individual whose faith is a little unsure, and who carries his nostalgia for the pagan world rather too far: but you will find no one, I think, who has deserted the Christian faith for this reason. You would be more likely to find men whose excessive devotion to philosophy has brought them to this pass.

51   The speaker names Marullus at this point.[12] Very well, I dislike the fellow too. But our author has forgotten the promise he made a moment ago, to mention no names in his criticisms. He has to justify the exception by adding that Marullus' position is made quite clear in the books he has published. That, at least, lets me off completely. I never attached a name to anyone's mistakes, unless they were made in published works and obvious to everybody.

52   Having thrown all the others out, Latomus' speaker proceeds to show which poets and orators he thinks particularly suitable for boys to read. He mentions Juvencus, Paulinus, and Prudentius [as poets], then Lactantius and Cyprian [as orators]. As if a child whose expression has still to be formed is going to learn much from Juvencus! Or Paulinus, for that matter, for he only wrote one or two poems! As if one would choose Prudentius as essential reading for anyone except a theologian! People who are suspicious of Lucian or Homer never read authors like these at all, let alone teach them. When children are very young and first learning to read, they need something attractive to beckon them on to serious studies: as if authors like Paulinus would provide suitable reading! Apart from the fact that Lactantius is hardly suitable for children at the first stage of their education, his works contain gross errors on matters of faith. I am amazed that our old scholar did not list Cicero, or Quintilian, or Seneca, who contain nothing in the least bit improper and have the further advantage of providing a completely sound moral foundation for life. They positively urge us towards well-doing.[13]

53   Those who suspect that Latomus' next point applies to me have some reason for doing so. I think it was in my pamphlet De pueris instituendis that I wrote suggesting the poets as our best source for the first principles of Greek and Latin grammar.[14] I followed the advice of Quintilian in naming Homer and Virgil. But our old moralist finds a distinct lack of discretion in those who take this view. 'Can we not find a grammarian who was a Christian?' he adds ponderously, as if Christians and pagans did not use the

same mode of speech, or as if pagan models should not be preferred to Christian in this field, for many reasons. If young Christians are to be forbidden to read pagan poets and orators, then Augustine is going to have some charges to answer, for he called Licentius away from the love-elegies of Ovid 'back to his own poetry.'[15] Jerome should be reprimanded too: he expounded the pagan orators and poets to the young noblemen who were sent to him for education. When Rufinus tried to turn the fact into a charge against him, that holy man despised the attempt so utterly that he did not think it worth refuting.[16]

54   The conclusion which the old gentleman draws from all this is also thought by readers to apply to me: he considers it improper for one who is set on a career in theology to spend time in the preliminary study of fiction, similes, and allegories, as I appear to have advised in my *Methodus* – though when dealing with legends I go on to add 'especially those which encourage good conduct.'[17] But if my critics think it so dangerous to spend some initial time and effort on the orators' devices or the poets' legends, and if such moral poison lurks in pagan authors, as Latomus' speaker says, then why do he and people like him spend not only their first years but most of their old age as well poring over the texts of Aristotle? He was a pagan too. Why do they spend so long on Averroes, who was something worse than a pagan? I am not looking for a quarrel with anyone who may disagree with me, but I do not in the least regret having made the original suggestion.

55   Latomus next turns to a point raised in his previous book, and tries to draw a distinction between perfect and imperfect piety – as if any man could achieve perfect piety! Then he differentiates between the theological reasoning by which we know God and that by which we teach others about him, making two mental processes out of one. Next he adds that 'one who is holy, is not automatically a theologian: there is such a quality as "holiness" in peasants.' As if anyone had ever said that all holiness was the same! I should certainly not feel inclined to apply the terms 'peasant' or 'man in the street' to one whose mind was radiantly pure with the sacred gleam of faith, and whose heart glowed with Christ's eternal light. But there is no passage in which I have said that being a theologian means no more than being set ablaze and carried out of oneself by the power of love. If I had said any such thing, I would not entirely regret it. Seneca and Plutarch deny the title 'philosopher' to those who can do no more than recite the principles of a good life by rote: they bestow it on those who can carry out those principles in the conduct of their own lives. In the same way I deny the title of 'theologian' to those whose understanding of the Holy Scriptures

goes no deeper than the intellect – and I have seen all too many of them. It belongs to the person who feels within himself what he reads in those sacred books and who is affected by it to the very core of his being. This is why it was necessary to say so much to explain my view of what is essential to the understanding of theology.

56   Latomus' lengthy discussion of languages affects me not at all. Can anyone deny that men of different tongues and races are capable of achieving the same knowledge, when all the observed facts declare this to be the case? I am not advising anyone to grope his way back to some basic, primordial ideas, when the help of language can reveal the meaning to him in far less time. But it is well established that many have made mistakes in the Scriptures through their lack of linguistic skills – and that is enough for me. I am not leading anyone towards despair, in fact I am even giving the elderly good grounds for hope. Lastly, I am telling those who cannot, or have no time, to learn the languages for themselves, that as far as I am concerned they can rely on other people's work, and, furthermore, it is up to them to decide what is least important, what is best, and what comes in between. Often what seems lowest turns out to be the most important. I am not saying outright that languages are so vital to a theologian that no one can be a theologian without them: only that in explaining the Holy Scriptures and unravelling their mysteries a theologian risks running into serious trouble if he has no languages to help him. Relying on other people's eyes is not safe enough, and you may not always have someone nearby whose advice is trustworthy. Sometimes you may not even realize that you need advice, if the stress of the words does not put you on the alert. So let us grant that one or two theologians may not need languages: as a general rule languages are certainly necessary. Particular care must be taken by individual theologians who deal with mystical texts, where there is always a risk of error, and no guard against it except the help of languages. So it seems that individual theologians must strive to learn them. Lastly, everyone knows that this word 'essential' often means no more than 'highly relevant.'

57   In the passage which I cited, Augustine does not call a knowledge of languages 'essential': he assures us that it is a very great help when the precise significance of a concept is not clear; but he soon goes on to add that we 'need' languages, which is practically the same as calling them 'essential.'[18] Latomus' old scholar tries to water down Augustine's statement by making him mean that up to his time two languages besides Latin have been necessary, so that when the different readings of his Latin manuscripts

embarrassed him, he could fall back on Greek or Hebrew texts as a last resort. The implication is that now different readings have been eliminated as well. My first reply to this is that our Latin manuscripts still show very considerable differences. I could go on to show many other reasons why we may still be compelled to hesitate in our explanations of the Holy Scriptures. We may find a passage where the text is corrupt, the expression ambiguous, the phraseology complex or unfamiliar, or where the commentator is less than wide awake. Whatever the cause of our uncertainty over a scriptural text, we need to go back to the sources. And since texts are still being corrupted today and new problems constantly coming to the surface, it is worth the trouble of keeping the cure which Augustine pointed out to us ready at hand at all times.

58   The fact that certain problems of language happen to be found very commonly does not mean that the original language will not help us to understand them.

59   The fact that Augustine speaks disjunctively and seems to leave us free to choose one of three options does not help their case very much. Since every possible method is not available to everyone, he indicates a selection of cures in case we should find ourselves without any cure at all. His first suggestion is that we should consult linguistic experts. But if we hiss our lecturers in the languages off the academic stage, as some writers try to make us do, then we shall have no one to consult. In any case, when a man is writing or expounding, he does not always have an advisor ready to hand: and even if he does, not everyone can safely be trusted. Finally, Augustine is not discussing a full version of the Bible at this point, nor is he speaking in general terms about the phraseology and stress of a foreign language, nor even about the corruption of the manuscript tradition: he is speaking only about the few alien words which have found their way at times into the Latin text. I have many more reasons for saying that languages are essential even if I pass over the fact that Augustine, whose own grasp of all the relevant languages was somewhat less than adequate, tried to excuse himself from learning them by suggesting to others, as far as he could, that they need not do so. It is a common human failing. Unless he is talking of a time one or two centuries gone by and referring only to Greek literature, I do not think Latomus' old gentleman is correct in saying that there are now more experts whom you may consult than there used to be. Augustine saw the same problem and did not completely trust his solution: for he immediately went on to add 'or else you should learn the language yourself, if you have the time and intelligence to do so.'[19]

Augustine was busy with the affairs of his diocese and must be excused for not doing so. But if a young student, a schoolboy even, who is determined to become a theologian and has no other duty than that of learning, still finds that he has no available time, then who ever will have it? So if no one denies that a knowledge of languages is the surest solution to the problem by far, why do we not make it our very first choice? The third solution – that of relying on commentators – has been snatched from us at the present time for there are not enough commentators available, except perhaps on St Paul's Epistles.

60   Augustine knew no Hebrew, but wrote on Genesis and the Psalms.[20] He explained the text as best as he could, with the help of earlier commentators who had known Hebrew. A man who was prepared to make a rather close scrutiny of these works might well find that Augustine ran into the difficulties of which Jerome warned him. Let us grant that he made no actual mistakes: perhaps he missed many points which he would have been able to explain if he had known Hebrew. It is quite certain that anyone who embarks on scriptural commentary without a knowledge of language runs a serious risk of error. I mean no disrespect to those who give the best explanation they can, working without pretence and showing themselves ready to follow improvements if anyone offers them. But if you are convinced that languages are not necessary just because Augustine dared to write on Genesis and the Psalms, why cannot others be convinced that they are necessary, since famous doctors have fallen into error in discussing mystical texts because of their ignorance of languages, and they have done so quite frequently?

61   Now let us grant that Augustine examined much of both the Old and New Testaments more searchingly and explained them much more effectively than many others have done with a wide array of languages at their disposal. Perhaps their other resources were as inferior to his as their linguistic resources were superior. In any case, if Augustine had been a skilled linguist, he would have done his job with greater effect and less difficulty. Or he would have done so, had not all his writings been the product of divine inspiration rather than human industry.

62   I cannot understand how Latomus' readers manage to turn his next point against me. I am not raising questions about how the early Christians brought the Gospels into being, how their message was spread in the languages of all the church's different members, or what rule was applied in approving the four Gospels. It is certain that, as the situation stands at

present, we must look for the true teaching of our Gospels in Greek and Latin manuscripts. I have replied before to his objection about the corruption of texts. The fact that heretics base their notion on doubtful passages and sometimes use the same manuscripts as orthodox believers does not prove that linguistic knowledge cannot help us here and there. I admit that many questions cannot be decided by language. It is enough for me that languages can help to resolve some problems which used previously to puzzle us.

63   I accept the comparison which Latomus makes between the light, or grace, which gives us some share of the divine nature, and the natural enlightenment by which we secure our knowledge of human learning. But in our pursuit of human learning we embrace whatever forms of assistance will sharpen or develop our natural understanding. We should do the same in our pursuit of theological learning, for the truth of the Gospels is not so closely linked to grace that it can turn away the disciplines which prepare the mind to receive it. In either case what point could there be in a future theologian sweating for so many years over the philosophy of Aristotle? I shall not repeat what I have said before – that it is one thing to have a sufficient knowledge of the gospel truth to ensure your salvation, but quite another to take on the discussion of mystical texts with authority. I confess to seeing some risk of everyone claiming this state of grace for himself, if we lay too much stress on a rule which I still prefer not to criticize. But the pillars of early Christian belief felt that they should rely chiefly on the evidence of the Scriptures. When will it be safe for us to rely on this conviction of 'grace' when Ambrose and Augustine, to say nothing of the others who were helped by it, if anyone was, still wander occasionally from the gospel truth?

64   As to Latomus' plea that individuals may fall short of the truth, but the whole body of the church can never do so, I accept that on all questions concerning what is needful for our salvation. Heaven forbid that God should desert his own church: he would doubtless make himself its teacher if it should lack a man whose counsel could guide it. But this train of reasoning does not excuse those who are not prepared to learn what they do not know from another man but choose instead to make malevolent comments about work which they neither read nor understand because they are ashamed of letting themselves appear in any way ignorant. These are the people who are opening a split in the body of the church, not those who are striving to use languages to help the development of sound learning.

65   So if knowledge of languages helps us to keep a foot on the ground, those who attempt to amputate so vital a limb are acting foolishly. I do not feel affected by the warning given by Latomus' old scholar, that the foot or the hand should not consider themselves the eye or the ear. I have often said that the post I claimed in my *Annotations* is the lowest in the study of theology. It is as though I were sweeping the floor in the Lord's temple.[21]

66   The point which Latomus draws from Paul's experience of the gift of tongues does not apply to our discussion at all. Nowadays a teacher of languages does nothing more than explain sounds: it is not a matter of divine inspiration, but of human application. Nobody is claiming that a knowledge of languages is sufficient on its own to let a man explain the Holy Scriptures: in fact it has never been sufficient even to provide an explanation of human knowledge. But Paul does not reject the help of linguists, so long as he has advisors to judge between them and explain their precise meaning. Yet I think we are in debt to George of Trebizond for giving us a translation of Chrysostom, even though he was not a theologian himself. I do not claim any advanced knowledge of theology: on the other hand I do not think myself so utterly ignorant of it as to have been unable to translate the Gospels and the Letters of the apostles, especially when I had so much help from the writings of the early commentators.[22]

67   Whether the neglect of languages is partly to blame for Christendom's being reduced to its present straits is not a question I am discussing at the moment. But I must say in all sincerity that the main responsibility lies in the personal faults of those who govern the Christian community. I certainly believe it is the case, as I have written on several occasions, that the decline, the neglect, the ruin of learning is a disaster which we must attribute to the neglect of languages.

As long ago as Pliny's time some subjects were out of fashion because they were honourable rather than profitable. This does not make it any less true to say that in the centuries since his time writers and entire fields of study have been neglected or perished because language has been neglected. Pliny deals mainly with agriculture. For he calls even those 'liberal arts' because they were once thought worthy of a free-born citizen. I wish people thought the same of them today.

68   Before he has completely dismissed this point, Latomus' old scholar goes on to map out a course of study for his future theologian. He disagrees with me on almost every feature except in approving the New Testament as a starting point. But I am not taking this as an insult. I pleaded

conscientiously for what I believed to be best, so let him tell us what he thinks is better still.

69   In the interest of brevity I am going to pass over points that do not apply to me in any way: but I do wonder why he finds that particularly subtle and ethereal form of theology which he seeks in Origen, of all people. No one was more active in historical research, whether in examining the languages, comparing the evidence of the commentators, or in offering a popular version in his *Sermons*.

70   I also wonder why he considers it a particular quality of Augustine never to have put a foot wrong in either branch of theological studies. Perhaps he thinks Augustine was the only theologian who never wandered off the point into the realms of history and allegory. Easy enough for Latomus to say: very difficult indeed to see the evidence.

71   He admires Augustine because he clings closely to the letter of his text: the implication is that Origen destroys it. But a commentator who says that the text is dull and tasteless if deprived of spiritual meaning is not thereby destroying it.

72   Latomus' old scholar disagrees completely with my feeling that the highest place among the commentators must go to Origen. He is scarcely prepared to allow even a seasoned theologian to read that Father's works. Yet everyone, without exception, recognizes that Origen had the profoundest knowledge of the Scriptures and there are very few passages in his surviving books which are suspect. It is pretty well agreed that the *Sermons on Luke* are not Origen's work.[23] If anyone was prepared to do the arithmetic exactly, he would perhaps find more mistakes in the works of Peter Lombard than in those of Origen which have come down to us. Yet we hand the Lombard to our theology student at the very beginning of his course.

73   Origen has none of that feigned effusiveness that makes us look fearfully for the hidden trap: his language is entirely straightforward and churchmanlike. None of his poisonous doctrines are extant except in Jerome, who made it his business to see that the world knew about Origen's errors, but not about the sound points he made.[24]

74   A few moments ago our old scholar seemed to be saying that the rough groundwork of theology lay in understanding the text, while the refined

and spiritual side lay in interpreting allegories, and he was accusing Origen of concentrating too much on the second. Now he seems to have forgotten himself: he tears me to pieces for suggesting that the student who wants to set his hand to the groundwork of theology should begin by spending time on the outlines laid down in poetry and rhetoric. But in the meantime he seems to have confused 'outlines' with 'commonplaces.'

75   This is what he says: 'This fellow who discusses virtues and vices with the man in the street, who preaches faith and strives with his whole heart to build it up, shows very little interest in defining what faith is: he thinks it quite irrelevant to decide what subject feels it, towards what object it is directed, whether that object is true or false, divine or human. He urges me to be charitable: but he cares little what the subject or object of that charity may be, whither it is directed, what its species may be, or if it has a species at all. He does no more than bend every resource of his mind and speech to making his readers pious, faithful, and loving, and they end by thinking that this is the mark of a perfect theologian.' So far, these are the jolly old fellow's very words.[25] Now, honest reader, I appeal to you – could any of you possibly suspect that this applies to me? If someone wants the aspiring theologian to spend his first years of study looking at rhetorical figures for the sake of recognizing theological allegories or at certain commonplaces because of the light they shed on theological exhortations, is he thereby advising his student to take little account of anything else? Or is he convinced that a man is a perfect theologian, if he does no more than urge people to trust in God and do the right? Could you find even an orator who would be stupid enough to fall silent as soon as he had said 'Love one another' when he was to address the people on the subject of loving-kindness? When Chrysostom is discussing rhetorical commonplaces does he have anything to say of these Scotist hairsplittings of subject, object, and the like? They may teach something: but they do nothing to arouse the emotions. In my *Methodus* I tell readers of the Gospels to notice how much importance Christ attaches to faith and love:[26] should I have added 'and notice his wonderful academic definition of faith'? Should I have shown what can be found there under the heading of type, of difference, and of inherent quality? Should I have run through the different views on the subject and object of faith? Granting that such things can usefully be discussed and passed on in the schools, they cannot but seem boring to a wider audience, especially when you are dealing with rhetorical commonplaces. These are a matter for the speaker, who is more concerned with kindling the heart than instructing the mind. Should I have produced a Scotist definition of loving-kindness when the people would not even be

able to understand it? Should I have made a fine definition of terms, to show that everyone values his own money, his own life, his own reputation and his own advantage more highly than the next man's? I beseech you – on the many occasions when Christ and his apostles exhort us to trust in God and love one another, can we say that they are simply bawling and acting the fool because they do not season their plea with any of these subtleties? Some think they have made this kind of point clearly enough if they have done their best to roar as loud as thirty thousand devils. To put my opinion frankly, I do not think that Latomus has shown a sense of propriety in this passage, especially when he endows his old speaker with such an aura of dignity and respectability.

76   It remains to examine the methods by which he proposes to educate his angelic and daring theologian. First, he wishes him to be thoroughly grounded in the main tenets of Christian belief. Well, has he any reason to fear Origen's books once that has been achieved?

77   He thinks that a reasonable knowledge of grammar is sufficient to provide this grounding. Beyond that, he wants his pupil to keep his nose to the grindstone of true dialectic, as he puts it, hinting by the way that there is a kind of false dialectic as well. I take it that he is referring to the widespread and debased methods used to teach dialectic. I also note that men do not allow me to make the most modest protest about the corrupt methods used to teach theology.

He thinks that the student should have at least a moderate grasp of the natural sciences, but through dabbling in them rather than through an exhaustive study: I on the other hand would prefer the student of theology to spend some time on other works besides the eight he mentions.[27] Apart from arithmetic, he thinks it is enough just to touch on the mathematical disciplines.

Latomus' speaker hopes for a conscientious study of moral and metaphysical philosophy, which will equip the student for the speculative flights of theological reasoning.

This is certainly not a syllabus which I would wish to criticize, even though it is somewhat different from mine. My aim was to produce a theologian who would not only know Christ's doctrine but understand it as well, and whose learning would give him true holiness of character rather than an inflated salary and an inflated opinion of himself. Latomus' old scholar seems to have thought rather of swelling the number of those whom they called bachelors, masters, and licentiates. It is for that reason that he gives most attention to the subjects which are normally taught in universities. And it is clear that he has argued in this way more to make today's accepted practices in those universities appear in the best possible light, than to devise what would be the best possible syllabus. Perhaps it was in the old theologian's own best interest to put this kind of a case. I neither care for nor take account of any factor except the common interest of all. I am not trying to stand in anyone's way. In fact, if I had done more to bring it about, far more people would be seeking those academic titles than do so now. I never dissuaded anyone from embarking on this course of studies: I have urged quite a few to try it. So if numbers have declined it is unfair (if I may use the old gentleman's words) to make a cause out of a non-cause. Such declines often come about through lack of income, or other reasons – even through sheer chance. But I cannot help feeling some surprise that Latomus' speaker never so much as mentions rhetoric when he attaches such cardinal importance to dialectic. The two are so closely related that some theoreticians actually identify them, but consider that they have been taught in different ways. It is of special interest that rhetoric is reckoned among the seven liberal arts, whose teachers are known as masters.[28]

78 So far, there is not a word about the books of the Old or New Testament, on which I laid particular stress in my *Methodus*.[29] The old teacher does not want to let it look as if he has forgotten the matter entirely so he allows his student, given the opportunity, to spend a little time each day reading the Scriptures. First he should read them through, just skimming the contents: then he should devote some part of each day to learning certain sections by heart. If during his reading he finds any passage which puzzles him, he should turn to the glosses rather than submit himself to the torment of translation and linguistic study. As though all the relevant information could be drawn from glosses! As though the translation, and the linguistic skill which I advise, shed no light beyond that provided by glosses! Further, I hardly understand how a student at this stage can be helped by other scholars' works, unless he compares translations to one another and looks to the languages to help him. That hideous word 'torment' – the old fellow speaks almost as if he was persuading his student not to put himself on the rack – fails to disturb me at all. In fact he wants issues over which the greatest theologians have hesitated, and sometimes stuck fast, to be passed over as matters of relatively little concern.

79 Latomus' speaker eventually allows his student to touch the works of the early commentators such as Origen, Ambrose, and Augustine, but only after he has become thoroughly acquainted with scholastic writers. So

completely does he prefer these authors to their predecessors that our old scholar wants his theologian to study them before he touches the books of either the Old or the New Testament. He is concerned about the risk of a student's reading Cyprian, Hilary, Jerome, and Ambrose before Scotus, Durand, and Holcot, then being unable to stomach these modern writers without feeling sick.[30] I cannot reject the old fellow's chain of reasoning, but another thought concerned me: if a theologian grew old among these cunning, emotionally sterile, and frankly childish writers, I saw a real risk of his never finding time for the early commentators or else coming to them too late in life, and deriving no profit from them when he did. I know that this was common experience among many students in Paris a few years ago, and Latomus was acquainted with quite a few of them. So his old speaker disagrees with me, and I with him. I leave others to weigh the relative importance of the arguments we have put.

80   There is a further difference of emphasis between myself and Latomus' old gentleman. I think that I advised the student to read the best of the early commentators first, and to choose them with some care: we must not be deceived by a mere title, or take the dronings of some complete charlatan to heart like the words of a prophet. The old scholar thinks that no real danger lies in running up against the occasional spurious work among the writings of Jerome, Ambrose, or Augustine: his lynx-eyed theologian will take no account of the weight behind any man's name but submit everything to that die-straight rule which he carries around everywhere with him. However celebrated the writers, he does not think that we should carry respect to the length of trusting them on every point: we should go no further than trying to excuse them when they have fallen into error, or twisted the meaning of the language, and so keeping up the appearance of our high esteem for them. But meanwhile that sage of ours seems to have forgotten that theologians are stressing the weighty opinion of Augustine or Jerome in serious debates and citing a few words from some attributed work of theirs to prove that what so-and-so wrote is heretical. There is no danger to the man who quotes the passage, but any amount of it to the so-and-so against whom he quotes it: and if by any chance their positions are reversed, all the danger can rebound on the head of the fellow who found the passage. No names mentioned: I am too sensible for that. This is a matter of 'tiptoeing through the hot coals under those innocent-looking ashes,'[31] as Horace has it. Meantime, I shall not mention the fact that not all academics agree on this 'rule of scholars' to which our old speaker wishes to submit everything. There is a real risk of mistaking false conviction for rule, so that everyone becomes sure that his rule is the right one.

81   After all this, our old scholar expands on a popular theme and urges us to go and listen to our teachers in terms which suggest that I approve of nothing except reading, or that I have not advised, in several passages, that we should mingle the written with the spoken word and prefer the lively sound of the spoken word to the teaching of dumb masters, as they say.[32] But when a suitable teacher does not happen to be available, the next best thing is to seek your information from books. And even when a teacher is available, how important is what we learn from him compared to what we learn for ourselves through our own reading? A neat point of his, to set Jerome's example against me because the great man spent three months, I think it was, in close company with Nazianzen, and once met Didymus. Compare that with all the years he had for reading! Then he adds: 'Jerome writes to Paulinus and does not urge him to read the text of the Gospel or Origen, but to hear the teaching of his master.'[33] It is as though I and my colleagues were tempting people away from listening to their teachers, when we suggest that they read authors who are not studied in the universities, or are not studied carefully enough. Why did he not rather quote the numerous passages in which Jerome urges us to read through the Holy Scriptures and the commentators? Is it not clear enough that what the old professor had in mind was to keep the lecture-rooms chock full of students? It is not an aim I would criticize, but there are surely other arguments which so venerable a greybeard could more properly have used. Why did he not mention Bernard, who took the oaks and beeches as his instructors? Or Antonius, who studied in a glade, then afterwards emerged from it to rescue the Christian faith?[34] Or Ambrose, who never spoke to Origen but studied with him and became as learned as we know? Or Augustine, whose reading made him so great but spent no more than a few days listening to Ambrose haranguing the people?[35] Suppose – just suppose – that what reading could teach me was more ample and more worthwhile than what some dull, sleepy, and perhaps ill-educated professor could?

82   But our old teacher has a quick tongue, and back he comes again: in his own lifetime, he says, he has seen a number of writers fall into obvious blunders because they have neglected the established scholastic authorities or made light of them. I hope others can find the examples as easily as our sharp-eyed old observer. Personally, I think it is easier to find people who have tumbled into obvious pitfalls by paying too much attention to scholastic authorities. And he speaks of scholastic authorities as if they all held the same views and were all free from error themselves. In fact some follow Aquinas and differ so violently from Scotus and Gerson that they regard them almost as heretics.

83   But now our old censor starts to treat us a little more gently: he follows Gerson's view in allowing the theologian to glance quickly through the historians, orators, and poets in odd spare hours. In fact he allows them almost as much time and importance as he allows the Old and New Testaments.[36]

84   He gives a sound bit of advice, when he urges the speculative theologian not to look down on the man of less refined intellect, but rather to give him the help of his own advice, and his own pen. Today most people do the exact opposite, using both speech and writing to tear apart men who for their part are only trying to advance the study of literature.

85   There was one passage which I could hardly read without a smile: the old fellow attacks only greed and vainglory in a theologian, saying nothing at all of their other vices. I do not know if he has reached the conclusion that the majority of theologians really do have a special propensity for these two vices. No one has ever judged me so harshly as to fix the charge of greed for money on me. Far more have criticized my neglect of material things. Nor do I see why I should seem especially vainglorious, when I have taken the last place in every literary enterprise and always taken care to behave so as not to push in front of anyone whenever I have become involved. Even if I have not allowed anyone to overtake me so far, I hope many may do so in the future.

86   There is another passage which no one could read without a flash of amusement: Latomus' sage does not want his theologian to spend too long on the basic rules of rhetoric because it is an art which is learned quickly, or not at all. It is as though Quintilian meant ten days when he said 'quickly.' But the speaker continues 'in declamations that are appropriate to boys,' as if declamation was in itself an easy exercise or as if men of the most profound learning, and old men at that, have not concerned themselves with it. Or, for that matter, as if the *Declamations* of Quintilian and Seneca were intended only to be read by boys.[37] I do not agree with those who think this shot may have winged me, because I have published one or two *Declamations* which I would allow to be called 'elementary' if this old man could get through them. Finally, Latomus is arguing as if setting a theme, and stating the arguments on one side and the other, was not declamation, or as if this old fellow's speech was not, in its way, the very same exercise. It was a neat point to say that eloquence is not something to be learned because, as Augustine says, it follows its mistress Wisdom without prompting – a single, serious comrade attached to her

from birth, needing no summons but obeying no dismissal.[38] Very well: but I see a further risk here: some writers lack all trace of this controlled, inborn eloquence, and find that their every word falls flat and frozen on its face; according to this argument one might deprive them of all claim to wisdom too. Again, I am naming no names for I have no wish to anger anyone. I know some speakers whose temperament is so awful that they can bear neither compliments nor criticism. But if there are people who dislike rhetoric so much, even though they themselves have accepted her among the liberal arts, then let them reject her as far as I am concerned: but at least let them substitute an art of striking false attitudes, to keep the number up to seven. But this whole comparison of ancient and modern authorities is so vast a field that I propose to keep it for another time, especially since I do not entirely acclaim the ancients or reject the moderns. But many suspect that the old theologian's comparison contains a number of points whose real meaning conveys slightly more than they say, in the fashion that the Greeks call 'sycophancy.' Personally, I can hardly believe it.

87   They think that people of this kind have the same sort of characters as those who used the slanderer Rufinus' evidence to blacken Jerome, on the charge that he buries the heretical opinions of others so deeply in his own commentaries that the reader can barely decide whether they are his own, or those of others.[39] This is Latomus', or his speaker's, reason for preferring the moderns: they define everything, while ancients discuss rather than define. But I prefer one who discusses with caution, even with honest doubt, to one who lays down his meaning with a boldness which amounts to bravado, especially since such people's statements do not agree and are often diametrically opposed to each other.

88   Who has ever denied or doubted that the original sin occurred just because Origen failed to mention it in his first book De principiis?[40] This was certainly not the source of Pelagius' error.

89   Suppose that, for the sake of argument, one were to assemble a few points from the early commentators which were once matters of doubt but which some critics now consider more certain – I almost said than the Gospels. Is such conduct prejudicing the moderns in any way? Dear reader, you must understand how foolish Latomus' old scholar is to devote himself so completely to them, and to fear for them at every turn, even when the road is perfectly safe.

90 Whoever said that marriage is not a sacrament just because Dionysius mentions all the others in his *De coelestibus hierarchiis* without saying a word about this one? Suppose we do assemble a few such points from the early commentators in our discussions: why should this make our opponents any more suspicious of us than we are of them, with their arguments raked in from every side to batter at points on which it is heretical even to feel some doubt?[41]

91 The speaker presses for a thorough study of philosophy, so that the errors made by the philosophers can be refuted: so why not bring the study of Platonic philosophy into the universities? But it is one thing to know what the philosophers believe, another to swallow a complete system. A rough outline of the main ideas can be conveyed in just a few sessions, so this is no reason for the future theologian to spend all those years exhausting himself in the study of Aristotle. I am not saying this because I am convinced that it is true, but because I want to establish it as a debating point. The old gentleman's argument may have had its place in Jerome's time, but now we need have no truck with the philosophers unless we want it for ourselves. And if this is the case, I could press exactly the same argument for a thorough study of the poets: we need to refute the false fantasies about the gods, which they hand down in their works.

92 But whatever view we take of this point, I find the next almost intolerable. The speaker pictures Paul preaching of Christ to the Athenians in terms which include allusions to the relative and the absolute, to nature and to quality. Paul had never read Scotus and Aquinas! He himself declared that he did not preach the gospel to the learned in the words of human wisdom, lest the glory of the faith be thought a part of some philosophical armoury. It is most unlikely that he would have revealed to the Athenians, who were still unacquainted with such ideas, the mystery that Christ was both God and man and the means by which this was possible. Paul himself declares in this passage that he knows nothing but Christ crucified. We do not need to know the exact justification for every article which we accept by faith. It is perfectly clear from Luke's account that Paul is speaking in that passage about God the Father as creator of the whole human race. When he has passed on to Christ, he calls him the *man* through whom God decided to save the world through faith. The proof of this faith is that he has raised the man concerned from the dead. Furthermore, both Origen and Chrysostom teach that the doctrine of God in man was not preached immediately and everywhere lest it should prove a stumbling-block to minds which were still not attuned to such a mystery

and incapable of accepting it. In the Gospel itself the disciples are at first forbidden to proclaim Jesus as Christ.[42]

93   The next point is very similar. The speaker argues that the apostles could have given no account of their faith unless they had preached the Word made flesh with a running commentary on the individual, the nature, the properties of the individual in question, the general qualities, and the number of possible combinations. As if the apostles could have converted the world by philosophical reasoning! Was it not rather the simple force of their message, lest the glory of Christ's cross be brought to nought, the miracles which they wrought, the holiness of their lives, and lastly the most potent witness of all – the manner of their deaths? Of course we may grant that Paul used philosophical methods against philosophers. So if we need to learn the same methods now as he used then, it seems more suitable to our purposes to thumb through the works in which Cicero argues from Greek[43] philosophical sources for the immortality of the soul against the views of Epicurus, than to turn to the works of Aristotle. Lastly, you may remember that a little while ago our reverend advisor excused his theology student from buying some little Greek's efforts, lest he be forced into the torment of learning languages. Well, perhaps we could hire some little philosopher to reduce all these distinctions and definitions to a simple guide, give this to the aspiring theologian, and so allow him in the same way to be spared the vast labour of spending all those years learning the whole of philosophy. Again, I would not say such a thing because I really believe it, but to set one argument against another like a couple of nails.[44] But my next point is quite serious: it is not clear whether the apostles used philosophical methods, but it is clear that they used the poets to illustrate their message. Certainly Peter, the first of all the apostles to proclaim Christ to ordinary people, brought no philosophical concepts into the speeches recorded by Luke.[45] Finally, I do not know how others feel. But I am delighted to have learned my faith in Christ from the Gospels, the Letters of the apostles, and the early teachers of the church. The finely drawn syllogisms of a few philosophers, which many think are self-evident anyway, never made much appeal to my spirit. I state my feelings as a simple fact, whether they are right or wrong.

94   Latomus then proceeds to show that certain problems, whose oddity I may have quipped about in some other work, have an interest of their own in certain contexts. Take, for example, the question: 'Could the divine nature, according to our idea of its nature, have become one with an irrational creature or even with an inanimate body?' It may seem a pointless

inquiry in itself. But it has a certain relevance when we come up against the problem of Christ's burial and the issue of divinity being one with a dead body, or separated from it.[46] Suppose one were to say that even this does not affect Christian theology very much, especially since the proposition certainly cannot be proved or disproved and theologians do not agree in their view of it?

95 Men may ask questions like 'Does the simplicity of God exclude absolutely every sort of composition: of form and substance, act and potency, subject and accident?' But we may feel that these are the sort of whom it was written 'He who looks too closely at the divine majesty will be crushed by its glory.'[47] No one objects to the sober discussion of such questions in universities. But some take them to widely advertized public debates and many who nod off to sleep at any other spectacle hurry eagerly to this one sort of show. Examples of this kind may well seem inappropriate to one reader or another. But no one, not even Latomus' old speaker, can deny that theologians are discussing a number of questions which have not the slightest relevance to real theology. Yet a speaker who can justify the usefulness of these questions to theology by such subtle reasoning finds only languages, poetry, and rhetoric impossible to justify.

96 We certainly find nothing to criticize in turning the philosophy of Aristotle to the needs of our study of theology. What we resent is rather setting the whole corpus of Aristotle's works at the very core of theology, and giving almost as much, if not more weight to his authority than to that of the Gospels. If only we were content with Aristotle's *Dialectic*: but what a supplement we have added to it, and how we add to that every day! But this is not quite the point that concerns Latomus' old scholar. He lets us choose any one of the more recent authorities, so long as we have no dealings whatever with the old ones. I wonder why he could not find a place for Augustine in his list? For I shall pass over the fact that he says, offering an example of an unqualified statement, this is like calling the ancient authors heretics – as if modern authors contained no heretical statements.

97 Latomus' theologian takes the example of Pico, who spent six whole years on the study of Aquinas, Scotus, and Albert the Great. He expressed his regret at wasting all this time, for he says quite plainly at the end of the letter that it is an exercise rather than a considered opinion, in case any more gullible reader should be deceived.[48] But I have heard the best theologians making the same complaint as Pico, and lamenting not that they

had spent time on scholastic theology but that they had spent so much time on this one field of study and this alone. But I cannot keep back my amazement at this wonderfully gentle old professor: he excuses his theology student from the study of grammar, languages, and the orators; he does not want the poor boy to be 'tormented' by the poets, by reading the Holy Scriptures, or even the early teachers, whom the church numbers amongst its holy doctors; then, as soon as he reaches the moderns, he overwhelms the unhappy youth with a pitiless flood of required reading, demanding that he read every page of authors such as Peter Lombard, Alexander of Hales, Thomas Aquinas, Scotus, Bonaventure, William of Paris, Maurice of Armagh, Isidore, Holcot, Pierre d'Ailly, Gerson, Ockham, Durand, Aymon, Gabriel, Nicholas of Lyra, Carrensis, Aegidius, Adrian, Tartaretus, Bricot ... in short, every one of those who ever have taught this form of theology, are teaching it now, or are likely to teach it in the future.[49] He does not spare a single book, though a whole human life would not be long enough to read them all. He might at least have been generous enough to allow his pupil to allot the time young men usually waste on games, sleep, parties, or gossip, to the study of languages, the orators, and the poets.

98   I suppose truth has its own form of beauty wherever it is found. All the same I should prefer to see a beautiful shape naked, or simply and neatly dressed, than fouled by shabby rags. I would prefer to pick jewels from a golden vessel than from a muck-heap. I would prefer to eat fine food from a clean plate than a dirty dish. But these are points which I shall discuss elsewhere.[50]

99   There are passages in my works where I have given Aquinas the highest place among modern theologians. But I do not think there is one where I have said that he is the only modern theologian who is worth reading. Latomus' argument that you cannot compare the more modern authors either to each other or to their predecessors unless you have read them all is a mere quibble. Someone could just as well respond and ask whether he has read all the ancient authors to whom he prefers the moderns or, last of all, whether he has read all the moderns. That, I think, is something that no one will dare to claim, however inexhaustible his appetite for reading. For that matter, who can compare poet with poet, as Latomus' speaker does, unless he has read all the poets? Finally, what is the objection to judging some works according to the general impression they make on you, even if you have not read through them all? All around us we see theologians condemning works which they have not read at all. I could name quite a few of them.

100   While he is giving reasons under this heading for the moderns' being compelled to bring Aristotle's philosophy into their theology, the speaker cites the example of some commentators who are trying to go beyond the practice of the ancients in bringing grammatical evidence to bear on the study of the Holy Scriptures. While establishing this point, he does not seem to count Augustine, Jerome, or Origen among the ancients, though they often describe the figurative sense, and explain the force of a word, and so keep the language well in hand.

101   If you removed from their works all that they had borrowed from the ancients and brought in from Aristotle, would you find as much true theology in the works of Aquinas and Albert the Great[51] as in any one of the early theologians? This is too large an issue to settle in a few words, so it is better to keep it for another time.

102   It is quite true that Augustine brought in various ideas about the parts, the powers, and the actions of the rational soul in order to explain the mysteries of the Trinity. But if we decide on that ground to learn the whole of metaphysics then we should be still more strongly obliged to learn the whole of astronomy, since the Holy Scriptures make frequent mention of the stars. But I am no enemy of philosophy, provided it is employed with a proper restraint and control. Since I gave a few words of advice on this point in my *Methodus*, I thought there was little need for me to draw any further attention to it, as it drew more than enough attention to itself.[52]

103   I do not believe that his tracing the passage of the divine law through many stages down to the professors in today's universities has anything whatever to do with me.

104   Latomus' theologian makes some quite scathing comments about the sound beliefs of the early commentators, whose extravagant and florid style of discussing sacred questions could have driven Christian society to the brink of destruction, had not more recent thinkers brought the discipline of their schools to its rescue. This seems to suggest that no false doctrines have emerged since these schools were founded, and that none have ever emerged from the schools themselves: by association, to hint that nothing is discussed in the courts which does not concern the case in hand. He compares the example of the change in legal practice.[53]

105   In the final section he gives a list of the various different methods by which philosophy can be pursued. Some might think the various turns of

phraseology more suspicious, but what delighted me was that he turned the full force of his invective on logic. This is precisely the form of philosophy which boys are compelled to learn in the public schools, and when its importance was called into question during my time in Basel the theologians raised such an outcry that it almost came to a riot. I leave others to guess what he means by that riddle about the 'surgical sophist.' That has nothing to do with me.[54]

106   As he runs through the faults of those whose philosophy leads them to dabble in speculative theology, the speaker notes with scorn that they attach little importance to poets and orators. This proves clearly enough that he thinks a theologian should attach great weight to them, and cuts directly across all he has said before.

107   But now the old gentleman seems to receive a breath of inspiration. His style suddenly changes as he draws the complete picture of his practitioner of superficial theology, so much so that you would think another person was speaking in his place. Some suspect that this is directed at me. I do not agree, because there are so many charges which do not stick to me. I would not take it entirely as an insult to hear someone count me among foolish theologians, since I never counted myself among theologians of any kind. Nor do I promise a new theology, as some maliciously but quite falsely allege. I am trying, to the best of my ability, to restore an old theology which until now has been far too widely neglected. Where it has been restored, I am trying to help it develop.

108   Wisdom is a quality I have never even claimed for myself, let alone assumed that all of it is embodied in me. It is not the quibbles and definitions in the discussion of the Scriptures that I condemn, but the individuals who fall into the trap of wrong definitions – in fact just the people whom Latomus' old theologian condemned a moment ago.

109   Who was ever foolish enough to treat theology and rhetoric as the same subject?

110   I confess to having said that there are some passages in the Scriptures which make flat, chilly reading if they are studied without the help of sound literary methods. It would be very easy to prove the point, if anyone demanded proof. But our eager, young-at-heart old fellow throws in a proof of his own, and one which is hardly worthy of him.

111   To bring the early theologians to the attention of those who think that the cunning of Scotus encompasses the whole of human knowledge, and do not give a straw for poetry or rhetoric,[55] I put it to them that those ancient masters like Cyprian, Ambrose, Augustine, Victorinus, and Jerome were all products of the rhetorical schools, not the philosophical academies of the Stoa or the Lycaeum. As further proof, we would no doubt be able to make the same point about Paul if he had not taken a jump ahead of us by saying that his message could not be founded on the persuasive power of human knowledge, lest the cross of Christ be made vain.[56] And so he makes himself the greatest of the prophetic bards. What Paul said about the language of the philosophers Latomus tries to twist towards the orators, even though Paul's style is far closer to the rhetorical than the philosophical. Augustine too shows the word-play of the orators, but never the subtleties of the dialecticians.

112   Others must guess at the target of his next attack, for it cannot even appear to be directed at me. In my works language and rhetoric do not 'fill every page.'[57] I declare that languages are the foundation, not the topmost pinnacle, and that rhetoric is no more than a preliminary exercise to equip us for theology.

113   Who praises Origen to the skies because he was an orator and a skilful linguist rather than because he has shown himself the most penetrating investigator and careful interpreter of the Holy Scriptures?

114   What is the crime, if a book gets a good reception because it is sound, decent, and well written? Does Latomus prefer a work to be crude, immodest, and badly written? Is there some disgrace in an author's being respected and defended because of his good literary work? Does he deserve a stouter defence for writing something bad? Is there anything surprising in a book's being set aside, because it is crudely expressed, unless it has useful qualities which excuse the barbarity of the language? The apostles use a crude language, but no one casts their work aside.

115   The force of this speech makes the 'old professor' who pronounces it an unconvincing character: you might say that this was more the style of a poet carried away by his own frenzy. But the old fellow presses on: 'These people,' he says, 'would rather not be understood when they speak than turn by so much as the skin of their nails from classical Latin usage.' He talks as if crude expression was automatically clearer, or as if Latin speakers should pay more attention to those expressing themselves badly and

conciliate them by unlearning their Latin and talking like barbarians. It should be the other way round. The other side should learn to speak Latin correctly, and get rid of their barbarous expressions. But I must say that I have yet to meet anyone whose spoken Latin has got into such a rut that he cannot adapt it to catch the attention of his audience.

116 Next our witty speaker – such a stalwart admirer of the Latin language – turns against Hebrew and calls it into suspicion on two counts. First because Jerome calls it 'barbarous' – as if Plautus had not said the same thing about Latin[58] – then because (he claims) that Jerome's attention to Hebrew involved a consequent loss to Latin. As if the same thing would not happen of its own accord, since he spent a good deal longer on the Greek authors.

117 On he rants ... 'These people,' he claims, 'do not want the course of learning about spiritual matters and the dogmas of the church to be kept within certain limits like a stream within its banks, for that would prevent the free assertion or denial of any proposition by any person. They disapprove of canon law, even of the penalties decreed against heretics and schismatics, and they say that the church defends its beliefs not by reasoned argument but by terror.'

Well, what a childish old man the old fellow turns out to be, though I do not see what any of this has to do with me. Of course it is the theologians' right to teach that proper measures should be taken against stubborn heretics, whether by the stern censures of their bishops or by intervention of the secular magistrates. Yet in his letters Augustine by no means approves of heretics being simply forced to conform, rather than taught to do so. He pleads for the Donatists with some energy and on a number of occasions, urging the authorities not to use violent physical measures against them though they were not only the most ferocious of heretics but brigands into the bargain.[59] Lastly, what we personally want to call heresy does not automatically become so. As we often see, a proposition that stinks of heresy to one theologian does not offend another: one university condemns what others approve.

118 But why should writers of the present age be denied a right that the saintly Aquinas demands for himself, though his very learning entitles him to less consideration? Why, when we review opinions, should we be denied the freedom of commenting on them? Not only Jerome claims this freedom, but every more modern writer takes advantage of it.

119   And why do our critics demand that what is put forward merely as a point for debate should be treated as an article of faith? Why should men who are only toiling to carry research one step further not be granted the same indulgence as any other writer? Perhaps those who seek to deny them that right think that they themselves are gods, and that they therefore need no such indulgence.

120   In one particular passage I urged that in our reading of the Holy Scriptures we should pay the greatest attention to the ideals which would make us most like Christ, rather than fence endlessly over questions such as 'Is sin merely a lack, or does it produce a positive change of quality in the soul?' I think it is more the theologian's task to see that everyone hates sin and flinches away from it. This idea, it seems, offends Latomus' old scholar, who argues that sin cannot in any sense be treated as an entity, and that the logical conclusion of my view would be to treat God, who is the source of all good things, as incapable of being the source of sin because good is an absence of evil ... so we should argue endlessly over tiny issues like these rather than pay real attention to the ideals which would make us worthy of heaven. Excellent reader, I beseech you: tell me if you think it is better to spend some time on the books of Cicero, and make some initial study of the Christian apologists or the fables of the poets – or to read such fanciful fables as these? If the truth was as some suspect, and if Christian modesty meant as little to me as it does to some, I would show them what sort of engineer they have brought into battle against them and make them understand that this gentleness of mine comes from a Christian spirit of forgiveness, not from the fear of any men. But I have found that there is another person, a creature tacked together, alloyed, and compounded from mere guile, craft, and deceit: one who was born, then fashioned to lie, slander, flatter, and insinuate; who will sink to any contrivance to win himself notoriety among future generations and make other men remember him; who harms those whose only aim is to do good to others. It may be an amazingly quick way to make a name for yourself, but it is the most disreputable that can be imagined. I am not saying who he is, where he is from, or where in the world he is working, nor will I ever do so, unless he declares himself.[60]

121   But now our young-at-heart old gentleman has got himself in hand again so let us, too, take what follows in a lighter style. His suggestion, that a man should spend more time and effort on keeping his own views sound than on telling others where theirs have become unsound, is very good advice. But the whole direction of this book is very different indeed.

122   The old scholar has another good point when he says that theology treats all other sciences as its handmaidens. Those who err are people who set some handmaidens on the same level as the mistress or even prefer them to her, or – crueller still – hiss and maltreat her. It does not concern me whether they depend on theology or theology depends on them, so long as it is admitted that theology cannot be understood or discussed without them.

He makes another point which pleased me by suggesting that if any faults have found their way into the system of scholastic education they should be trimmed or pruned away as useless to allow room for what is sound. But so far a few academics have been reacting far too violently against attempts to carry this plan out, wanting the 'useful' and 'essential' to be simply what they have come to know by habit, while refusing to allow promising young men a better chance than they had themselves. But to conclude: since Latomus' old scholar admits that there are two different kinds of theological sophists, why are some so eager to apply what is said against them to all theologians? You see, most gentle reader, that though there are some points in this dialogue which might possibly be thought to apply to me in some sense, by far the great part of it cannot be attached to me. But I saw some danger of the reader's noticing one or two passages referring to me, and so concluding that every single word was aimed in my direction. I thought I might have to confront the sort of charges that Latomus had directed against Luther, perhaps, or Petrus Mosellanus, or Hutten, or some other quite different person. So those who put this suspicion on me are doing a bad turn to us both: to Latomus, by hinting that he wanted to sting me in this dialogue; and to me, by inferring that I am the sort of person to whom all the charges might apply. In fact those who spread the rumour that this pamphlet is not the work of a single author called Latomus but the joint production of a team of theologians are doing the worst possible turn to that entire faculty. I could make some very lengthy answers to some of the charges. But the truth is that it did not seem worth taking much trouble over the business, nor, reader, did I wish to be guilty of keeping you away from better pursuits any longer and wasting your time on these foolish little problems of mine. Farewell.

Louvain, 28 March 1519

DESIDERIUS ERASMUS OF ROTTERDAM:
THE DEFENCE OF THE
DECLAMATION ON MARRIAGE

Desiderii Erasmi Roterodami Apologia
pro declamatione matrimonii

translated and annotated by
CHARLES FANTAZZI

The piece that set this controversy in motion appeared first as the third of four declamations printed by Dirk Martens, Louvain, 30 March 1518.[1] It bore as its title in this original edition *Declamatio in genere suasorio de laude matrimonii*. Erasmus thus cleverly presents his eulogy of marriage in the guise of an oratorical exercise, in which while denying responsibility for the opinions expressed, he grants himself the liberty of saying more than he might otherwise have said.[2] He will remind his opponents repeatedly of the rules of this literary fiction, in the course of the declamation.

As Erasmus states in the letter to Botzheim (Allen I 18:6ff), he originally wrote this declamation in praise of marriage to please his student William Mountjoy and from various indications from the letters and elsewhere it must have been written some time between April 1498 and April 1499.[3] Less than two months after the Martens edition, it was reprinted in Cologne by Nicolas César (20 May 1518) and at the end of August by Froben with the new abbreviated title of *Encomium matrimonii*. More important for its future history is the fact that the declamation, now in the form of an *epistola suasoria*, was included in the treatise *De conscribendis epistolis* published by Froben in 1522.[4] Although it continued to be published independently as a declamation until the year of Erasmus' death, it appears in the Froben 1540 *Opera omnia* only as a part of the longer book.

The first attack against the treatise came from Jan Briart, doyen of the Louvain faculty of theology. In January of 1517, during a brief visit of Erasmus to Louvain, Dorp had invited him to a dinner together with Jean Desmarez at which he said Briart would also be present (Ep 509), anxious, as it would seem, to reconcile Erasmus with the Louvain theologians. Erasmus later reports to Gillis that he succeeded in making peace with them (Ep 516:7), but in a letter of 24 February 1517 addressed to his good friend Ammonio he intimates that the encounter was none too pleasant, and that he remained wary of Briart: 'You would hardly credit, dear Ammonio, how close I have come to a blazing outburst of hostility from the theologians here. In Louvain they were creeping up on me with knives drawn, in a conspiracy (what is more) led by Atensis [Briart], who is all the more dangerous because he was an enemy disguised as a friend' (Ep 539:1–6). In subsequent letters he seems assured that the theologians of Louvain and specifically Briart are now well disposed towards him. He writes to Joris van Halewijn in late August of the same year that with the support of Briart he was being considered for an appointment to the faculty (Ep 641:13–15). He repeats this news to several of his friends, and praises Briart in a note to Tunstall of 17 September, released for publication: 'I find the theologians in Louvain fair-minded and friendly and among them especially Johannes

Atensis, vice-chancellor of the University, a man gifted with incomparable learning and exceptionally civilized' (Ep 675:24–6).

But suddenly the axe fell. In a discourse pronounced on 21 February 1519 at the awarding of the licentiate to a young Carmelite, in the presence of the crowded academic assembly, Briart declared certain propositions concerning marriage and celibacy as heretical. No overt reference was made to the recently published *Encomium matrimonii*, but the insinuation was clear to all. Erasmus wasted no time in responding. The *Apologia*, in the form of a six-leaf quire, was added to some copies of the *Paraphrase on the Epistles to the Corinthians*, published by Martens with the date of 1 March 1519, which itself contained some censorious remarks on virginity and celibacy in the commentary on 1 Cor 7:39 (LB VI 692E–702F). It was printed separately on May 15 by Froben and again as part of the *Apologiae omnes* (1521–2).

Erasmus was very disturbed at this public condemnation by the vice-chancellor of Louvain. He knew that this pronouncement would set off a whole series of attacks, as indeed it did. He was already under heavy attack from Edward Lee, Latomus, the inquisitor Jacob van Hoogstraten, and the implacable papal nuncio, Aleandro. The *Apology* itself is very mild-mannered, although not without its subtle accusations of Briart's naïveté in listening to his fellow theologians without having read Erasmus' work carefully himself.

When the assault was renewed by Briart's disciples, Erasmus wrote another polite letter (Ep 946) to 'a certain theologian,' obviously Briart, asking that he put an end to this plague. Relations between the two men remained strained until Briart's death in the following year, after which Erasmus insisted that the vice-chancellor had always approved of his writings.[5] The memory of the public denunciation before the academic audience remained a rankling one with Erasmus, for he returns to it frequently in his later correspondence.

Erasmus continued to be plagued for the rest of his life by criticisms of his views on marriage and celibacy. The scene changed from Louvain to Paris where in 1525 the faculty of theology of the Sorbonne singled out for attack the translation of the *Encomium* made by Louis de Berquin, the *Declamation des louenges de mariage*. Erasmus responded to their censures in a letter to Noël Béda (Allen Ep 1581) and to Béda's own criticisms he wrote a letter to the Paris faculty sent on 6 February 1526, followed by a formal refutation of Béda's *Annotationes* in the *Prologus in supputationem calumniarum Bedae*, published in August 1526. To this he added an *Appendix de scriptis Clichtovei*, responding to the oblique criticisms made by a Flemish theologian teaching at the Sorbonne, Josse Clichtove, who had taken umbrage at the views expressed by Erasmus on priestly celibacy, a subject dear to him. In the meantime Erasmus had also written a longer treatise, the *Institutio christiani matrimonii* also published in August of 1526, which far from being a retractation is a reconfirmation of his views on the sacrament.

The controversies dragged on with formal condemnations from the Sorbonne and point by point refutations by Erasmus, who never deviated from his views both on matrimony and clerical celibacy. The last lengthy refutation on the subject was the *Dilutio eorum quae Jodocus Clithoveus scripsit adversus Declamationem Des. Erasmi Roterodami suasoriam matrimonii*, published in 1532 but probably written much earlier. It did not appear in the Basel *Opera omnia* of 1540 or in the Leiden edition.

CF

THE DEFENCE OF THE DECLAMATION
ON MARRIAGE

ERASMUS GIVES GREETINGS TO THE EMINENT SCHOLARS
OF THE ILLUSTRIOUS ACADEMY OF LOUVAIN

Since the matter is too well known to be ignored, having been the subject of a public address before a crowded and open assembly, and the suspicion has sunk too deeply into everyone's mind for it to fade away of its own, especially since there are those who attempt by their talk and adverse interpretations to impress it still further into people's minds, I have seen fit by this apology to remove every shadow of suspicion and protect at one and the same time the honour of the excellent theologian, Jan Briart,[1] vice-chancellor of this most renowned school, and my own innocence. In a public ceremony that took place a few days before a certain Carmelite theologian[2] was to receive the honour known as the licentiate,[3] a word now generally accepted but rather poor Latin, Briart gave a speech, as is the custom, which in the opinion of many was stuffed with various insinuations that were purposely directed against my person. Although this was reported to me verbally by several learned men, who agreed both in their suspicions and in their reports, and although this coincided with numerous plausible conjectures from other sources, all of which I shall here prudently omit, nevertheless, I did not allow this suspicion to influence my own feelings. The reason for this was partly my own state of mind, which was not conscious of anything that could implicate me in any such charges (for innocence is not prone to be suspicious); and partly the fact that the character and temperament of Jan Briart were long well known to me. I certainly did not think that his integrity would allow him to sully the reputation of an innocent man in an important public address, nor did I think him capable, given his humane character, of charging publicly with the heinous crime of heresy a friend who had implicit trust in him, even if such a friend were guilty of some error, as men are wont to be, especially since the person concerned was readily available and was not only willing to be admonished but also had frequently and insistently asked for advice.

Even supposing it is possible that the written word may either not be understood or may be interpreted differently than the writer intended, similarly, to say nothing else, just as we as fallible human beings may fall into error in writing, so others can err in reproving, seeing that they are men also. Lastly, it did not seem to befit the prudence of such a great man to open up this loophole[4] and introduce a dangerous precedent into the school of theology, which would allow that in future oblique attacks could be made on anyone's reputation, and that what first began as an attack against one who deserved it, to admit of that possibility, would later be turned against the undeserving, especially in a solemn public oration. This sort of thing would be more excusable in the disputations to which they give the name *quodlibetica*,[5] or in the introductory lectures called *vesperiae*,[6] in which in a custom that is more traditional than worthy of respect the candidate for the doctoral degree is exposed to insulting comments – a tradition, it appears, that was passed on to us from ancient pagan rites, in which one who was to be initiated into the mysteries was subjected to these light-hearted jokes. Plato's *Euthydemus*[7] and Apuleius' *Golden Ass*[8] give ample testimony of this custom.

But since a serious matter was at stake and the person responsible was a man of such prestige, I was fully disposed to disagree with the common opinion. Maarten van Dorp confirmed my sentiments, when, seeing me on the next day, he attested in the presence of Gillis van Delft,[9] a person worthy of respect, that there was nothing in the oration aimed against me. He said that the only thing that could perhaps pertain to me is that he branded as heresy the preference of marriage to celibacy. In this matter, he said, Briart had been falsely informed concerning my encomium of marriage because in some people's opinion I seem there to prefer matrimony to celibacy. And in this also I recognize the politeness of Jan Briart, in that although he was convinced that this was the case, still refrained from mentioning my name, content to condemn the belief. Nor is it surprising that one man should be persuaded when there are so many who urge him on,[10] while there is no one to recall him to the opposite position with well-founded advice.

It remains, therefore, for me to say in a few words that Dorp's report was absolutely correct, namely, that Briart was wrongly informed about my book, which, as I am told, he had not yet read, since he was occupied with more serious concerns. Thus the one who informed him, whoever he was, acted no less wrongfully against Briart than he did against me, in my opinion. Unless I can demonstrate by very clear proofs that I neither say nor believe anything of the kind, I do not wish any arguments in my favour that would protect me from the charge of heresy, even if there were no other defence. The first proof, to begin with the weakest, is that I wrote this insignificant little book as a young man twenty-five years ago, if I am not mistaken. Jerome gives this same reason for excusing his early *Commentaries on Abdias*,[11] a highly serious theological work. 'All right,' they will say, 'you wrote it when you were a young man, but you published it when you were an old man.' I did indeed, but I published it as a work of my youth and on that account to be read with greater allowance for its shortcomings. Moreover, I saw nothing at all in it that should have been suppressed. Unless you claim that if Virgil had published the *Gnat*[12] as an old man or Homer the *Battle of the Frogs and the Mice*[13] so that their first literary experiments would not perish, they would have to be judged by those writings even as old men. I wished to provide young men with a sample of my youthful writing so that in treating similar arguments they might exercise their writing ability and their inventiveness. And I wished this to be noted in my preface and in Froben's.[14]

When I call it a declamation, for that is what it is, does not that very title sufficiently exempt me from all risk, even if throughout the whole book I had preferred marriage to celibacy? Who is not aware that declamations deal with imaginary subjects for the purpose of exercizing one's ingenuity? The Greeks demonstrate this more clearly in the very word they use, μελέτας, which is to say 'exercises.' The nature of these exercises is to treat the argument from both sides, as for and against a tyrannicide, for and against an abductor, for and against war, for and against Alexander. By thus comparing statements and proofs, judgment and invention are developed, the two things that are of most importance in acquiring the power of eloquence. If I had praised fever or drunkenness, it would have been unjust to speak of heresy in a theme that is merely simulated. But if there are some who do not know what a μελέτη is in Greek or a *declamatio* in Latin, I do not think it fair that I should be made to suffer because of someone else's ignorance.

To make it even more apparent that this little treatise was written by me for no other purpose, I have in my possession, as do many others, a work that I had begun a long time ago, *On the Writing of Letters*, in which this subject will be found treated as an example of a letter of persuasion. And there you will also find the opposing argument,[15] which discourages one from taking a wife. There was no other reason for my not publishing it save that being long wearied of the task, I merely collected propositions and arguments and indicated to the casual reader in what ways that aspect of the question might be treated. Since it is a much more prolific topic, it required a more extensive treatment, especially since I saw that it was the subject of declamations by several Greek and Latin authors.[16] Accordingly there was no time to treat the subject for the volume about to be published, and since it had been treated by many writers, it held no attraction for me. If someone should maintain that it is not permitted in any form of writing to say anything that is contrary to Christian truth, on what grounds will we defend almost all modern theologians, who produce proofs to affirm that simple fornication,[17] to use their terminology for a moment, is not a sin.

Then, adducing other reasons, they conclude that it is a crime punishable by death. Let that be cited as an example, in spite of the fact that in this case there is a very great danger that many may find the arguments of the first part too much to their liking. And they do this in a serious work while I merely offer a declamation. What if I had criticized virginity in a declamation in order to provoke others to praise virginity as Glaucon[18] in Plato feignedly criticizes justice and praises injustice for the purpose of inciting Socrates to defend justice? It could perhaps be called rashness or frivolity, but not heresy. Whoever professes to give a declamation disclaims all responsibility for the opinions stated; thus one's ability may be at stake but not one's credibility.

In praising marriage I am dealing with a subject that has received much praise, and if I should succeed in proving my case, there would be no danger to faith and morals involved. I extol marriage so greatly in order to extol virginity even more, which is something I attribute to angels, apostles, and apostolic men. But what I prefer in others I do not approve in the personage whom I invent. I shall not mention for the moment the fact that I do not treat a general question, but one limited by specific circumstances. I envision a noble young man of excellent lineage, on whom depends the sole hope of propagating his race. I prefer marriage for him, not for everyone. This is made explicit in many passages but especially in the division of the discourse at the very beginning when I say: 'But I shall show by the clearest of proofs that this alternative would be far more honourable, profitable, and pleasant for you, and, one might add, necessary even in this day and age.'[19] No one is so rigid in his beliefs, I think, as to deny that there are those for whom marriage is more suitable than celibacy. Moreover, if the argument for the propagation of the race is of such importance that the compiler of the *Sentences* book 4, distinction 33,[20] 'The investigation of ancient practice,' does not hesitate to equate the polygamy of the patriarchs with our institution of marriage, and compares the fornication of those times to our wedlock; and if he uses the same argument to excuse Abraham's sleeping together with his maid-servant and the incest of the daughters of Lot, which Origen[21] all but prefers to some forms of marital union, why should we hesitate to draw a similar conclusion when a similar reason for marriage is proposed? For in the declamation, as we have said, we describe a case in which we argue that marriage is even necessary, in the circumstances, but still do not prefer marriage to virginity, but to celibacy.

Perhaps the one who made this accusation, or rather calumny, thinks that *caelebs* in Latin means one who leads a pure and undefiled life, while the truth is that pimps and debauched nephews, not to mention more obscene examples, could be called celibate, as long as they do not have a lawful wife. And conversely, there is nothing to prevent virginity from existing within wedlock. Once again I should like the impartial reader to allow that I should not be held to blame for someone else's poor knowledge of Latin, especially in such a charge. This is what I plainly discovered in Briart, who after delivering his oracular utterance in the schools admitted to me[22] that he thought *caelibatus* meant a heavenly and chaste vocation and *declamatio* a sermon. I for my part willingly forgive human errors, but I wonder how these persons compel others to make a recantation for mere trifles while in such grave accusations they do not deign to conciliate their brother with a single word or repair the reputations they have recklessly damaged. It is as if they would rather plunge the world into flames than retreat one iota from their authority. I do not think it is a dangerous thing to praise especially when the marriage I praise is very similar to virginity, a marriage in which one has a wife for the production of offspring, not the satisfaction of lust. I shall not pursue single points that this or that person chooses to criticize, according to his intention and inclination. The fact is that I plead the case with arguments drawn from every source, but to give one example, they take offence at the passage in which I say that the reproductive instinct does not come from sin, but from nature (CWE 25 136), since it is a question of those instincts that are not opposed to reason. Likewise the statement, 'I should call one who is not affected by sensual pleasure to be more like a stone than a man' (CWE 25 140), although I plainly indicate I am speaking of licit intercourse, since I add: 'especially if it can be granted to us without giving offence to God' (cf CWE 25 140).

I shall come to the passage which I suspect gives them most offence, in which the one whom I represent as giving the advice says: 'The holiest kind of life is wedlock, purely and chastely observed' (CWE 25 137). For here I seem clearly to prefer marriage to any other state of life. First of all, I could respond that the word 'holiest,' used hyperbolically, means nothing more than 'especially holy.' Secondly, one must take into consideration that marriage is not predicated in an absolute sense but is qualified as 'purely and chastely observed,' so that it is not so much a way of life that is being discussed as the morals of those who live both kinds of life. Nothing prevents us from calling those assembled together 'the assembly,' or patricians and knights the 'patrician' or the 'equestrian order.' Similarly those who follow this or that way of life may be referred to as 'a way of life.' The words that immediately preceded and led to this discussion would remove any doubt that might exist: 'But nowadays conditions and times are such that you would not find anywhere a less defiled purity of morals than among the married' (CWE 25 137). I beseech you, my excellent reader, what could be said more clearly? The words that follow shortly after are consistent with these: 'I only wish those who conceal their vices behind the high-sounding name of castration, and under the pretence of chastity gratify worse lusts, were truly castrated. I do not think that it becomes my sense of modesty to describe the disgraceful actions which those who oppose nature often fall into' (CWE 25 137). Does not this language proclaim clearly enough that I am not speaking of a way of life, but of the corruption of morals? There are great numbers of Christians who have embraced celibacy in such a way as to have debarred themselves from the use of marriage forever. The great majority of them attach themselves to this way of life not so much through love of chastity as for the sake of gain or ease. The hideous and wide-spread lusts which are found among them are known to those who have occasion to listen to the daily accounts of their secret transgressions. Again and again I implore you not to force me to become eloquent on this subject. I do not wish that any race or any class of men be sullied by my words. The prudent reader will recognize my meaning and understand what I so deplore. Let it be sufficient to have alluded to it. Moreover, if I had treated the subject seriously, and in my desire to eulogize marriage had disparaged the dignity of virginity at some point, what difference would there be between my predicament and that of Jerome? While he battles with all his strength in the cause of virginity, he is often quite unfair, not to say unjust to marriage, to such a degree that he was called upon in the letters of many men to recant.[23] St Augustine,[24] too, so extols the blessings of matrimony that I think there would be no lack of things to be censured. If the prerogative of antiquity and authority were removed, he would have judges as unjust as those who confront me, who even calumniate things they do not understand. It is not a harmful distinction to disagree on certain points in an argument debating the more probable of two possible actions as long as you have an excellent opinion of both sides, just as if one person were to prefer the Carmelite mode of life and another the Dominican, but each would express such admiration for the other that the degree of difference would be very slight. Then one must also weigh carefully whether what may be called an error, if one prefers marriage to celibacy without reservation, may also be called a heresy. I shall not discuss this question for the present but reserve it intact for another occasion. Just as according to the saying of Tychonius[25] 'whatever we wish is not necessarily holy,' so whatever we do not like is not necessarily heretical. Christ does not call those who castrate themselves blessed without qualification; he adds 'for the kingdom of God's sake.'[26] Likewise Paul[27] does not prefer celibacy in absolute terms, but for certain reasons, and if they are removed or turned to an opposite purpose, perhaps the order of comparison will be reversed. But we shall neither discuss nor affirm anything in this regard for the moment.

With those few words for the time being we have thought that this false suspicion, unworthy alike of the prudence and dignity of Jan Briart and of our innocence, should be removed from everyone's mind. Concerning other matters which certain people were seizing upon as directed against me, he, as well as Dorp, Delft, and Bintius[28] were quick to come to my defence although I had already made ample defence of myself previously. Concerning the preference of marriage to celibacy, even though this opinion was attributed to me, Briart condemned the belief, not me, for he had not yet found out whether I was guilty of error. Why, then, should I not quote here what Archelaus[29] said when he was doused with water by mistake; 'He didn't douse me but the one he thought me to be.' And yet, it cannot be denied that it is much less serious to be doused with water than to be branded with heresy. My foes will be indignant, I think, at the fact that I ascribe thoughtlessness to a theologian of this academy for having publicly condemned something he had not read. He should have taken care that it could not deservedly be said of him: 'This came from those who put the old man up to this story.' And those who instigated him will be the most indignant, unless perhaps they think it fair that I should prefer to be a heretic rather than expose inaccuracies in those who profess open hatred for me. I don't think there is anything in my books by which anyone could be made worse. I acknowledge that I am a man. I have shown my sincere interest in furthering the cause of piety: I cannot guarantee the outcome. I ask in all circumstances an honest and fair reader. If such is lacking, then neither in Cyprian, nor Hilary, nor Jerome, nor Ambrose, nor Augustine, nor Scotus, nor Thomas, nor Peter Lombard, nor Gerson – in sum, in no writer ancient or modern, will there be anything that can escape the charge of heresy. I won't mention the fact that we read Lactantius, Poggio, and Pontano without uttering a word of criticism. Whoever makes himself the censor of other men's books must first have a thorough understanding of the subject-matter and be guided by reason, not emotion. For envy is no judge, and hatred and anger do not have sound vision.[30] Last of all let him be mindful of Christian civility lest the requital of an unfair judgment fall back upon him some day. For what mortal was ever wise all his days?[31] Who has written so circumspectly that he pleases everyone everywhere, especially since even among a few the variety of opinion is so great, as I have discovered more than once? But let there be a limit both to my apology and to false suspicion. To be sure, I would have preferred to spend this effort on the *Paraphrase on the Epistle to the Galatians*,[32] which I had begun.

Farewell, good reader, whoever you may be.

Louvain, March 1519

ACTS OF THE UNIVERSITY OF LOUVAIN
AGAINST LUTHER

BRIEF NOTES
OF ERASMUS OF ROTTERDAM
FOR THE CAUSE OF THE THEOLOGIAN
MARTIN LUTHER

MINUTE COMPOSED BY A PERSON
WHO SERIOUSLY WISHES
PROVISIONS TO BE MADE FOR THE
REPUTATION OF THE ROMAN PONTIFF
AND THE PEACE OF THE CHURCH

Acta Academiae Lovaniensis contra Lutherum

Axiomata Erasmi pro causa Martini Lutheri

Consilium cuiusdam ex animo cupientis esse consultum
et Romani pontificis dignitati et christianae religionis tranquillitati

translated and annotated by
MARTIN LOWRY

Though all of the short tracts which follow have been attributed at one time or another to Luther rather than Erasmus, and though none of them is precisely dated, the stylistic evidence for attributing them to Erasmus is overwhelming and the three form a natural sequel to the early controversies with which we have been concerned until now. The skirmish with Latomus and the Louvain theologians had been fought in March 1519. It concerned biblical studies and the use of language. Luther's name was only mentioned. The events which form the background to these three tracts took place about eighteen months later, in the autumn of 1520. Luther now fills the entire horizon, and the writer's principal worry is that the reformer and humanist studies may be engulfed together. What had brought the change in direction?

A letter from Luther, obsequiously phrased but designed to enlist Erasmus' prestigious support, carries the same date as the humanist's own reply to Latomus – 28 March 1519. Erasmus replied from Louvain on 30 May, distancing himself from the reformer with a double-edged assurance that he was delighted to make this new acquaintance and urging moderation, but including his usual criticism of academic theology and declaring a 'particular liking' for Luther's commentary on the Psalms. By the end of June the letter had been published. Erasmus' enemies were as quick to pounce on the implied association as he was anxious to deny it.[1] For a while the matters of state mentioned in both the *Axiomata* and the *Consilium* were sufficient to ensure that Luther's ideas remained a matter of academic rather than European politics. By 7 November 1519, the Universities of Cologne and Louvain, both apparently prompted by the inquisitor Hoogstraten, had pronounced against a number of Luther's propositions. But with the imperial election in the autumn and the Field of Cloth of Gold in May 1520, the rulers and their councillors had other things to occupy them. It was the arrival of Charles V in the Low Countries on 7 June, his coronation on 22 October, and the preparations for his first Diet at Worms the following January, that thrust Luther into the limelight. Dealing with the imperial princes now meant dealing with him as well.[2]

The papal bull *Exsurge Domine*, excommunicating Luther, was promulgated on 15 June 1520 and reached the new emperor in the Low Countries. It provided the occasion for Erasmus' declared enemies within the theology faculty at Louvain to plunge into the manipulation of committees, the inflammatory sermons, and the sporadic book-burning which are denounced and ridiculed in the *Acta* (102). The same passage makes it quite clear what tactics the writer was following: he hoped to drive one wedge between Rome and the universities, by suggesting that the text of the bull had been tampered with in Cologne or Louvain, and another between the different faculties at Louvain itself, by showing that the theologians had failed to follow the correct procedure. It was only playing for time: but time might give a more moderate faction at the curia the opportunity it needed.[3]

But for Erasmus, the events of October 1520 were given a harder edge of personal bitterness by the papal official who brought the bull. Girolamo Aleandro was an old friend of his. He had helped Erasmus to gather Greek material for the Venetian edition of the *Adagia*, and Erasmus had spoken to him of the opportunities that waited in France. Since then, the adroit pursuit of patronage had raised Aleandro to an eminence which Erasmus found hard to accept in the poor student with whom he had once shared Andrea Torresani's limp lettuce and reeking shellfish.[4] He felt a profound sense of betrayal, both of his own friendship and of the humanist principles which he and Aleandro had once shared. Was there also, perhaps, a tinge of jealousy behind the malicious fictions of the first paragraph of *Acta*? Language as extreme as that no doubt made it safer to publish anonymously in 1520, and may account for the polemic's being included in editions of Luther's *Opera omnia* in 1546, 1556, 1562, and as recently as 1865. But as early as 1521 Cratander had recognized Erasmus' turn of phrase and the repeated verbal echoes both of contemporary letters, and of the *Axiomata*, place the identity of the real author beyond reasonable doubt.[5]

The *Axiomata* themselves belong to the next stage of the political process, when Elector Frederick the Wise, who had not attended the coronation, met the imperial court at Cologne in early November and was urged by Aleandro to respect the bull and have Luther arrested. Genuinely puzzled by both the theological and the jurisdictional aspects of the problem, Frederick sought the advice of Erasmus through his secretary Georgius Spalatinus. The list of points, simplified in deference to the elector's indifferent Latin, was delivered on the evening of 5 November and may well have played a crucial part in tipping Frederick's judgment towards continuing to protect his subject. It also aligned Erasmus once again with Luther, and, against the humanist's express desires, was published immediately and under his name, probably in Leipzig. Two more editions, one definitely from Worms, appeared within a year. Thereafter the sheet ceased to have topical interest, and remained unedited until it was included in texts of Luther's *Opera* from 1546.[6]

Though the *Consilium* belongs to the same period of anxious lobbying between the arrival of the bull and the meeting of the imperial diet which would decide how to respond, its tone differs markedly from that of the other two tracts. The venom of the *Acta* and the haste of the *Axiomata* are discarded. Instead, we have a carefully argued scheme which aimed, first, to placate and strengthen the moderate group in the curia to whom Erasmus had gestured in the *Acta*, and second, to suggest definite plans for the way of arbitration which he had indicated to Elector Frederick in the *Axiomata*.[7] Erasmus had discussed the idea of an international committee of arbitration in detail with the Dominican liberal Johannes Faber at Louvain in October 1520. Prior of Augsburg, vicar-general of Upper Germany since 1512, and an imperial councillor since 1515, Faber was admirably placed to influence the diet and his plans for the foundation of a Collegium Trilingue in his own cloister made him a natural ally of Erasmus at this moment. Both were in Cologne during November. A letter from Erasmus to Conrad Peutinger, dated 9 November, urges that councillor to support the plan at the coming diet: and the appearance of the first edition of *Consilium* in Cologne early in 1521 suggests that the publication may have been part of the two authors' strategy for their scheme. By then it was too late. Luther had his own plans for influencing the diet, and *The Babylonian Captivity of the Church* demolished any idea of cool theological appraisal by a learned tribunal.[8]

The *Consilium* was issued five times in quick succession, two of the editions being dated 1521, the remainder lacking evidence of date or place. It was included in the editions of Luther's *Opera* in 1562 and '64, then – more surprisingly – in a complete edition of Zwingli's works which appeared in 1832. Given the studiously moderate tone and the possibility that the first edition was printed direct from an author's manuscript, the anonymity of this tract is less easy to understand than that of its two companions.[9] Aleandro's suspicion of Erasmus may have made it seem politic to circulate the scheme without the humanist's name on it. Or the known co-operation of Erasmus and Faber may have given the document a dual authorship which both preferred to respect. One critic, arguing from Erasmus' later assertion that Faber had shown him a draft of the scheme in Cologne, has attributed the whole work to the Dominican. But the stylistic evidence of Faber's other work, of Erasmus' letters, and of the two related tracts, once again puts the matter beyond any reasonable doubt.[10] The polemic, the brief notes, and the elaborate scheme build up a coherent picture of Erasmus' last effort to settle the religious problem according to the principles of reason and moderation that he had been preaching for the past two decades.

ML

ACTS OF THE UNIVERSITY OF LOUVAIN
AGAINST LUTHER

I shall be delighted to convey the latest news to you, as it is in everyone's interest that the facts should be as widely known as possible. A few days ago Girolamo Aleandro arrived. He thinks himself by far the greatest of men and not only because of his knowledge of languages, profound though it is – if Hebrew was his native tongue, he grew up with Greek from boyhood and learned Latin by teaching it incessantly: but the antiquity of his tribe seems also to do wonders for his self-esteem. He is a Jew by birth, and that race boasts beyond all measure of tracing its descent from the most ancient patriarch Abraham. Nobody knows whether Aleandro has really been baptized. He certainly cannot be a Pharisee, for he does not believe in the resurrection of the dead and there is not a single vile habit which he avoids, living indeed as if the whole of him were going to rot away with his body. The least offence will provoke him to a fury that verges on insanity: his conceit is uncontrollable, his greed insatiable, his lust as unspeakable as it is unbounded: a total slave to his own self-advancement, he lacks the determination to build his own reputation by refining his style and the moral qualities even to attempt it in straightforward argument.[1]

Well, just to leave none of us in doubt, he has chosen a perfect moment to abandon his pretence of a desertion to us Christians. For he has snatched up his pen with the aim of celebrating his master Moses and darkening the glory of Christ, which is just beginning to blossom again at the present time as superstition and the futile but deadly old rites of mankind lose their force. So he arrived recently armed with papal letters, and set on doing his utmost to destroy all the most promising developments he can find. Farewell.

This is simply what I wanted you honest readers to know.

Now the tyranny of blockheads and maniacs is seething to its height. Aleandro had a number of books burned in the market-place by the public executioner and prosecutor on the very day when the king left Louvain. In fact I could say that the deed was done in the king's presence. They tried the same trick at Antwerp, but it failed. Hoogstraten is back in his old job of inquisitor and makes frightful threats to all who have not bowed down to that beast of his.[2] The Louvain theologians are threatening Dorp that they will throw him out of their synagogue unless he retracts a speech which he recently published, and in which he praised linguistic knowledge.[3]

The affair has been conducted according to the procedure which theologians usually follow. The university council was summoned under oath to the rector's residence. The residence was not big enough to hold the council. Rector Rosemondt is unwell, and is now showing the sort of man he was before this. Though the university had been solemnly assembled to hear proposals put by the envoys of the pope, the only people to show up were two lecherous, bearded little clerks who waved the copy of the tremendous bull as it had been produced at Louvain, set the original alongside it, and said 'compare the two.' The bull was read. And there they sat for two hours. The council took no other decisions than to take the bull as read. On the following day the theologians proceeded through their subcommittee as if the whole issue had been dealt with by the university, although Aleandro had as yet said nothing about his commission and the bull had neither been examined by the appropriate authorities nor approved by all, as should have been the case in a matter of such importance. A few books were burned in the market-place, but everyone stood laughing.[4]

On 9 October Baechem preached a sermon to the people in a style which was worthy of him – that is to say, it was savage and idiotic. He said more against Erasmus, who was in the congregation, than against Luther, and it was the most shameless pack of lies. Luther, he said, had fallen into these frightful heresies of his because he was greedy for new and revolutionary change – all this in spite of the fact that Luther has drawn all his ideas from Augustine, Bernard, Gerson, and Cardinal Nicholas of Cusa. Erasmus, he claimed, had done all in his power to favour Luther's cause – this in spite of the fact that Erasmus has never had anything to do with Luther's cause at all but has only blamed the fashion in which attacks have been made on him.[5] Those who could not or would not try to refute him have tried simply to shout him down before audiences of ordinary people. Baechem had a good deal to say in the same vein, including a sidelong criticism of linguistic studies and the New Testament. Almost everybody had a laugh at his performance.

The following Sunday, 14 October, he worked over the same arguments as he displayed the bull to the people. 'Look at the seal,' he urged, as if waving the seal at a great distance was the same thing as securing approval for the bull. Among his new points was an offensive mention of Erasmus. 'They will come to the stake themselves sooner or later,' he bawled, 'unless they relent.' As if the bull were not enough, an ordinance was issued by the rector which added many points not contained in the bull, including a ban on the sale of pamphlets defaming the universities and their worthy members. This was the theologians' defence against the speeches of Dorp and Mosellanus.[6]

There was a rumble of discontent from the lawyers, who now have a serious disagreement with the theologians. Few theologians appeared when one of the lawyers defended his propositions:[7] when he received the licence to practise which resulted from this defence, there were no theologians at all except for Dorp and Erasmus. For on that very day the theologians had banned the meeting at which the licence was to have been granted: but there was an immediate appeal, and it was shown that they had no power to issue such a ban. They still refused to withdraw it. But they agreed among themselves that no theologian would appear and, apart from Dorp (whom nobody told), none did so. As far as Erasmus was concerned, they decided not to invite him to any meetings. What a terrible fate!

How could one's amazement do justice to men's stupidity? This is an issue so serious that it could disturb the entire world: yet they tackled it in this thoughtless, short-sighted manner. It is common knowledge that the matter was handled in Rome without proper procedure, and in the face of determined opposition from the cardinal of Santa Croce and many others. The bull was hatched at Cologne and Louvain, printed before it had even been promulgated: and the printed version differs from the bull which Aleandro is bearing. Experts by whom the bull has been read confirm that many of its clauses rouse suspicion of forgery. The style is that of the friars, which is poles away from that of the Roman court, and it contains a great many vulgarisms. No one accepts it as authentic, except the theologians. It has never been examined. Nor does it specify the errors which it mentions.[8]

Now look at those who have been in charge of this splendid business. The first was Cardinal Cajetan, and it would be impossible to find a more hardened and arrogant rogue than this Dominican. After him came Karl von Miltitz; Marino Carracciolo took over from him;[9] and last of all came the marvellous Girolamo Aleandro, a man who has no sense of shame and one whom general gossip, his face, his speech and his faith openly declare to be a Jew. The Jews recognize him as one of them. It is fated for Christians to be plagued by Jews. It was a Jew who prodded Pope Julius towards destroying the world. In Cologne Pfefferkorn threw the Christian world into confusion.[10] And now Aleandro, the blood-brother of Judas, is outdoing even his ancestors and is set on betraying the future of the gospel for only three pieces of silver. His reputation in Padua and Paris was such that instead of spending his time burning other people's books, he should be burned himself.[11] You cannot call somebody who believes in nothing a heretic. Someone or other put out a royal edict for the bull to be carried out – the king either knew nothing of it, or had been badly briefed – and along came that notorious and unprincipled glutton Remacle to do the job.[12]

Now, if you like, let us look at the beginning of it all. The affair sprang at first from the hatred of languages and literature that Reuchlin attracted. It was pushed along by that maniac Hoogstraten, assisted by his idiotic fellow-maniac Baechem. Then came Latomus, a Frenchman whose considerable learning had taken the wrong turning. The mendicant orders joined in, fearing that someone might tell them to fast or work with their hands if the dominion of the Roman pope, which allows them their present reign of ease, was to be weakened. No single theologian condemns all the articles mentioned in the bull. But just as Octavius, Lepidus, and Anthony joined forces and, as part of their scheme to crush public liberty, agreed that each would allow some of his friends to be killed, so these theologians of ours have sought favour with one another by allowing one man to condemn some points so long as the other keeps his side of the deal by condemning what the first hated or thought would run against his interests.[13] The Louvain school does not condemn the point to which Luther attaches the greatest weight, that is that the primacy of the pope is not a matter of divine law. Jan van Turnhout, in preparing his rejection of Luther's *Conclusions*, indicated that he wanted this point to remain untouched.[14] So they show clearly enough that on this point they agree with Luther – yet they have still allowed it to be condemned in the bull. There are others at Louvain who wanted to exclude particular articles from the general condemnation. So here are just two universities which are in on the same plot but still do not agree.

Now these theologians admit that the works of Aquinas, Scotus, Peter Lombard, Augustine, and all the rest of them contain errors and the same errors that they condemn in Luther. Yet they find no cause for offence in these cases. This is sufficient proof that their own action stems from hatred of Luther rather than a zeal for the faith in which these idlest of men, who love only themselves and are eager only for power, do not possess. No one has given Luther a brotherly word of advice, though he is ready enough to learn. No one has shown him where he is wrong. No one has refuted his arguments. They have begun, at long last, to examine arguments against him in the schools, but within such narrow limits that no bachelor would be allowed to speak to any theologian who produced an argument (in favour of Luther) which they could not refute. They were greatly incensed, and summoned a meeting to throw the individual out. Turnhout and Latomus have begun to refute Luther in their lectures but they have scarcely completed two headings – just enough to give them an excuse for gaining the sort of short-term advantages that we can see they have gained in the eyes of fools.

Suppose the matter was taken to the point where the theologians were given a free chance of saying, without reasoned evidence, 'This is false, this is heretical, this is offensive.' There are no books in which you cannot find something that might attract this sort of charge, so anyone with whom Hoogstraten is the least bit displeased will be summoned off to the stake, while good literature and good men will be betrayed to the whim of an uneducated, impulsive rogue. In his prefaces he rolls out those bragging syllogisms which he is going to use to whip us into line, whether we like it or not. And straight after that he brings in the executioner with his faggots ... as if this executioner in a cowl needed any assistance.

Everything that has been written against Luther up to this time shows an obvious strain of madness. All the writers flatter the pope with the most disgusting extravagance. The first in the field was Cardinal Cajetan: then came Sylvester Prierias; Thomas Todischus was third, the fourth a Franciscan named Augustinus.[15] Unless I am mistaken, the Louvain theologians are not going to publish their dreary tracts. Christ did not think it was beneath his dignity to teach even the lowest and most ordinary people: these fellows think themselves too grand to teach a man of high character and learning. If all the bishops go on winking an eye at this sort of conduct, as some are doing at present, they will soon find themselves in a position where the friars have seized absolute control and joined hands with the pope to trample like tyrants on the heads of their bishops.

Someone is going to say, 'So what? It's hard to stand up to the pope.' First, it is a very safe supposition that all this is being done without the pope's knowledge, or certainly without his being properly informed. Let Aleandro be questioned, and he will be proved a criminal and a Jew. Let the bull be examined, and it will be proved a forgery. Even if it did come from the pope, immediate action should not be taken. The pope should be given time to hear sounder advice: otherwise, there is a danger that this affair will provoke serious disorders throughout the Christian world. It's easy enough to remove Luther from the libraries. It's not going to be nearly so easy to remove him from men's hearts, unless those unanswered criticisms of his are met, and unless the pope states the opposing argument with the evidence of Holy Scripture behind him. These drones have been imposing their views on the world for quite long enough: from now on, the world wants some plain answers. There is no lack of minds which can be persuaded by the truth, and they cannot be scared by a whiff of smoke. Truth will not be crushed, even if Luther is.

BRIEF NOTES OF
ERASMUS OF ROTTERDAM
FOR THE CAUSE OF THE
THEOLOGIAN MARTIN LUTHER

The matter has sprung from a tainted source, the hatred of literature and the claim for spiritual domination.

The means by which it has been pursued are in keeping with this source – wrangling, conspiracies, bitter passions, and poisonous libels.

The persons by whom it is being pursued are suspect.

At the same time it is said that the best authorities and those closest to the doctrine of the Gospels are least offended by Luther.

It is well known that certain persons are taking advantage of the pope's good nature.

This makes it the more important to avoid hasty decisions on this question.

More is at stake on the issue than some realize.

The severity of the bull strikes all reasonable men as quite out of keeping with the very gentle character of Christ's vicar.

For this reason, the bull should have been far more carefully scrutinized by unbiased persons who are experienced in questions of this kind.

So far, only two of such an innumerable crowd of universities have pronounced against Luther: they have done so in general terms, without advancing specific charges, and they do not agree with one another.

In offering to submit himself to a public disputation before unbiased arbitrators, Luther seems to all reasonable observers to be making a reasonable request.

Luther's critics are using arguments which no Christian audience can tolerate.

But anyone who sets himself up as a judge or critic should be above reproach.

Since he has no personal ambitions, Luther should be the less subject to suspicion.

Other parties are trying to forward their own interests.

The pope should set Christ's glory before his own, and the gaining of souls before any shorter-term gain.

Even granting the profound importance of this issue, it would have been more fitting to tackle it at a different time.

Pressing matters of state are under discussion, and the beginning of Charles' reign should not be shrouded by ghastly debates of this kind.

Since the pope's reputation is under discussion, it seems best to settle the issue through the sane advice of unbiased and discreet persons. This will provide the best defence of the pope's position.

Those who have written against Luther up to this time are being criticized even by theologians who oppose Luther on other grounds.

The world is thirsting for the gospel truth, and seems to be borne on its way by some supernatural desire.

So this desire should perhaps not be resisted by such hateful means.

MINUTE COMPOSED BY A PERSON WHO SERIOUSLY WISHES PROVISIONS TO BE MADE FOR THE REPUTATION OF THE ROMAN PONTIFF AND THE PEACE OF THE CHURCH

It is part of the Christian spirit to give sincere support to the vicar of Christ, and to wish that his standing be unimpaired. Conversely, it is a sign of the pope's devotion to his duty to let no private interest come so close to his heart that he would not gladly set the glory of his captain, Christ, and the general peace of the Christian church before it. Yet those who support the pope's status and dignity should do so with discretion. They will do that if they protect it with reasoned arguments which are likely to receive tacit support from men of sound character and judgment. On the other hand, no one does more to injure the pope's reputation than the man who wants to keep it safe and sound with no defence other than the intimidation or bribery of his fellow men. So whoever is most committed to the well-being of the Christian faith is most grieved at the confusion which has been caused by a few individuals who goaded Luther into writing in rather too free a vein, and stirred the pope's normally mild disposition into dealing rather more severely with Luther than was perhaps best for the peace and repose of the Christian community. No attempt is being made here to weigh the rights and wrongs of Luther's writings: but we are being advised to take account not only of what Luther deserves, but of what is best for the peace of the church. It is often best to take no open action against injuries, in case that action leads in its turn to some more serious disturbance.

First of all, it is sufficiently clear that the issue had ugly origins – that is to say, the hatred of the good literature which is just beginning to come of age among the Germans, and the resentment of the study of languages which is coming to life everywhere these days.[1] Those who, until now, have been able to pass themselves off as teachers of the most exquisite scholarship without the help of these disciplines fear that their authority may be outshone by the lustre of literary studies. So a few have taken certain measures to crush them. They differ greatly in this aim from the Roman pontiff, who has always treated literature with the greatest respect. As far as the case of Luther is concerned, by far the greatest part of this trouble should be blamed on those who, both in sermons and pamphlets, made claims about the nature of indulgences and the power of the pope which no educated and religious audience could tolerate. So, if we look at the beginning of the trouble, Luther seems to have been stirred by righteous indignation and zeal for the Christian faith. Afterwards he may have begun to write in sharper terms: but even those who cannot excuse him for this lighten their reproach by admitting that savage provocation and invective from several directions gave him some reason for acting in this way. Before they had even read his books, people were shouting to one and all 'Heretic, antichrist, schismatic!' – and taking care to do so before papal authority could intervene in the matter. Nobody troubled to give the man a word of advice, or to refute him, though he offered to take on all and sundry in debate and is still doing so. All they could do was condemn him. Even those who secured the bull against Luther do not approve of the replies of Prierias and Augustinus.[2]

Though the discussion with Eck was committed to the decision of the school of Paris, it had been preceded by judgments from the Universities of Cologne and Louvain, which had received no such commission and confined themselves to condemning Luther. And although they took this course in collusion, they still do not agree on the articles they select for condemnation – and they are the most important articles.[3] Finally the persons who have been dealing with the matter up to now are characters whom one might reasonably suspect, for their own interests are at stake. Their lives and learning are not of a quality to give much weight to their judgment, especially in a case of such gravity.

Observers of the highest character and scholarship are rightly critical of the means that have been followed in proceeding against Luther: even if Luther had written open heresy, such tactics would have been excessive. Criticizing the method and origins of the case does not mean one is favouring Luther, any more than insisting on the proper course of trial and verdict means arguing that a parricide should not receive his just punishment. The bull against Luther is being published in a form that lacks all mercy and is viewed with displeasure even by those who support the claims of papal power. It smacks more of the uncontrollable hatred of a few monks than of the peaceful character of the person who now fills the role of our most gentle Saviour, and has none of the sharp intelligence of our lord Leo, who so far has appeared the most mild and approachable of men.[4] This creates a strong suspicion that certain parties are taking advantage of his naturally pleasant, easy-going temperament to forward their own private ambitions. But the more sacred we all consider the position of the Roman pontiff, the more carefully we should strive to prevent anything being dispatched from his court which might seem unworthy of him in the view of good men. They may not express those views, but no prince, however great, can afford to neglect them. So the more widespread and dangerous this issue becomes, the more care should be taken to see that no hasty decision is made.

Everyone knows that Christian behaviour has declined steeply from the pure gospel truth of Christ's own message, as standards slipped gradually. In fact there is nobody who does not admit the need for a widespread, general revival of law and morality. But if it is important to avoid rash experiments, it is as important to refrain from snarling thoughtlessly in the face of those who make well-intentioned suggestions, even if they do seem rather too free-spoken. It may be beyond doubt that Luther has wandered from the truth: but a humane school of theology would first have given him a word of brotherly advice,[5] then refuted him with sound arguments based on the evidence of Holy Scripture and only treated him as we usually treat a desperate case if he refused to recant in the face of this proof of his error. Those who suggest this course of action are not supporting Luther, but the theological profession and the reputation of the Holy See. By this means, if any, Luther's threat could be completely demolished: but he would have to be removed first from men's minds, and then from the libraries. The present policy of book-burning will destroy his influence in the libraries, up to a point: but in the meantime his ideas will have become fixed in many people's minds, for they can see those ideas are not being refuted.[6]

Laymen too who are gifted with intellectual powers can exercise their own judgment: even among the learned, judgment is very largely an inborn quality. There are many men of advanced learning and high moral character whose devotion and commitment to gospel truth shows them little, if anything to criticize in Luther's writings. Intellects of this kind want to be taught. They ought not, and do not want to be compelled. To submit to nothing but compulsion is a quality of donkeys: to apply nothing but compulsion is the mark of tyrants.[7] The appropriate course for theologians is most certainly to instruct with all possible mildness, not to press things ahead with shouts of abuse, bribery, and cabals.

What Luther really deserves is not the only question these men should have in mind, and I am not venturing any premature judgments on him here: they should also be thinking what policy is most likely to promote the peace of the Christian community in the present crisis. We can see that Luther is saluted on all sides as a man of unimpeachable character. He has gained such a place in the minds of his fellow Germans, especially, but of other nations as well, that those whose judgment is least tainted, that is furthest removed from all considerations that usually pervert it, are also least hostile to Luther.

There is no single reader who does not admit that he has profited from

Luther's books, even if they do contain some points of which, perhaps rightly, he does not approve. We know the character of the German people. We can see how Bohemia remained stubborn for so many years, and that the neighbouring regions are not far from this way of thinking.[8] Every day we hear serious complaints as many growl that the yoke of the Roman see can be borne no longer. They do not, perhaps, blame this on the pope, so much as on those who use the pope's authority to turn themselves into tyrants.

Anyone who has any sense can easily see that less serious issues have often brought the most frightful divisions into the world: it is easy enough to guess what confusion could result from this, if the matter is handled with violence and abuse; and it is just as easy to see the value of good sense. The world seems also to be tired of a theological method which has sunk too far into the niceties of formal logic, and to be athirst instead for the message of the Gospels.[9] If the doors are not opened to it, the Christian world will break in by force. So even if Luther's ideas are completely rejected, changes should still be brought into this sophistical theology.

So the matter started badly and errors seem to have been made on both sides: but the first came from those whose unholy provocations roused Luther's anger, then embittered him more and more by hateful, ferocious ravings. The worst point is that these people appear to be furthering their own interests while no such suspicion falls on Luther, who is quite content with his humble position. The conclusion must be that the whole matter must be settled by persons who are far above all suspicion.

The truth is that investigating matters of faith is the particular function of the Roman pontiff, and what is his by right should not be taken from him. But for the public good he ought to allow this question to be passed to others – men of outstanding knowledge, proven virtue, and unstained honour, whom no one could possibly suspect of wishing, whether through fear of punishment or hope of advancement, to flatter the pope and forget the truth of the Gospels, or of favouring the other party for some purely human motive.

These arbitrators should be chosen from their subjects by each of the three kings who are themselves furthest from suspicion – the emperor Charles, the king of England, and the king of Hungary.[10] They should read Luther's books through and through with care, hear him in person, and pronounce their decision in his presence. And that decision will be final. Luther will recognize his error when it is honestly pointed out to him, and will take care to produce definitive editions of his books once they are cleansed of all errors, so that the great profit of this scriptural harvest will not be ruined because of a few small blunders. Many feel it is both unjust and inexpedient to let what is right be included in the condemnation of a few human mistakes. Even the books of Augustine contain passages which, when pointed out and read aloud by clerks, seem like heretical opinions, full of blasphemy and impiety.

But if Luther stands by the points which have been condemned by the arbitrators, then extreme measures will have to be taken. But no one will support Luther when he has been so properly vanquished: and if he recants, the affair will be settled without any confusion in the Christian commonwealth.

Such a course will do nothing to lessen the authority of the Roman pontiff, rather it will take care of the suspicion of those who perhaps think that the pope's judgment on this matter is not quite so weighty, because he could seem to be biased as it concerns indulgences and the primacy. In fact the pope's sense of duty will gain universal approval, if he concedes some of his prerogative to advance the truth of and the peace of the Christian world.

But if some do not approve of this method, the next best course is evidently to pass the matter to the next general council: and the state of the Christian community, which is rotten in many parts, seems for many reasons to demand such a conclave.

It seems quite inappropriate to deal with such a difficult question almost as a side-issue in the turmoil of important state business. There is uncertainty on every side, especially in Spain and Germany, so it is not the time to throw on the stuff of which new upheavals can be made.[11] Besides, it is only right that the installation of a new emperor should be completed in a favourable atmosphere, and that the proceedings should not be made miserable and unlucky by an unpleasant business such as this.

I do not want this document to anticipate anyone's verdict. But I have said, with an unbiased mind, what seems to me the best course to follow. And my main reason for doing so was the invitation of the highest leaders in church and state. I long for the truth of the gospel to conquer, and for all things to give way to the glory of Christ. Amen.

May the knowledge of Christ's truth be victorious.

MANIFEST LIES

Manifesta mendacia

translated and annotated by
ERIKA RUMMEL

In March 1525 there appeared in Antwerp a book under the pseudonym 'Godefridus Ruysius Taxander' in which Erasmus' views on confession were attacked in vicious terms.[1] Erasmus knew of the publication within a month of its appearance and identified it as a collaborative effort by four Dominicans, among whom Vincentius Theoderici played the leading role.[2]

Theoderici (1481–1526), a member of the faculty of theology at Louvain, had been critical of Erasmus' theological positions for some time and had had a personal confrontation with him in 1520.[3] He was eager to publish his criticism of Erasmus, but was restrained by his vicar, whose orders he eventually circumvented by publishing under a pseudonym.[4] Erasmus' first defensive action was to dispatch a letter of protest to the faculty of theology at Louvain.[5] He saw the attack as the latest development in an ongoing battle with the Louvain theologians, which had already prompted exchanges with Maarten van Dorp, Briart of Ath, and Jacques Masson.[6] He was also preparing a rejoinder to 'Taxander's' book, but in the end decided to suppress it. His reply, entitled *Manifest Lies*, is however preserved in manuscript in the Royal Library at Copenhagen.[7] Although the existence of the manuscript, an Erasmian autograph, was pointed out by C. Reedijk in 1966, it has languished in obscurity until now because Erasmus' scrawl is difficult to decipher. For the same reason the apologia was wrongly identified, first as a polemic against Diego López Zúñiga, then as a reply to Jacques Masson, until my own, more detailed, analysis showed that it was addressed to 'Taxander.'[8]

We can only speculate on the reason for Erasmus' decision not to publish his apologia. One factor may have been Theoderici's death in August 1526. However, Erasmus had ample time to reply in the interval, and the demise of an opponent did not necessarily keep him from continuing a polemic, as the notorious case of Alberto Pio shows.[9] A more cogent explanation for Erasmus' discretion in this case would be the intervention of higher authorities. Erasmus himself had petitioned both pope and emperor to intervene on his behalf in the controversy with the Louvain theologians and to prevent them from further attacks. Both authorities responded to Erasmus' pleas and issued pertinent instructions to the faculty of theology. Erasmus complained that these directives were ineffectual,[10] except for keeping Masson from adding a fourth hostile pamphlet to the three published already,[11] but the efforts made on his behalf by the authorities put him under a moral obligation to keep the peace himself. Two reasons may therefore have combined to keep the *Manifest Lies* in limbo: It was impolitic to publish a polemic while negotiations for peace were going on; and when it became apparent that the negotiations had failed and Louvain was not keeping its side of the bargain, it was no longer appropriate to publish the apologia since the adversary had died and a new enemy, Frans Titelmans, had taken over the stage.[12]

Although Erasmus did not publish *Manifest Lies*, he remained implacable towards his late critic and his collaborators. In 1529 he sarcastically referred to the pseudonymous authors as 'those four elect champions of the church' and their leader, 'Professor Bucenta.'[13] He recalled Theoderici's attack once more in 1534, noting his own discretion: 'I turned a deaf ear to Vincentius and his Dominican cronies' (Allen Ep 2956:32).

I would like to take this opportunity to thank Dr J. Trapman and Joseph Wey CSB, whose assistance has greatly improved the transcription of the text on which this translation is based. The page numbers preceding each paragraph are Erasmus' cross-references to the relevant passages in 'Taxander's' book. Since that publication has signatures only, Erasmus must have paginated his private copy for the sake of convenience.

ER

MANIFEST LIES

At the beginning of his charming preface he says that I make assertions about or cast doubt on what has been decided by the church, indeed by Christ himself.[1] He is referring to my *Exomologesis*.[2] Indeed, in my dispute with Lee[3] I state that this confession must be accepted no differently than if it had been instituted by Christ himself. These are my words: 'We do not read that Christ has instituted secret confession, yet these people believe what they have not read, and I believe what the church has ordained and what is by general consensus approved as handed down by the Spirit of Christ and through him by Christ himself; and I believe that [the practice of confession] must be observed no less than if Christ had handed it down to us.'[4] Is this statement not sufficiently clear? And yet I speak not of confession in general, but of 'this' confession, that is, of confession as it is practised today. I have added the pronoun to include all the circumstances of this form of confession. I conclude my discussion thus: 'If the church affirms in an unequivocal decree that this form of confession is based on divine law, if she believes that it was instituted by Christ himself, if she believes that it cannot be abolished, I do not contest the judgment of the church, but adapt my view to her certain pronouncement, however different it may be.[5]

According to Masson's book, *De generibus quaestionum*,[6] it is sufficient for a person to state that confession is necessary either because it is taught in Holy Writ or because it is handed down by Christ or because it is prescribed in canon law through a general edict of the church. In his book *De confessione*[7] he admits that it was instituted by men, as far as incidentals are concerned.

Nor do I call anything into doubt in my *Exomologesis*. On the contrary, I say that I do not wish to discuss the many points called into doubt by others.[8] And I explain to the reader the subject I undertook to treat there.

But, he says, I should have stated that confession is necessary. I have already stated that elsewhere. That confession, as practised today, was instituted by Christ I shall state when I have heard it in the certain pronouncements of the church or when I have convinced myself of it and can demonstrate the corresponding position to others as well. If I had not thought that confession is necessary, I would have written my book *De modo bene confitendi* in vain. And I am being thanked for reassuring some people who were uncertain in this respect. I myself practise confession and shall do so till I die, nor am I suggesting to anyone that it is right not to go to confession.

1   But I do not, at present, intend to respond to the cavils of Masson. I merely want to show what an impudent lie it is to say that there are in my books 'insane assertions, impiety, and scurrilous blasphemy against the Holy Spirit and his bride, the church.'[9]

page 4
2   No less impudent is the lie that I may myself be 'the champion of a false liberty,'[10] when all my writings have a very different message. Moreover, he casts into my teeth words from the *Spongia*, in which I criticize those who make a bad job of vindicating evangelical freedom,[11] whereas I praise ceremonies and human constitutions and obedience toward superiors in more than one place.

page 4
3   Everywhere he calls Luther my disciple,[12] although no one has so far been able to point out in my books a proposition that is among the condemned Lutheran propositions. Certainly Luther would never acknowledge such a teacher.

page 5
4   But it is even more impudent to say that in my books I lash out against the chastity of priests, that I want confession among Christian laymen, that I condemn fasting which I praise everywhere, that I condemn feast days and the distinction between foods. Concerning the celibacy of priests I have answered Ath.[13] In the tract to Christopher, bishop of Basel,[14] I merely discuss whether it would be expedient to permit priests to marry, which in any case I would not want to happen without the authority of the church. And I speak of the future for the most part. I have never even dreamt of the idea of a confession among laymen. And my book on confession shows that I think otherwise. In the same tract I discuss fasting, whether it would be expedient to make the rules more lenient – not to abolish them. And I adduce reasons that are not altogether frivolous. Nor do I want anything changed here without the authority of those in charge. It would not be absurd to abolish a good institution because many people abuse it, just as the rule of excommunication is relaxed so that people will not leave off going to mass. In the same tract I treat of the choice of foods and feast days.

page 6
5   This, too, is completely false, that I take away the authority of superiors over those in their charge;[15] and all my writings proclaim the opposite. I

disapprove of the tyranny of those in charge, which I want to be borne however, provided this does not engender impiety.

page 6
6 Regarding warfare I have replied at sufficient length to Zúñiga.[16] And my book on the prince[17] shows clearly that I do not totally condemn war, since there I teach moderation in undertaking and waging war. If Luther teaches that [war must be condemned totally], how does that concern me? And if [Taxander] does not say this against me, what is the point of the words that follow about 'the raving pen of Erasmus'?[18]

page 7
7 Perhaps the following may seem only a small misrepresentation: [He says] that I called the Carmelite an impudent showman,[19] and that I say the same thing about Masson and Vincentius[20] whom he neatly joins as a pair of learned theologians.

ibidem
8 It is equally false that I praise foul villains for the sake of monetary gain,[21] unless he means to describe in this manner the pontiffs, bishops, and princes to whom I dedicate my books. I have many friends whose lives are not entirely blameless, but I certainly never praised anyone's moral turpitude. And if some men, who were at one time praised by me, have turned to sin, I cannot be blamed for it, since I have no foreknowledge of the future. Finally, I praise even now many qualities in Luther, although he has been condemned.

page 8
9 It is especially impudent to say that I want to 'bring disgrace on Christ,'[22] to whose glory I am devoted with all my heart and shall be to my last breath. What can be more wicked than to call it 'bringing disgrace on Christ' if a Christian is admonished to become a better man? No less impudent is his claim that I 'defile the meadows of Scripture'[23] – I treat it more fittingly than many so-called great theologians. If he who makes a mistake 'defiles' Scripture, there is no one among the orthodox exegetes who has not defiled it.

page 12
10 He says that I overthrow the sacraments of the church. As far as matrimony is concerned, I believe I have given an account that is satisfactory to all good men. Concerning confession I have already replied. I

discuss confession, but I submit my views to the verdict of the church. So far no one has produced such a verdict. Yet I profess that confession, as practised today, is necessary for salvation. On page 14[24] he makes equally impudent remarks, repeating that the sacraments of the church are torn to shreds.

page 16
11   He carries on as if I wanted to do away with confession on account of the disadvantages [attaching to it].[25] On the contrary, I list them so that they may be avoided as far as possible. The person who warns people <not> to accept being baptized by a drunken priest does not want baptism to be eliminated completely. As for abolishing [confession], I relate the opinion of others, not my own. And there may be reasons why the church could abolish sacramental confession, at least as far as the practices are concerned that were added by men.

page 17
12   He calls it 'slander' that I mention in my *Exomologesis* someone who had illicit intercourse with many virgins,[26] although I indicate neither the person nor the place, and the subject itself required that I adduce this example, lest the priest cast those confessing carnal sins into despair.

page 17
13   In my *Colloquies* there is nothing that poisons young people; rather there are many things that offend the Lutherans, for example, concerning the invocation of saints and confession (of which I approve) and the mass. I have answered concerning the passages criticized.[27]

page 23
14   He says 'it is not far removed from blasphemy' to claim that confession, as practised now, is 'more burdensome than the whole of the Mosaic law,'[28] although it is in some respects very true that the gospel law is harder than the Mosaic law. I, however, am speaking of confession encumbered by human constitutions and human faults. It is certainly a legitimate topic of inquiry which law is more burdensome. Thus my words are very far removed from blasphemy, especially since I cite the arguments of those who do not approve of confession.

page 27
15   He says I deride those who respect the decrees of the Catholic church.

In fact, I derided the stupidity of one man who was worried about a matter of no account.[29]

ibidem

16 It is vain speculation to say that as a consequence of what I say mass will be said by drunks, and the host will be consecrated 'at public banquets.'[30]

page 28

17 'Concerning general confession, which' etc: He speaks as if I rejected it, although there is no such thing in my writings.[31]

page 26[32]

18 He says that I speak most irreverently about the veneration of the Virgin Mother and do not much differ from Luther.[33] On the contrary, I am very far from his view. And I deal most reverently with the Mother. Anyone who inspects the passage in my *Exomologesis*, sig C recto,[34] will recognize that I speak the truth. For I treat of the matter at length.

page 29

19 'Erasmus,' he says, 'claims that this was originally a matter of church consultation and council.' What he calls 'council' here, I do not know.[35] 'To claim' means to assert; I simply gave my opinion, which I submit to the judgment of the church. Nor do I speak of confession in general, but of the confession we practise now, the enumeration of sins and the detailed account of all circumstances. If all of this was there from the beginning, and if none of it can be changed by the church, I admit my error. If this is not the case, his accusations are empty.

Ibidem

20 He misquotes my words and writes: 'Confession is a matter of habit rather than a remedy.'[36] What else do these words imply but that perfunctory confession serves no purpose? My actual words are as follows: 'Some people greatly approve of frequently repeated confession – general confession, that is; and they suggest that confession be repeated for the slightest reason. I very much disagree with them. I consider it a very weighty matter when a person reveals his sins to a priest once and in good faith, washing them away with a shower of tears, then instead of growing old in perpetual sorrow, takes courage, and with gladness and joy zealously embarks on a better life. If he happens to relapse, let him relate to the priest only the sins he committed since the last confession. Otherwise confession

becomes a matter of habit rather than a remedy; and some even begin to take pleasure in something that is in itself unpleasant: to sift through the dirt repeatedly. And modesty, the safeguard of innocence, will gradually be forgotten.'[37] I ask you, dear reader, where in these words is the 'insanity' of which he accuses me?[38] If it is right for a healthy person to take a daily dose of medicine to become accustomed to it, I shall admit that it is likewise correct to confess frequently without any need, so as to become accustomed to confession. Medicine taken repeatedly and turned into something customary is no longer a remedy. So it is with confession.

And this lie he concludes with another one. 'Why,' he says, 'does Erasmus teach wrongly and scandalously that the same sin should never be repeated in confession?'[39] I am speaking of frequently repeated confession and confession repeated for any frivolous reason. I am not teaching that a sin should be confessed only once; rather I say that it is a weighty matter to go to confession once and do it well and to wash away the sins with a shower of tears, then, with the grief put behind, joyfully and with zeal embark on a better life.

He adds a third lie: that by such reasoning I try to disparage confession. Does one disparage confession who advises a man to confess well rather than often?

page 35
21 Because I wrote that the anxious enumeration of genus and species of sin, and the aggravating circumstances leading to other sins draws man away from the charity of God, he says that I agree with the condemned position of Luther,[40] who says that contrition on the basis of discussion and consideration of sins makes a man a hypocrite. How false this accusation is can be seen from my book in which I show that contrition of the heart is enhanced by such things. But, [he says], I criticize anxious enumeration. 'Anxious' means with excessive solicitude. I criticize this failing elsewhere in these words: 'And here as in many other respects men worry disproportionately. They torment themselves with anxiety over the bona fide enumeration of sins, lest they omit a species or overlook a circumstance, and of course these things must not be overlooked. And while they are completely occupied with this, they neglect the principal point.'[41] Is this in agreement with Luther's teaching? Finally, when he himself earnestly recommends that he who is grief-stricken be relieved lest he despair, how dare he reprehend me for criticizing anxiety and thereby dimming the light of charity?

page 39
22 Here he gathers together much from Holy Writ and from the orthodox

writers about lamentable and despicable sins. He declares that these passages are at variance with my views, although in this very book I teach hatred and detestation for sin, and this to him is 'dimming the light of charity.'[42] And he repeats this lie several times.

page 45

23   He says[43] that by calling to mind the disadvantages of the sacrament of confession I discourage everyone from confessing. How many lies there are in this. First of all, nowhere in my books do I say anything about the sacrament of confession. I recognize the sacrament of penance. Many call confession sacramental, and I do not quarrel with that. Secondly, I do not call the disadvantages of confession to mind; rather they develop from human failings on the occasion of confession. Nor do I call these disadvantages to mind so that confession be abandoned, but that the disadvantages be eliminated and confession become better and more useful.

page 46

24   From this he deduces an equally false proposition: 'Whoever criticizes [confession] denies that it has been handed down by Christ.'[44] I praise confession, I show how the vices of those who abuse it can be eliminated or corrected. The examples he adduces go against himself. It is true that he who criticizes baptism denies that it was handed down by Christ; but he who reproaches priests who are drunk and baptize, who mispronounce words, who don't understand what they are saying, does not criticize baptism. Just as he who detests adultery does not criticize marriage and he who exhorts priests living in sin to mend their ways does not criticize the clergy.

page 46

25   I don't know whether to call this a lie; it is ridiculous at any rate to conclude that I want to destroy confession, and that because I list nine disadvantages, but only eight advantages[45] – as if it were a novel observation that there is a greater variety of vices diverging from what is right than there is of virtue, which is onefold; and as if it could not be the case that one advantage has more significance than ten disadvantages; finally, as if I contrasted the advantages of confession with its disadvantages, when I listed the disadvantages arising through the fault of those who abuse confession.

page 47

26   I said to Ath that I was not willing to assert that confession as practised

in our time was instituted by Christ.[46] I never denied that some type of confession was instituted by Christ. He makes a similar mistake in the passage he cites from my *Methodus*. I adduce the example of confession, but add this clause: 'although what I say must not be interpreted in any other sense but as an example added for the sake of demonstration.'[47] Moreover, one who says that confession originated with our forefathers does not by this token deny that it originated with Christ. And there are not a few men who openly state that confession was instituted by the cardinals. Nor has anyone in all these years accused them of heresy. Indeed, not even the theologians say that confession, as practised today, was instituted by Christ.

page 48

27 He rejects as wrong the opinion of some who attribute to the Roman pontiff the authority to do away with purgatory,[48] whereas Scotus has attributed this power to him[49] ... And after much talk, he himself admits that the pope can do what he denied was in his power. For the words 'at his nod' are his addition.[50]

page 59[51]

It is true that I wrote somewhere else[52] that I have doubts whether the books bandied around under the name Dionysius are the books of Dionysius the Areopagite. It is not true, however, that I thereby slipped the noose of arguments. Perhaps he attributes to me what belongs to Luther.

page 65

28 'No one,' he says, 'denies that confession is denoted by this figure – no one except Erasmus.'[53] It is false at any rate to say that no one denies it. And my words are: 'I deny that a figure of speech has such weight in a matter of such great significance, especially since the old exegetes, among them Augustine, interpreted leprosy as heresy, not just any spiritual vice.'[54]

page 74

29 He says that I assert that in Jerome's time there was no confession,[55] although I assert so many times in my books that confession existed even before Jerome's time, though I doubt that it was this kind of confession. Similarly lacking in substance are his frequent accusations that I object to the authority of the church. Let him show where the church declares that this confession was instituted by Christ, and if he has proof, let him bring it out into the open. For what is he doing now but 'brandishing his sword in the darkness'?[56]

page 89

30 'None, however, etc':[57] Here he links two lies. For neither do I assert anywhere that all aspects of confession were instituted by the pope, nor is it true that the canon of confession is nothing but an affirmation of Christ's institution. He himself said so a little earlier, justifying Panormitanus,[58] who thought that confession was not instituted by Christ, saying that this must be taken to refer to annual confession.[59] And did Christ institute annual confession?

page 90

31 I don't know whether to call it vain or false when he says that I wrote: 'What the Catholic church institutes on the inspiration of the Holy Spirit must be accepted as if God had instituted it.'[60] And he objects to my contending somewhere that the pope can err, as if the pope were the church.[61] And from this he deduces most impudently that I said the Catholic church could err in matters of faith (rather than of devotion). After all we read that Peter in the Gospel was wrong and was reproached on this account by Paul[62] – would it be strange then if the Roman pontiff <committed> an error? ... Here he cites my annotation on Matthew 19, although I say nothing of this kind there.[63]

page 91

32 He imagines that I wish to do away with annual confession,[64] which has never been my purpose. Nor do I advise that it be done away with. I merely argue that man can abolish what was instituted by man, with the exception of that which was instituted on the authority of the first apostles.

Ibidem

33 Similarly lacking in substance is what he adds: 'That fellow, who begrudges us the light of divine love, tries to extinguish the lantern of confession.'[65]

page 92

34 Once again he insists that I discredit devotion. Next, because I declare that I say some things that are not my own but other men's opinion, he says that I am playing games.[66] He says my hiding behind the characters in the *Colloquies*[67] is the same sort of trick. He hints at the same, but in a meaner fashion, on page 97,[68] adding that I [attack] confession in all my books.

page 97

35 He says that I openly deny in my *Colloquies* that confession, as practiced

today, was instituted by Christ.[69] And if I had denied that it was instituted by Christ, what risk would there have been? But I do not even say that in the *Colloquies*. Indeed, the whole page is full of lies: that I make disparaging remarks about indulgences in the *Colloquies*, that my purpose in doing so is to have confession abandoned, that in my apology against Lee I do nothing but attack confession.

page 98
46[70] He does not understand what I say about 'theatrical money,'[71] yet he speaks insultingly. And under no circumstances does he want those who hear confession to be deprived of their money. As if charity ought not to overcome the tedium of hearing confession.

page 99
47 This whole page is full of lies and insults about 'false Christian freedom.'[72] He likes Hutten's book against me. I don't object, as long as he likes all of it.[73]

page 104
48 It is completely false that I praise Panormitanus because he denies confession.[74] I merely cite him because he is rightly considered a man of some authority among theologians. It is equally false when he says that I reject Thomas [Aquinas] because he supports confession.

Ibidem
49 'The truth is shown to Erasmus on the basis of scriptural evidence,' he says, 'and he disdains it.'[75] This is a twofold lie. Neither does he offer proof, nor would I disdain it, were it offered. Indeed, this whole argumentation does not accord with his preface and contains insults. I do not assert that this confession was instituted by men, I proffer an opinion; yet I submit my interpretation to the verdict of the church. Nor does he cite a verdict of the church that contradicts me. Rather he admits the truth of what I am saying: that the mode of confession was imposed by men. Yet he celebrates a triumph over Erasmus. Although I added 'in other words,'[76] he is the orthodox believer, I am an enemy of the church. I wish confession, which is attacked by many, had better champions.

page 108[77]
60[78] He says that I exhort everyone to abolish ecclesiastical institutions, just because I cite the example of a bishop who instituted a feast day for an insignificant reason.

page 109

61   When I refer to the particular devotion that each person feels towards his own saints,[79] he falsely says that I want us to disdain the veneration of the saints as a whole. If that human devotion towards individual saints, from which strife and blasphemy often take their rise, is removed, would it inevitably follow that all veneration of saints is done away with? For in that passage I do not condemn that kind of devotion, rather I do not want it being given such weight that anyone can demand a feast day on the strength of his devotion. I have written so much in praise of the Virgin Mother; in my book *De orando Deum* I do battle with those who condemn the veneration and invocation of saints;[80] I have written a new liturgy for the Virgin Mother[81] – and that man claims that I am totally doing away with the veneration of saints! What an impudent lie! And he adds what is in fact even more impudent: 'Shall we all together with Erasmus adore Luther?'[82] Do I adore Luther – I, who in published books disagree with his teachings? What can be more absurd than these words?

page 110

62   He repeats the old lie: that Luther took his doctrines out of my books, although he has yet to cite a single one (I am referring to the condemned doctrines).[83]

ibidem

63   He says that I wrote that 'indulgences have no foundation in Holy Writ.'[84] Whether I wrote that, I don't know. I don't recognize my turn of phrase.[85] But let it be. Does this mean that I agree with Luther, who writes that indulgences are worthless because they are not in Holy Writ? Is what the Catholic church instituted beyond Holy Writ worthless?

ibidem

64   He says I wrote that 'nowhere in the old sources or in Holy Writ is it stated that the Roman pontiff has more power than other bishops.'[86] What can be more impudent than this lie, when I say everywhere that the Roman pontiff is the head of the church, when I cite some passages out of Jerome and Cyprian which attribute to the Roman pontiff the highest authority, when I say the same thing in my *Annotations*, when my paraphrase on John 21 runs as follows: 'meaning that he should have first place among the teachers of the gospel because he is first in his love for the Lord's flock and excels the others.'[87] Finally, when in an epistle ... I defend the primacy of the Roman pontiff.

page 111

65   It is a great lie to say that I 'pretend to submit myself to the pontiff, so that I may do more harm.'[88] What licentious language!

ibidem

66   He makes two false assumptions: first, that it is my purpose to have all feast days abolished; and [secondly] that there will be no good works, once feast days are abolished.[89]

page 112

67   Again he says what he has said before: 'The veneration of saints bothers Erasmus just as it bothers the disciples' – because they were indignant about the ointment poured on the feet of the Lord.[90]

ibidem

68   He states that I should have written about this to the pope,[91] as if I had not done so; for I have written about these matters to Adrian, to Clement, to Cardinal Campeggi, and to several others,[92] and perhaps we would not have this confusion if attention had been paid to me.[93]

ibidem

69   He adds that I foster strife in the community,[94] when there is no man who gives more encouragement to concord and who is more averse to every kind of faction.

page 112

70   He says, if I could, I would abolish Sunday as well[95] – as if Sunday were abolished if men are permitted after mass, if they so wished, to work with their hands to support their families rather than to drink and gamble.

page 114

71   He casts into my teeth that I wrote that it is superstition to venerate Christ in the veneration of the crown.[96] On the contrary, it is correct to venerate him in all aspects of the suffering he took upon himself for our sake. But there is no necessity to create new feast days for each single aspect. Or else the nail, the spear, the reed, the sponge, the cloth, the lamp, the staves and ropes, and all the other countless implements would each require its own feast day. I am not sure that the pope instituted the feast of the Lord's crown, yet some popes rather indulge and have indulged the inclinations of princes. Concerning the foreskin and the Virgin's milk he thinks I am derisive because I added 'as they say.'[97] Someone who says 'as

they say' indicates doubt. How irrelevant it is therefore to say that I 'rush into derision of the saints with uncircumcized lips'![98] Does a man deride the saints, who shows the way to true and pious veneration?

page 115

72   He says that 'two-year-old children have learned from me that prayer does not consist in many words but in piety and sincere inclination.'[99] What could be truer? But I should have added 'as the heathens do.' And I do add it in my *Annotations* and in my book *De modo orandi*.[100] Nor do I pass over the fact that Christ said long prayers.[101] Yet there ought to be moderation in public prayers. Is this agreeing with the teachings of Luther, who simply condemned the canonical hours?

page 116

73   These are the passages on the basis of which he shows that I am in agreement with Luther, whereas there are none in which we disagree more.[102]

ibidem

He says that I wrote the *De libero arbitrio* under false pretenses and that I secretly am on Luther's side.[103] He stops at nothing in his bold invention.

ibidem

74   I wrote that the peasants are forced to let the harvest rot in the fields because of the great number of feast days[104] ... This he calls a deliberate lie,[105] saying that all theologians teach the opposite. What the theologians teach, I do not know. The parish priests at any rate, and the officials who have often been petitioned, deny them leave [to work] and punish those who dare to go ahead ...

page 119

75   With surprising impudence he declares falsely that I taught 'all fasting was to be abolished completely,'[106] whereas I approve everywhere the Christian practice of fasting. In the letter, which he criticizes, I discuss the possibility of abolishing obligatory fasting, because it seems to me that more evil than good comes from it on account of human vice. How few there are who fast! Perhaps more people would fast with sincere feelings, if the precept became a counsel, whereas now they either act hypocritically or violate the precept.[107]

page 121

76   He casts into my teeth that I said the Jewish practice of fasting was less

burdensome, for they were allowed to eat the meat of all animals. He says that I am totally wrong.[108] Indeed, what he tells us is totally wrong. My words run as follows: 'The Jews were allowed to eat the most wholesome of every kind of fish, quadruped, and bird.'[109] The man has no shame.

page[110]
77 He is lying when he says that I prefer marriage to celibacy in my declamation about marriage. I prefer a chaste marriage to an impure celibacy, and I compare virginity with the life of the angels, whereas marriage is a feature of human life.

ibidem
78 I do not permit wives to priests and monks. I say that 'in such a crowd of priests and monks it is better to permit marriage to those who cannot control themselves rather than have so many thousands of priests who are more libidinous than if they had legitimate wives.'[111]

ibidem
79 He says that the pope can permit marriage to priests, but never to monks.[112] I don't know whether that is true. It is certainly false that my purpose in permitting wives is to abolish monasteries. And it is also false that I want monks to take wives on a large scale.

ibidem[113]
It is also false that I believe the Christian community would be more pious if feast days were abolished and if priests took wives.[114] I spoke of the excessive number of feast days, and I spoke of priests who lead impure lives.

page 123
What follows is not only false but insane and scurrilous: he adds that in my opinion the priest would 'celebrate the holy mysteries in a more sacred manner if he came to them straight from having intercourse rather than if he prepared for them by fasting and observance.'[115] Whoever heard such scurrilous talk? Rather, whoever comes to [the altar] after intercourse with a concubine ... is less pure than one who comes from his wife.

page 127
He adds a similar phrase: 'It seems preferable to Erasmus if they be admitted to the altar straight from intercourse' ...[116] Do I not teach the exact opposite wherever I mention the holy mass? My comparison is between the

fornicating and the married priest, not between the chaste priest and the married man.

ibidem

He says that I 'call all laws "human" except those that are in the gospel.'[117] If by 'gospel' he means all of Holy Writ, what crime have I committed? I have called human laws 'human'! It's no worse than calling men 'men.'

ibidem

As for the rest, when he adds that laws do not make a man guilty of sin, 'unless they are derived from divine law'[118] – that is not my teaching. Perhaps Luther or Gerson[119] said so.

page 129

He says that Luther learned from my writings ... that it is difficult to distinguish between mortal and venial sins.[120] It is true that in many cases it is not easy to distinguish them. But it is false that Luther learned this from me, when every theologian knows as much. If Luther learned the rules of distinguishing sins, he did not learn them from me, for I have never spoken or written about such things. Nor did I say that no human law makes men guilty of mortal sin.

page 131

He says that we progress from precepts to habit – 'these too Erasmus condemns.'[121] Here we have a twofold lie. In that very tract I wrote that some customs introduced by bishops are necessary for humans, nor do I ever condemn praiseworthy customs. And he pretends that I condemn both precepts and customs.

page 135

He says that I am not afraid 'to eat meat on Fridays even among those who do not know that I have a papal dispensation.'[122] I do not think that I ever wrote or said such a thing. Indeed, I often took a risk to avoid giving offence, although I do have a dispensation. I remember writing that 'I would not be afraid to eat in the presence of Christ what I eat among men.'[123]

ibidem

He adds perjury to his lie. 'I speak before God,' he says. 'He and Luther together defile the whole [church], for they think that one need not respect the authority of the pope, or convention, or the decrees of the church.' On the contrary, the whole tract expresses the opposite view. It so displeases the Lutherans that they have sharpened their pens against me on account of my showing too much regard for papal authority.

[What a] heap of lies I have collected in this small booklet, [for I will not] pursue the solecisms that should make [the authors] the laughing stock of schoolboys. [They believe they do honour] to the University of Louvain and the Dominican order by writing such a book ... and as if they had done a praiseworthy thing, they dare to dedicate their vapid nonsense to Lee[124] and think they have done well in praising in this book what should be condemned.

Notes

Works cited frequently in this volume are referred to in the notes in abbreviated form only. A list of the abbreviations and full bibliographical information are given in Works Frequently Cited (pages 174–5). In these volumes references to the Correspondence are to the English translation of the letters in CWE, when these have already been published, or to the Latin edition of Allen. Since Allen's numbering of the letters has been adopted in CWE, letters are cited by epistle number and, where applicable, line number. References to the works translated in this volume refer to page numbers.

Introduction
ix
1 Ep 172. The incident is also mentioned in Ep 171. K.-H. Ducke, in the article on Adrian VI in CEBR, suggests that a prior familiarity may have existed between Erasmus and Adriaan. The only evidence for this is a brief reference in Ep 1304:8–9 Allen V 100, 'ut quondam tuae doctrinae theologicae auditorem et integritatis admiratorem.' This is in a letter of dedication of *Arnobii opera*, to Pope Adrian VI, 1 August 1522. It is impossible to assign a specific date to the reference, but it is unlikely to have been so early. Allen suggests 1502–3. There is no evidence that he knew Adriaan before coming to Louvain in September 1502.

xi
2 Ep 126, the dedicatory epistle to William Blount, Lord Mountjoy. This first edition was entitled *Adagiorum collectanea*.

xii
3 de Vocht MHL 125–6 suggests this possibility and Dorp himself in Ep 304 notes 'we have known each other well for a long time.'
4 See especially Ep 180, which is a kind of apologia for writing the *Panegyricus*. See also the account of its composition in the introductory note to the printed text in CWE 27 3–4.
5 Allen Epp 179, 181 introductions reproduce the documents from Philip's treasury authenticating the amount, which Erasmus calls 'a very generous reward' Ep 179:18–19. See also CWE 27 2–3.

xiii

6 Before leaving Louvain in the summer of 1504, at the Premonstratensian Abbey of Parc near Louvain, Erasmus discovered a manuscript version of Lorenzo Valla's *Notes on the New Testament*. He subsequently edited the work which he gave to Bade to be printed as *Laurentii Vallensis ... in Latinam Novi Testamenti interpretationem ex collatione Graecorum exemplarium adnotationes*, 13 April 1505. It was a clear presage of Erasmus' own work on the New Testament. See the long dedicatory letter to Christopher Fisher, Ep 182.

7 In the adage *Festina lente* from the 1508 Aldine edition, in Margaret Mann Phillips' *The 'Adages' of Erasmus: A Study with Translations* (Cambridge 1964) 180.

xiv

8 On this latter point see the important article by Andrew J. Brown 'The Date of Erasmus' Latin Translation of the New Testament' *Transactions of the Cambridge Bibliographical Society* 8 (1984) 351–80. From the time of Allen (cf vol II 182–3), it has been assumed that Erasmus had made a Latin translation earlier in England, prior to his departure for Italy, and that Colet had had it copied by Pieter Meghen, on the evidence in the colophons of the manuscripts. Brown has re-studied these manuscripts and has concluded that the Erasmus version was not written until at least the 1520s and was probably copied from the printed text of the second Froben edition. On the preparation of Erasmus' annotations see Jerry H. Bentley *Humanists and Holy Writ: New Testament Scholarship in the Renaissance* (Princeton 1983) 112–93 and especially Erika Rummel *Erasmus' Annotations on the New Testament: From Philologist to Theologian* (Toronto 1986) 3–33, 89–121. The definitive critical edition of the Meghen New Testament is H. Gibaut *Un inédit d'Erasme: La première version du Nouveau Testament* (Angers 1982). See also Erika Rummel *Erasmus as a Translator of the Classics* (Toronto 1985) 89–102.

xv

9 He stated the case somewhat more strongly in his *Apologia ... qua respondet duabus invectivis Eduardi Lei* (1520) *Opuscula* 237–8 'sic enim visum est Principi Carolo, in cuius concilium tum eram recens ascitus, ut in Brabantia sedem figerem ubi vellem, sed maxime Lovanii.' And in 1521, in a letter to Pierre Barbier, he refers to his moving to Louvain 'for such was at that time the emperor's wish' Ep 1225:30–1.

xvii

10 The process of co-optation continued into the fall of 1517. On 7 September the process was still not complete (Ep 651:25–6) but on 2 November, writing to Pirckheimer, he states 'I have been co-opted a member of the faculty of theology, although I am not a doctor of this university' Ep 694:2–6. Perhaps for this reason, perhaps for another, Erasmus was only admitted to the *collegium largum* of the theological faculty and not to the *collegium strictum*. He never became a member of the exclusive eight-member council of regents of the faculty. See Epp 637:12n and 808:19n, de Vocht MHL 190–1,

and M. Nauwelaerts 'Erasme à Louvain' *Scrinium Erasmianum* ed J. Coppens (Leiden 1969) I 7.

De Vocht MHL 175 points out that this readiness of the Louvain theologians to come to terms with Erasmus may have been partly due to the scant encouragement they had found at court for their scheme of making Louvain and Cologne examine the orthodoxy of Erasmus' writings. The court nobility were, on the whole, more sympathetic to Erasmus than to them, as were the learned men of the court, led by Gianpietro Caraffa, the future Pope Paul IV, who was the papal legate to the Netherlands, a friend of Erasmus, and a champion of his ideas. Scarcely six month before, Erasmus had written to Ammonio that the head of this 'conspiracy' of the Louvain theologians was none other than Briart 'who was all the more dangerous because he was an enemy disguised as a friend' Ep 539:4–6.

11 Ep 800:32–4. This is a modest estimate of his annual income. His English pension alone would have produced something more than 300 ducats per year and, though it was regularly in arrears, his stipend from Le Sauvage for his councillor's position to Prince Charles amounted to almost that much. See Ep 621 introduction. He was also making a substantial income from the sales of his many books. A generation ago Jean Hoyoux in 'Les moyens d'existence d'Erasme' BHR 5 (1944) 7–59 first pointed out that by this time in his career, and much more so later, Erasmus was financially well off and by no means an impoverished Christian scholar. Hoyoux stressed, probably too much, Erasmus' profits from the sales and dedications of his books. A more recent study by Eckhard Bernstein 'Erasmus' Money Connection: The Antwerp Banker Erasmus Schets and Erasmus of Rotterdam, 1525–36' *Erasmus in English* 14 (1985–6) 2–7, places greater emphasis on his income from his several pensions. Bernstein observes that, at about this period, 'Erasmus drew annually from his pensions in England and the Low Countries fifteen times the amount that an Antwerp mason, a very well paid craftsman, earned in one year' (4). The inventory of his assets, made shortly after his death, reveals that he had resources amounting to the 'staggering' sum of 8000 florins plus almost another thousand in Schets' account, at a time when a typical university professor could command only 100–200 florins per year.

xviii

12 Louvain had been among several universities that condemned Reuchlin's *Augenspiegel*, declaring it suspect and not to be read. With the exoneration of Reuchlin and his book and the condemnation of the inquisitor Hoogstraten by papal sentence, 29 March 1514 (Pastor I 219–22), there was general alarm at Louvain, which had strong historic ties with Cologne. See Anton G. Weiler 'Les relations entre l'université de Louvain et l'université de Cologne au XVe siècle' *The Universities in the Late Middle Ages* ed Jozef IJsewijn and Jacques Pacquet (Louvain 1978) 49, 61. Even the magisterial Adriaan Florizoon wrote, on 21 April 1514, to Cardinal Bernardino Lopez de Carvajal, papal legate in the Netherlands, to advise him of the gravity of the event and to beseech him to influence the pope 'ut huic morbo cancraso sine mora litiumque ac processus dispendio, conveniens medicina paretur

seu remedium' de Vocht MHL 140. For the relations between Reuchlin and Erasmus, see Manfred Krebs 'Reuchlins Beziehungen zu Erasmus von Rotterdam' *Johannes Reuchlin 1455–1522 Festgabe seiner Vaterstadt Pforzheim zur 500. Wiederkehr seines Geburtstages* (Pforzheim 1955) 139–55.

13 Much later, in 1519, Erasmus wrote in a letter to Cuthbert Tunstall that Briart 'was the man who originally egged Dorp on ... I suspected as much long ago and now know it for a fact' Ep 1029:4–6. The same sentiment is expressed to Mountjoy in Ep 1028:21–4.

14 The fully annotated text is found in the Yale More Edition 15 ed Daniel Kinney 3–127.

15 More learned of Dorp's change of heart in a letter Dorp had sent to Erasmus who sent More a copy, Ep 1044. In response More wrote to Dorp, 'I easily foresaw that you would one day think otherwise than you thought then. But really that you would not only become wiser, but even in a most elaborate address testify that you had changed, and that so openly, genuinely, and categorically, this indeed went far beyond not only my expectation, but also the hopes and almost prayers of all, for your action manifested incredible probity and utter self-restraint ... I see quite clearly, my dear Dorp, and to my shame, that my letter had no power to change you, although out of courtesy or modesty you now yield to it praise which belongs to you and which, the more you avoid it, will all the more surely follow you' Yale More Edition *Selected Letters* ed Elizabeth F. Rogers Ep 82 112–3.

16 De Vocht MHL 151–3. De Vocht also suggests that Dorp had chosen a career in theology largely in the hope of receiving a better income, rather than from deep religious conviction. See Rogers *Selected Letters* 135.

17 Some two years later Dorp published the *Oratio*, with Michaël Hillen in Antwerp, 27 September 1519. A few months later he wrote Erasmus again proclaiming his friendship for him and his commitment to the Erasmian principles of biblical study. He also asked Erasmus to use his influence with Froben to have the *Oratio* published by his press – which Erasmus did, the edition being published in March 1520. Dorp's letter was added to it. See Ep 1044 and introduction. See also de Vocht MHL 216 and J.H. Bentley 'New Testament Scholarship at Louvain in the Early Sixteenth Century' *Studies in Medieval and Renaissance History* ns 2 (1979) 57–60. There is a recent edition of Dorp's *Orationes IV* ed J. IJsewijn (Leipzig 1986).

xix

18 De Vocht MHL 165

19 Ibidem 190–2, 244–5. See the *Acta Facultatis* in H. de Jongh *L'Ancienne faculté de théologie de Louvain* (Louvain 1911) 48, 51.

20 De Vocht MHL 151–2 points out, quite correctly, that the *Moria* is scarcely even mentioned in Dorp's second letter to Erasmus, Ep 347. Nor does it loom large in his later disagreements with other Louvain theologians. M.A. Screech in *Ecstasy and The Praise of Folly* (London 1980), however, makes the case for a continuing debate over the book, mainly because of its profound theological implications, pages 62, 193, 228.

21 Whether the Collegium Trilingue was actually the first such institution to
be founded is immaterial. The idea was widespread, an outgrowth of the
enthusiasm for humanist colleges and institutes and of the related enthusi-
asms for humanist biblical scholarship. The clearest parallel was the trilingual College of San Ildefonso in the University of Alcalá, founded by the
great Spanish churchman Cardinal Jiménez de Cisneros, which opened in
1508. Marcel Bataillon *Erasme et l'Espagne* (Paris 1937) 10, however, contends
that this was not a humanistic institution. Bentley *Humanists and Holy Writ*
71 agrees, arguing that Ximénes' motives were largely pious. See also Basil
Hall 'The Trilingual College of San Ildefonso and the Making of the Complutensian Polyglot Bible' *Studies in Church History* ed G.J. Cuming 5
(Leiden 1969) 114–46. The extent to which Erasmus was aware in any detailed way of the organization and goals of Ximénes' college remain problematic. He was, in all probability, aware of the Complutensian Polyglot
Bible being produced there and this project is likely to have hastened his
own publication of the Greek New Testament. We know that Erasmus was
invited by Ximénes to join the Complutensian project, Epp 582:11, 597:53–4,
628:62–3.
Erasmus was also aware of the founding in 1517 of Corpus Christi College,
Oxford, by his friend and former patron Bishop Richard Foxe of Winchester. But again, he does not seem to have been clearly informed of its aims
and structure. He regarded it as parallel to the Collegium Trilingue in Louvain. He wrote, two years later, to the president of Corpus Christi, John
Claymond, about its being consecrated 'expressly to the three chief tongues,
to humane literature, and to classical studies' (Ep 990:7–8). In fact it was not
a trilingual college: it provided three programs, in Latin, Greek, and Divinity. There may have been some study of Hebrew in the divinity program
but there was no formal offering in Hebrew studies.
As early, probably, as 1517 Erasmus' great French fellow-humanist Guillaume Budé was advocating a trilingual college in France. This goal was
only partially accomplished much later with the founding by Francis I of
royal lectureships in 1529 in Greek and Hebrew. A Latin lectureship was
added in 1534. These lectureships, still later, became the basis for the Collège de France, which was first called the *Collegium Trilingue*. See Budé's
preface to *Commentarii linguae graecae, Opera omnia* III foc 2–3 and *De
philologia, Opera omnia* I 94–5.
Erasmus was deeply committed to the idea of the trilingual college not
simply because of its technical goal of teaching the three languages basic to
biblical study. He always insisted that training in the liberal arts existed to
perfect the Christian man, the Christian scholar. Thus there was a linkage
between educational reform and moral reform. See, for example, CWE
xxviii–xxix.

xx

22 De Vocht CTL I 8 asserts Erasmus' role in the founding of the college '... the
most effective assistance, if not the very first idea, was offered
by Busleyden's friend, the great promoter of the literae humaniores,
Erasmus.'

23 De Vocht CTL I 25 ff reproduces the entire 'Testament.'

xxi

24 Adrianus was well known to Erasmus, having been the Hebrew teacher of the Amerbach brothers in Basel and of Wolfgang Capito, Epp 707 11n, 731:30–1.
25 De Vocht CTL I 280–1 and CEBR 'Barlandus'

xxii

26 The importance of Erasmus' role in establishing the college is assessed by de Vocht CTL I 61: 'Thus in compliance with Busleyden's wish, Erasmus became the promoter, the effective patron of the Trilingue: his inventive enthusiasm and his unfailing clear-sightedness, as well as his world-renowned erudition worked like a spell. For several years the College lived his life, and the managers and professors merely worked out his schemes and suggestions, until, under his impulse, it secured a creative spirit of its own, which was only the continuation of what he had been infusing by all the power of his soul and mind.'

xxiii

27 Published in late August 1517 by Dirk Martens
28 For the controversy with Lefèvre see Margaret Mann Phillips *Érasme et les débuts de la Réforme française 1517–1536* (Paris 1934) 23–46; Helmut Feld 'Der Humanisten-Streit um Hebräer 2, 7 (Psalm 8, 6)' ARG 61 (1970) 5–35; and John B. Payne 'Erasmus and Lefèvre d'Etaples as Interpreters of Paul' ARG 65 (1974) 54–82.

xxv

29 This translation is from his *Apologia ... qua respondet duabus invectivis Eduardi Lei* (1520) *Opuscula* 250 and is done by Erika Rummel in an article 'Erasmus and His Louvain Critics – A Strategy of Defense' NAKG 70 (1990) 5–6.

xxvi

30 Ep 1061:420–36. In spite of Lee's charge, Erasmus denied that Lee was the person lampooned in the work, *Opuscula* 289–90. Nevertheless the passage was expunged from the next and all subsequent editions, Ep 1061 n44.

xxvii

31 Ep 936:34–5 and Yale More Edition XV 152–95. Erasmus had also elicited support from Tunstall, Foxe, and Lupset Epp 886, 908, 1026, 1029, 1030. See also *Opuscula* 229–31.
32 These two works appear in LB IX 123–284. The earlier response to Lee was somehow overlooked in LB and was subsequently published by Ferguson in *Opuscula* 225–303.
33 Ep 1061:269; cf also lines 853–4, 855–6. This is the chief argument of Robert Coogan 'The Pharisee Against the Hellenist: Edward Lee versus Erasmus' RQ 39 (1986) 476–506.

xxix

34 The texts are to be found in LB IX 111–22 and 433–42. For a lucid discussion of the issues involved in them see Erika Rummel *Erasmus and His Catholic Critics I 1515–1522* and Bentley *Humanists and Holy Writ* 155–8.

xxx

35 Ep 948: 47–8. Latomus (Jacques Masson), a Frenchman from Cambron, was one of the most respected members of the theological faculty. He had been a pupil of Adriaan Florizoon. He had served as head of the Domus Pauperum which Jan Standonck founded at Louvain in 1500 and was devoted to Standonck's rigorous moral standards. He was a member of the council of the university and, after receiving his doctorate in theology in 1519, was immediately admitted to the *collegium strictum* of the faculty of theology and became dean in the following year. He had served as tutor to two young members of the great courtly Croy family, Charles and Robert de Croy. This eminence and high visibility made Latomus an ideal 'stalking horse' for the other theologians in their quarrel with Erasmus. And, for the same reason, Erasmus felt compelled to answer him. He recalled that in former times Latomus 'was not particularly against the humanities, and my good friend ' 'nor,' he continued, 'can I guess what has suddenly changed his whole nature' (Ep 948:40–1). Their relationship, however, steadily deteriorated, Latomus becoming one of Erasmus' most bitter critics (Epp 1088, 1113, 1123). As the animus against Luther in Louvain grew, Latomus tended, like others of Erasmus' opponents, to link him with Luther (Epp 1581, 1582, 1585). At the end of his life Latomus left unpublished both an attack on Erasmus' *De concordia* and a response to Erasmus' *Apologia*, entitled *Antapologia*. These were published posthumously by his nephew in his *Opera omnia* (Louvain: Gravius 1550). For Latomus see Bentley 'New Testament Scholarship' (n17 above) 60–3; J. Etienne *Spiritualisme érasmien et théologiens louvanistes: Un changement de problématique au début du XVIe siècle* (Louvain-Gembloux 1956) 163–86; Georges Chantraine 'L'Apologia ad Latomum: Deux conceptions de la théologie' in *Scrinium Erasmianum* II 51–76; and the CEBR entry.

xxxi

36 Cf the translator's introduction 35.

xxxii

37 The work is published at the end of CWE 7, the translation based on the text that Ferguson established in *Opuscula* 206–24. Although Ferguson had argued that 'Erasmus was responsible for at least a fair share of the dialogue; (198), the editors of the CWE edition have rejected the argument for any involvement in the work by Erasmus, CWE 7 330–2.

38 Erasmus had often indulged in exactly this same pun. See Epp 948:26–7, 991:66, 1029:3–10.

39 It had been quickly reprinted, anonymously, in Basel and by Lazarus Schürer in Sélestat. It was noted as circulating in Germany, Switzerland, and France. See the introduction in CWE 7 330–3.

xxxiii

40 See CEBR entry 'Wilhelm Nesen.'

41 In the *Apologia adversus debacchationes Sutoris* LB IX 770B

42 By Dirk Martens, dated 30 March 1518, titled *Declamatio in genre suasorio de laude matrimonii*, one of four declamations published under the title *Declamationes aliquot Erasmi Roterodami*

xxxiv

43 See LB IX 770B and Ep 946 introduction. These events are also reviewed in the opening paragraphs of the *Apologia pro declamatione de laude matrimonii* 1ff. For Gillis van Delft see the CEBR entry.

44 For example, Beatus Rhenanus, writing from Basel in 1515, urges him to finish the book for the Froben press, Ep 330:19–20; two years later he is still asking for the book, Ep 581:25. It was finally published by Froben in 1522. See CWE 25.

xxxv

45 See 93–4. This is probably a reference to the secrets heard by priests in the confessional, perhaps Erasmus himself, or certainly most of his fellow theologians at Louvain who usually held priestly livings.

xxxvi

46 Hans Voltz 'Die ersten Sammelausgaben von Luther und ihre Drucker, 1518–1520' *Gutenberg Jahrbuch* Mainz (1960) 186–92.

xxxvii

47 Luther had been led to this conclusion by their mutual friend Capito and by choosing to interpret two passages in the preface to the 1518 Froben edition of the *Enchiridion*, in which Erasmus had criticized the sale of indulgences, as approval for his own stand on that issue, Epp 933:22–6, 858:216–7, 430–1.

48 While asserting that 'I keep myself uncommitted,' he reports that there are some highly placed Englishmen 'who think well of what you write' and, rather incautiously, that 'some here too, the bishop of Liège among them, who favour your views' (Ep 980:42–3). The bishop of Liège was Erard de la Marck and the prompt publication of Erasmus' letter was a considerable embarrassment to him. Why Erasmus made this off-hand observation remains a mystery. Certainly it was not intended maliciously: only three months earlier he had dedicated to the bishop his paraphrases on 1 and 2 Corinthians, in a long and fulsome letter, Ep 916. Erasmus later published the letter himself in the *Farrago*, substituting 'an outstanding person' for 'the bishop of Liège,' Ep 980 introduction. He was eventually restored to the bishop's good graces. See the entry under de la Marck in CEBR.

xxxviii

49 Epp 972:10, 1119:14–6. In the course of the spring of 1519 the cost of Prince Charles' candidacy amounted to nearly a million gold gulden, almost half of it given as bribes to the electoral princes and their advisers. And there

was a comparable cost for secret agreements and understandings to defeat the candidacy of Francis I. Charles himself had been involved in the bribery and deal-making, as had his regent for the Low Countries, his aunt Margaret of Austria and her advisers. See the account in Karl Brandi *The Emperor Charles V: The Growth and Destiny of a Man and of a World Empire* (New York 1939) 106–13.

50 The poems are in Reedijk, items 109–10. The second, at least, was clearly intended to grace some sort of structure, probably one of the temporary facades erected as part of the pageantry of the occasion.

xxxix

51 This is noted in the famous adage *Festina lente*, where Erasmus acknowledges the help of Aleandro and his calling his attention to a collection of Greek proverbs by Michael Apostolius, LB II 405D, translated in CWE 33 3. See also Thompson *The Colloquies of Erasmus* 488ff.

xl

52 Erasmus broadly implies that Charles 'either knew nothing of it, or had been badly briefed' and states that its implementation was left in the hands of the secretary to Charles' private council Remacle d'Ardenne, an ardent anti-Lutheran. See *Acta* 104 below, CEBR 'Remacle,' and *Opuscula* 324 n78. There is no surviving copy of the edict: Ferguson speculates that 'probably the only copy was that given to the legate,' *Opuscula* n77.

53 He admits that it is only a matter of gossip (103), though he later mentions the charge in Allen Epp 2414:15, 2578:31–2 and in the *Purgatio ad expostulationem Hutteni* LB X 1645E. The charge may have originated in Aleandro's youthful association with a refugee Jew from Spain with whom he studied Hebrew. See CEBR 'Aleandro.'

xli

54 He was in Louvain as late as 19 October 1520, Ep 1153:255. This letter suggests that business with the rector of the university, Godschalk Rosemondt, over a hearing on Baechem's continuing charges against him, may have been more important to him than his presence at the coronation.

xlii

55 This famous epigram does not appear in Erasmus' own works. It was reported by Georgius Spalatinus, the elector's secretary, who was present at the interview. See V.L. von Seckendorf *Commentarius historicus et apologeticus de Lutheranismo* 1692 I 125 ff and *Georg Spalatins historischer Nachlass und Briefe* ed C.G. Neudecker and L. Preller 1851 I 164, as cited in *Opuscula* 332 n3. For an account of the incident see James D. Tracy *The Politics of Erasmus: A Pacifist Intellectual and His Political Milieu* (Toronto 1978) 115–17.

xliv

56 Ep 1162: 242–4, a letter to Thomas More detailing the entire confrontation, written sometime in November 1520. For another account see Ep 1173:29–109. The same ground is covered in his tract *Acta* 101–2 below.

57 Ferguson in *Opuscula* 341 n3 makes this assertion following Preserved Smith *Erasmus* (New York 1923) 230 and Allen Ep 1118 introduction.

xlv

58 See the case for Erasmian authorship that Ferguson makes in *Opuscula* 343–8.

xlix

59 See Erika Rummel 'Erasmus and His Louvain Critics: A Strategy of Defense' NAKG 70 (1990) 2–12, as well as her *Erasmus and His Catholic Critics*, especially I 186–90.

60 See C. Reedijk 'Three Erasmus Autographs in the Royal Library at Copenhagen' *Studia Bibliographica in Honorem Herman de la Fontaine Verwey* (Amsterdam 1966).

61 Reedijk 'Three Erasmus Autographs ...' 338 n2

62 H.J. de Jonge in ASD IX-2 43 identifies it as 'an apology against Jacobus Latomus' work *De confessione secreta, De quaestionum generibus quibus Ecclesia certat intus et fortis, De Ecclesia et humanae legis obligatione* Antwerp 1525.'

63 Rummel published the Latin text in 'An unpublished Erasmian Apologia in the Royal Library of Copenhagen' NAKG 70 (1990) 210–29. A descriptive article by her appeared in RQ 43–4 (1990), entitled '*Manifesta mendacia*: Erasmus' Reply to Taxander.'

64 Epp 1717:70–15, 1719:29–33, 1735:29–31, 1747:33–40. Erasmus did admit that the imperial ban had at least prevented Latomus from publishing one attack against him, Ep 1747:49–51.

LETTER TO DORP

2

1 The former in a letter to Johann von Botzheim Allen I 41; the latter in a letter to Hector Boece Ep 2283.

2 See CWE 25 liii.

3

3 The *Cato* was included in a volume *Opuscula aliquot Erasmo Roterodamo castigatore*, printed by Dirk Martens in Louvain, September 1514.

5

4 Cf Ep 337 page 112; Ep 347 page 155; Yale More Edition *Selected Letters* ed Elizabeth F. Rogers Ep 4 page 16 and another version in vol XV page 5.

5 Rogers *Selected Letters* xxii and Ep 337 introduction

6 Ep 337 introduction

7 This was pirated from an edition published in September by Schürer in Strasbourg and may well have been prompted by Dorp himself who, along with Erasmus, was a friend of Martens.

6

8 Allen II 91 is in error in asserting that 'it appears in all the early editions of that work from 1516 onwards.' On the contrary, 'Between 1516 and 1540 it was not included in at least twelve editions of the *Moria*. The early Italian

editions *never* included it,' Clarence H. Miller, review of *The Correspondence of Erasmus*, volume 3, in RQ 31 (Spring 1978) 59.

7

9 The text of this letter is reprinted from CWE 3 111–39, translated by R.A.B. Mynors and D.F.S. Thomson, annotated by James K. McConica.

10 This salutation was surely mildly satirical because Dorp was far from being a 'distinguished theologian' at this period in his career. He had received the licentiate in theology only months before the exchange of letters. He would not obtain the doctorate until the following year and be admitted to the theological faculty as 'magister noster' only on 30 August 1515. See de Vocht MHL 151.

11 Cf Epp 315:11, 323:31.

12 1 Cor 13:4–5

8

13 *Adagia* II v 86

14 The boastful soldiers Thraso in Terence's *Eunuchus* and Pyrgopolinices in Plautus' *Miles gloriosus*

15 Ugly, misshapen, and voluble, the very antithesis of a Homeric hero, Thersites is immortalized as a demagogue in the second book of the *Iliad*.

16 The celebrated Athenian orator against whom Demosthenes directed his speech *On the Crown* (330 BC)

17 The invective against Sallust preserved with attribution to him is spurious; for his other enemies see the speeches *In Pisonem, In Vatinium interrogatio, Philippics*.

18 *Invectivae in medicum quendam*, an attack on one of the physicians at the court of Pope Clement VI; see *Opera omnia* (Basel 1554; repr 1965) II 1199–1233.

19 On this controversy see Ep 24:34n.

20 A controversy on Latin usage with the chancellor of Florence, Bartolomeo Scala (1424–97), who was the target of certain members of the humanist circle around Lorenzo de' Medici. Antipathy between Scala and Poliziano degenerated into a violent literary quarrel in 1493–4; cf Ida Maïer *Ange Politien* (Geneva 1966) 377 n24.

21 A theological writer from Gaul, known from his controversy with Jerome over the cult of relics, which he declared to be an idolatrous adoration. Jerome's reply was the *Contra Vigilantium* of 406 AD (PL 23 353–68).

22 A monk who was a critic of celibacy and asceticism and to whom in 393 AD Jerome addressed his *Adversus Jovinianum* (PL 23 221–352). He is mentioned also by St Augustine in his *De haeresibus* (PL 42 45), *De bono coniugali*, and *De sancta virginitate* (CSEL 41 187–231, 235–302).

23 A fourth-century monk of Aquileia and sometime associate of Jerome at school and in the practice of asceticism. He became involved in a celebrated controversy with Jerome, chiefly over the doctrines of Origen; cf *Apologia adversus libros Rufini* (PL 23 415–514), written in 401–2 AD. Rufinus' own writings are collected in PL 21.

24 Horace *Satires* 2.1.30–1

9

25 *Enchiridion militis christiani*, published 1503
26 *Institutio principis christiani*, published 1516, cf Ep 393.
27 *Panegyricus ad Philippum Austriae ducem*, published 1504, cf CWE 27 1–75 and introduction, Epp 179, 304:165n.
28 *Laws* 649B–50B, 671A–73E. See also Aulus Gellius 15.2, Macrobius *Saturnalia* 2.8.5–6.
29 *Satires* 1.1.24–5
30 1.936–8

10

31 *De doctrina christiana* 2. 6 CCSL 32 35–6
32 Cf Ep 222 introduction.
33 *Adagia* II iv 29 and Pliny *Naturalis historia* 7.40.131

11

34 A farcical form of Latin comedy, played in masks, which is supposed to have originated at Atella in Campania and became a literary form in the last century before Christ. Erasmus would know of it from references in Livy and other authors.
35 *Phaedrus* 237A; cf 243B.
36 Ep 304:60–2
37 Jerome Ep 125:5 CSEL 56 122
38 LB IV 448B–E
39 *Adagia* I i 64; cf 24 below.

12

40 Ep 304:24–6
41 Persius 1.107–8
42 A bitter-tasting compound of aloes, sometimes used as an antidote, Scribonius Largus *Compositiones* ed Georg Helmreich (Leipzig 1887) 99, 156
43 2 Tim 4:2
44 Cf Horace *Ars poetica* 179–88.
45 Pyrrhus, king of Epirus; the story is told in Plutarch *Moralia* 184D and elsewhere.
46 Cicero *De oratore* 2.54.216 to 2.71.290; Quintilian 6.3

13

47 Cf Suetonius *Divus Julius* 73.
48 This probably refers to the *sotie*, a form of popular French satirical play. See *The Julius exclusus of Erasmus* ed J.K. Sowards (Bloomington and London 1968) 26–7.
49 Suetonius *Divus Vespasianus* 20
50 Cf Horace *Ars poetica* 281–4.
51 Ep 304:28–30
52 Ep 304:51–3
53 Terence *Andria* 663

14

54 St Eustochium (c 368–c 418) was the third of four daughters of St Paula of Rome. She led a life of consecrated virginity and was one of the noble Roman ladies who received spiritual direction from St Jerome. The letter here referred to (Epistle 22) – one of several addressed to her – is perhaps his most famous letter; CSEL 54 143–211.

55 St Nepotianus was nephew to the bishop Heliodorus of Altinum. Like his uncle, he had abandoned a military career for the clerical state. The letter is Ep 52, written in 394 AD (CSEL 54 413–41). Nepotianus died of a fever shortly afterwards; cf Ep 60 to Heliodorus.

56 A young monk of Toulouse to whom Ep 125 was written in 411 AD; CSEL 56 118–42

15

57 Alexandre de Ville-Dieu (fl c 1200), whose *Doctrinale*, a versified grammar for advanced students, was one of the most successful schoolbooks of the Middle Ages.

58 Cf Ep 26:100n.

59 A glossary to the Vulgate, the *Legenda sanctorum*, and other writings, compiled about 1300 by the Franciscan Johannes Marchesinus of Reggio, first printed at Mainz and at Lucerne in 1470, and often reprinted. The title is a corruption of the Greek *mammothreptos*, understood to mean 'a baby at the breast,' since when armed with this book even babes and sucklings could face difficult Latin.

60 Presumably in his *Liber facetiarum*, a collection of witty and often improper stories frequently directed against the clergy

61 Giovanni Pontano (c 1424–1503) of Naples, one of the most celebrated Latin poets in Renaissance literature. He was a prolific writer; this reference may be to his Lucianic dialogue *Charon*.

62 *Annals* 15.44.3ff

63 *Nero* 16

16

64 Pliny *Naturalis historia* 7.55.188–90 and Lucian *Dialogi mortuorum* 374, 404–5

65 An allusion to Erasmus' characterization of the vanity of theologians in *The Praise of Folly* CWE 27 130

66 Erasmus received his doctorate from the University of Torino in 1506. See the account in J.K. Sowards 'Erasmus and the "Other" Pope Julius' *Wichita State University Studies* 90 (1972) 11–15.

67 Plato *Apologia* 23A and LB 4 159A

68 This reference is not in the printed version of Ep 304 but must have been in the original draft of the letter.

69 Possibly Jan Briart, cf Ep 670 introduction.

17

70 *Adagia* I i 8 and Cicero *Ad familiares* 16.24.1

71 1 Tim 6:4

18

72 1 Tim 6:4

19

73 5.13.23 and following
74 Isa 64:6
75 CWE 27 111 and Plato *Phaedrus* 244A–5C

20

76 1 Cor 1:23–5
77 Allen suggests the source of this reference is St Thomas' *Commentarium super Matthaeum* 17:5. But it is not there. Only the phrase 'Petrus insipienter loquebatur' approximates the sentiment. See *Divi Thomae Aquinatis opera omnia* Stan. Fretté ed (Paris 1882) 19, 482–3. On the other hand, Clarence H. Miller, in his version of the Dorp letter in his translation of *The Praise of Folly* (158), correctly identifies the quotation as being 'from a sequence (hence sung in church) for the feast of the Transfiguration (*Analecta Hymnica* 54, 168–70 Number 110). The author is unknown; only Erasmus connects it with St Thomas.' Screech *Ecstasy and the Praise of Folly* 201 suggests that Erasmus may deliberately have made this misidentification to ally himself with St Thomas and thus give more legitimacy to his point.
78 *Precatio ad Virginis filium Iesum* LB V 1213A: 'Nam tu, dulcissime Iesu, pius ille es incantator et magus.'
79 *Translatio homeliarum Origenis in Lucam* 34, PL 26 316C
80 Gal 2:17, 3:13
81 Ie *Adagia* III iii 1
82 CWE 27 150
83 *Adagia* I iii 66

21

84 LB IV 504C
85 Plutarch *Moralia* 15D

22

86 One Herostratus, who in 356 BC successfully sought posthumous fame by burning down the great temple of Diana at Ephesus
87 Jerome Ep 115, CSEL 55 397

23

88 *Adagia* I. i. 48 and Terence *Eunuchus* 245

24

89 Ep 304:81–3
90 Plato *Philebus* 15C
91 Cf note 39 above.
92 Ep 304:90ff
93 *Adagia* I ii 46
94 Evidently Henry Standish, later bishop of St Asaph; cf Allen Ep 608:14n;

David Knowles *The Religious Orders in England* III: *The Tudor Age* (Cambridge 1959) 53–5

95 Guillaume LeBreton, the famous thirteenth-century Franciscan, wrote a work on St Jerome's biblical prologues, of which 45 manuscripts are recorded by F. Stegmüller in *Repertorium biblicum medii aevi* II (Madrid 1950) nos 2824–72.

96 Jerome *De viris illustribus*, PL 23 665

25

97 *Confessions* 1.12.19–1.14.23

98 The Council of Vienne was convoked by Clement V in 1311 and its legislation became part of canon law under the title *Constitutiones Clementinae*. Among other provisions was that stipulating that there be chairs of Hebrew, Syriac, and Arabic at Paris, Oxford, Bologna, and Salamanca. Cf Acta Clementis P.M.V., ed F.M. Delorme and A.L. Tautre (Paris 1955).

99 Cf Ep 182:194n.

100 Jerome *De viris illustribus*, PL 23 607–719

101 Cf note 70 above.

102 Ep 304:101ff

26

103 *Adagia* I viii 93

104 See note 87 above.

105 Ep 304:122ff

106 *Ad Quintum fratrem* 3.5.6

27

107 Ep 304:111ff

28

108 *Confessions* 8.12.29

109 Ep 304:99–100

110 Ep 182 introduction

29

111 Cf Ep 326:95ff.

112 Perhaps during Erasmus' visit to Paris in 1511; cf Epp 218–22

113 Aristotle *Nicomachean Ethics* 1096

114 *Adagia* I iv 27

30

115 Cf Ep 180 introduction.

116 Gerardus Listrius was a learned friend of Erasmus in Basel where he prepared a commentary for the 1515 Froben edition of *The Praise of Folly*. Cf Ep 495 introduction. That Erasmus himself had a hand in the commentary is indicated in Allen Ep 2615:171–6.

117 Cf Ep 298 introduction.

118 Nicholas of Burgundy, cf Ep 144 introduction.

119 Cf Ep 304:178n.

APOLOGY AGAINST THE DIALOGUE OF LATOMUS

Introduction

32

1 On the priority of the Complutensian version see D. Geanakoplos *Byzantium and the Renaissance* (Cambridge, Mass 1973) 239–46; and CWE 3 215–24 Ep 384 (Erasmus' dedication to Leo X) and introduction; CWE 4 44–5 Ep 456 (Bullock); 135–6 Ep 492 (Barlandus); 155 Ep 494 (Deloynes); 198–200 Ep 520 (Latimer). See also Bentley *Humanists and Holy Writ* 70ff.

2 CWE 4 115 Ep 481 (More's warning) and 298–9 Ep 560 (Mosellanus)

33

3 On Erasmus' view of Louvain see CWE 7 255–6 Ep 1111 (to Vives). On the new college see H. de Vocht *History of the Foundation and the Rise of the Collegium Trilingue Lovaniense, 1517–1550* 4 vols (Louvain: 1951–5) I 19–50; P.S. Allen 'The trilingual colleges of the early sixteenth century' in his *Erasmus Lectures and Wayfaring Sketches* (Oxford 1934) 138–63.

4 CWE 5 102–3 Ep 651 7 Sept (theologians well disposed); 155 Ep 686 19 Oct (hire of Hebrew lecturer); 413 Ep 836 26 April 1518 (approach to Lascaris). For the background see Vocht CTL I 241–53, 293–5, and CEBR I 28–32 (Aleandro), II 292–4 (Lascaris).

5 *Oratio de variarum linguarum cognitione paranda* (V. Schumann; Leipzig, dedication 1 August 1518), CWE 6 187 Ep 901.

34

6 CWE 6 220–1 Ep 910 (Melanchthon), 221–5 Ep 911 (Mosellanus); de Vocht CTL I 303–5

7 CWE 6 285 Ep 934; de Vocht CTL I 346–7

8 The most recent edition is in *Bibliotheca Reformatoria Netherlandica* (hereafter BRN) 3 ('s Hertogenbosch 1903) 43–84. On Latomus' background see CWE 6 285 n4, and de Vocht CTL I 325–48. On Erasmus' short period at the Collège de Montaigu see R. Bainton *Erasmus of Christendom* (London 1969) 47–51. On Erasmus' surprise at his attack see his introductory chapter (below), and on his previously cordial relations with the theologians CWE 5 102–3 Ep 651. On Guillaume de Croy see CWE 6 305 Ep 945, and CEBR I 367–8.

35

9 See especially ch 12–15.

10 de Vocht CTL I 326; CEBR I 195–6 (Briart)

11 CWE 6 283–5, introduction to Ep 934; de Vocht CTL I 334, and 537–41 for the full text.

12 CWE 6 312 Ep 948

36

13 Same letter, 312; 290 Ep 937. Compare CWE 5 342 Ep 794. For bibliography of *Apologia in Latomum* see introduction to Ep 934. Text in *Erasmi opera omnia* IX (Froben, dated 1540 but c 1542) ff 68f.

14 CWE 6 281–3 Ep 933

15 CWE 6 285 introduction to Ep 934; de Vocht CTL I 334. Nesen's dialogue is printed as an appendix to CWE 7. For Latomus' *Antapologia* and later writings see his *Opera omnia* (Louvain: Gravius 1550).

APOLOGY AGAINST THE DIALOGUE OF LATOMUS, BOOK 1

37

1 Echo of *Adagia* I i 95, CWE 31 137 (*Magis varius quam hydra* 'As variable as the hydra')

2 A mobile gladiator with a net was set against a static opponent whose heavy helmet was decorated with a fish. Pompeius Festus records the taunt quoted here: see *De significatu verborum*, under 'murmillo.'

38

3 Latomus dedicated his dialogue to Guillaume de Croy, and used pseudonyms which were easily recognizable: see ch 9 below. Erasmus mentioned advice from friends on April 2 (Ep 936), but did not name Latomus as an acquaintance before noting the publication of his dialogue on March 30 (Ep 934).

4 John Duns Scotus (c 1266–1308), Franciscan, died in Cologne after studying and teaching in Oxford and Paris. The close reasoning of his commentary on the *Sentences* (ch 41 below) and his Free Questions (*Quodlibeta*) earned him the title of 'subtle doctor.' Robert Holcot (d 1349), Dominican, also wrote on the *Sentences*. Both men were typical of the English philosophers whose adventurous logic strained language and attracted the scorn of humanists. See E. Garin 'La cultura fiorentina nella seconda meta del '300 e i "barbari Britanni,"' *Rassegna della letteratura italiana* 64, 2 (1960) 181–95. Erasmus developed the humanist 'topos' in *Praise of Folly*: CWE 27, especially 125–7.

5 BRN 44–5

39

6 Bartolus of Sassoferrato (b 1314, last mentioned 1357) and his pupil Baldus degli Ubaldis (1319 or 1327–1400) both lectured in several Italian universities including Perugia, Bologna, Pisa, Padua, and Pavia and were identified with the academic tradition of commenting on or 'glossing' the texts of Roman civil law. They were criticized by humanists such as Poliziano (*Miscellanea*, 1489) and Budé (*Annotationes in Pandectas*, 1508) for their neglect of the earliest texts. Erasmus was right in suspecting (ch 6, 28) that Latomus was attempting to spread suspicion of his critical method, as he esteemed both Budé and Poliziano (BRN 3, 44).

7 BRN 3, 44. Latomus selected the names to highlight the great tradition of mendicant theology. Alexander of Hales, Gloucestershire (d 1245) taught his fellow Franciscan Bonaventure (1221–74, canonized 1482) in Paris, where Bonaventure is supposed to have been awarded his doctorate on the same

day in 1252 as the Dominican Thomas Aquinas. Aquinas died in the same year as Bonaventure, just after completing his *Summa theologica*. He was canonized in 1323. Scotus represents the next generation of Franciscan theology. See ch 2 above.

8 LB V 76F

9 A vague passage, perhaps hastily composed. Reference may be to Paul's citation of Aratus *Phenomena* 5 ('We also are his offspring') in his address to the Athenians (Acts 17, 29), where the Jewish and Gentile literary traditions are set side by side. The phraseology of 1 Cor 11, 13 ('Judge for yourselves') is closer but the context less appropriate.

40

10 BRN 3, 47. Latomus describes a dialogue initiated by 'Peter,' who praises the attack made on 'scholasticos theologistas' by a new lecturer at Leipzig. The name and the occasion point to Petrus Mosellanus, who had reported his attack to Erasmus a few weeks earlier (Ep 911). See introduction to Ep 934 for further comment on the background.

11 Latomus' phrase 'certum est ... acturum' omits the subject of the clause in an awkward fashion which cannot be conveyed precisely. BRN 3, 47

12 Gratian's *Concordantia discordantium canonum* or *Decretum* was compiled c 1150 from patristic texts, papal rescripts, conciliar decrees etc. This passage can be found in *Corpus juris canonici* ed A. Friedberg (Leipzig 1879), pt I, dist ix, cap vi, col 17. No life of Alexander, including Lucian's *Pseudomantis* (ASD I-1 450–69) carries this exact form of words.

41

13 *De civitate Dei* 8.11; *Confessions* 7; Plato is described as 'coming nearest to the knowledge of Christ,' and as having helped Augustine to an understanding of St Paul.

14 Niccolò de' Tudeschi (1386–1445) was the most influential fifteenth-century commentator on canon law. Sicilian by birth, he was drawn into the service of Alphonso the Magnanimous in 1434 and upheld the rights of the Council of Basel against Eugenius IV. Rewarded by his king with the archbishopric of Palermo he earned the name 'Panormitanus.' See *Dictionnaire de loi canonique* VI (Paris 1957) 1195–1215 on his career and writings. Gratian, Camaldolese or Benedictine compiler of the *Decretum* (see ch 11 above) taught at Bologna in the mid-twelfth century. On the influence of his work Erasmus was correct: E. Will 'Decreti Gratiani Incunabula' *Studia Gratiana* 6 (1959) 5–280 identifies 44 editions before 1500.

15 BRN 3, 48–9. Peter mentions the demand of the Council of Vienne (1312) for chairs of Greek, Hebrew, Syriac, and Arabic in Paris, Bologna, Oxford, and Salamanca. John questions the inclusion of Greek. *Corpus juris canonici* II (Leipzig 1881), Clementinarum lib V, tit i, cap i, col 1179 confirms that only three manuscripts include Greek. R. Weiss 'England and the decree of the Council of Vienne on the teaching of Greek, Arabic, Hebrew and Syriac' BHR 14 (1952) 1–7 stresses that the aims were pastoral, not academic, and had little success.

42

16 LB VI 325, on Luke 23:23

43

17 BRN 3, 49. Latomus makes John apply 'reductio ad absurdum' to Peter's argument by claiming that Pilate's notice, which was pinned above Christ's head, could not have been as sprinkled with the holy blood as the lance which pierced his side: and were lances therefore sanctified? Erasmus points to the contradiction between this frivolous word-play and Latomus' introduction of a 'venerable theologian' in his second book. Hilary of Poitiers (c 315–67) stressed the sanctity of Latin, Greek, and Hebrew in the introduction to his commentary on the Psalms: *D. Hilarii pictavorum episcopi lucubrationes* (Paris: C. Guillard 1544) f 131v BRN 3, 49–50. Cf LB V 77–8.

18 Around 30 in both cases: Augustine, *Confessions*, bks 5–6 passim; P. Schaff and H. Wace eds *Select Library of the Nicene and Post-Nicene Fathers of the Christian Church* 10 (Grand Rapids: Michigan 1976 ed) xv

44

19 Basil the Great (c 330–379), bishop of Caesarea, pastor, controversialist, and champion of orthodoxy against the Arianism of Eunomius. Erasmus edited his works with Hieronimus Froben and Nicholas Episcopius of Basel, 1532. On Chrysostom see below, ch 31.

20 Hippocrates (c 469–399 BC), the most celebrated physician of Greek antiquity, was credited with a number of writings now thought to be later in date. On Galen and Erasmus' interest in medicine, see below ch 20.

21 Theodorus Gaza (died 1475) remained in Italy after the Council of Florence, 1439. Study at Mantua with Vittorino da Feltre (1442–6) and his work as a translator at the papal court under Nicholas V (1449–55) established him as one of the few native Greeks who attained an equal facility in Latin. Printed by Aldus (1495), his Greek grammar was re-edited by Erasmus for Froben (1518, 1520). Erasmus' defence of Jerome against Gaza's criticism can be found in *Hieronimi opera omnia* (Paris: Chevallonium 1534) I f 10v. In the dialogue Albertus is made to take up Erasmus' point and argue that, if Gaza had never reached perfection in Latin, there could be no hope for him. BRN 3, 50

45

22 Galen (129–c 200 AD) served as surgeon to the gladiators of Pergamum and codified the medical writings of antiquity in a series of writings which fill 20 volumes in the edition of G. Kuhn (Leipzig 1821–33). 'Methodus Therapeutice' fills vol 10. The work was edited by Erasmus' friend Leoniceno (see ch 27 below) as *De arte curatoria* (Paris 1528). Erasmus himself had written an *Encomium medicinae* in 1499 and published it in Louvain in 1518 (ASD I-4 147–86). He followed the publication of Galen's *Opera omnia* in Greek by Andrea Torresani (Venice 1525) with critical interest (Allen VI 142, 193, 249 Epp 1594, 1628, 1659) and later translated three of Galen's minor works (ASD I-1 629–69).

23 *Corpus juris canonici* II, Decretalium lib 1, tit 3, cap 11, col 20 'Falsa latinitas vitiat rescriptum papae.'

24 Augustine, *De civitate Dei* 16.4, 19.7. Hieronimi *Opera omnia* II f 7v (*Adversus Jovinianum*): 'Verum scriptorum tanta barbaries ... ut nec quid loquatur, nec quibus argumentis velit probare quid loquitus, potuerim intelligere.' Cf 70v–89r in the same volume for *Adversus Rufinum*.

46

25 Erasmus' strong interest in pronunciation (perhaps a legacy from the Aldine circle) emerges in this section: cf *De pueris instituendis* and *De pronuntiatione* in CWE 26 336–7, 387, 409. On the more distant background see M. Lowry *The World of Aldus Manutius* (Oxford 1979) 65–6.

47

26 The tense situation in Louvain is summarized in the introduction to Ep 934 in CWE 3.

27 Gunfounder of Nürnberg, based in Mechelen from 1510, died 1534 after supplying cannon to Charles V. Though this is the first specific reference to him in Erasmus' writings, Johann has been plausibly identified with the person addressed in *Enchiridion militis christiani*. See Allen VI 42 (Ep 1556): O. Schottenloher 'Erasmus, Johann Poppenreuter und die Entstehung des Enchiridion Militis Christiani' *Archiv für Reformationsgeschichte* 45 1 (1954) 109–116.

48

28 All (as the argument demands) were Greek scholars and all personal friends of Erasmus, who met Leoniceno and Leoni in Venice, Cop in Paris (1497), and Linacre in England (1499). Linacre and Leoniceno were both active as editors in the Aldine circle. See CEBR I 336–7 (Cop); II 322–3 (Leoni, Leoniceno); II 331–2 (Linacre) for biographies.

29 See ch 4 above and note. Accursius of Bologna, who codified existing commentaries on civil law c 1250, was proved wrong in several readings by Poliziano who had access to the early Codex Pisanus (*Miscellanea* lxxxiii). Latomus questions the value of this philological approach: BRN 3, 54. Erasmus' rather chilly allusion to Budé was typical of their relations at this time: CEBR I 215.

30 The allusion is probably to More and Alciato.

49

31 Cynic philosopher of the second century AD, known from a biography attributed to Lucian

32 *Laurentii Vallae collatio Novi Testamenti* ed A. Perosa (Florence: Sansoni 1970) 1–10 (preface). John's point (BRN 3, 55) is that Chrysostom commented on St Matthew's Gospel without knowing Hebrew, so there was no reason for Latin commentators to insist on Greek. Remigius of Auxerre (c 841–908), Hugh of St Victor (c 1096–1141), Aquinas (see ch 5), and Nicholas of Lyra (c 1270–1340) were selected to cover the widest span of biblical commentary. Nicholas of Lyra was in fact a Hebrew scholar.

50

33 John Chrysostom (c 347–407), patriarch of Constantinople, Doctor of the

church, author of homilies on Genesis, Matthew, John, and the Epistles. The reference here is to his *Homiliae in Matthaeum*, which were edited by F. Field, 3 vols (Cambridge 1839).

51

34 Jewish tradition held that Ptolemy II Philadelphus (285–246 BC) commissioned 72 scholars (*Septuaginta* 'seventy') to translate Hebrew literature for the library of Alexandria. In fact the version seems only to have been completed c 100 BC. Jerome (the 'most learned of them all') attempted to improve on this text by learning Hebrew, though his studies took place in the 370s, when he was in his thirties.

35 Origen of Alexandria (c 185–254) compiled a 'sixfold' (*Hexapla*) version of the Old Testament, with the Hebrew text set alongside Greek versions which included those of Aquila, Symmachus, and Theodotion. It survives only in fragments. His commentaries on the Gospels have been printed in the *Sources chrétiennes* series of Editions le Cerf (Paris: Luke 1962, John 1966).

36 See Field's edition I 60–70 for the text. Symmachus, Aquila, and Theodotion were Ebionite or proselyte Jewish commentators of the second century.

52

37 Cyprian, bishop of Carthage (martyred 258) wrote widely on pastoral subjects. Erasmus may already have been working on his text of Cyprian's *Opera*, which was printed by Froben in 1520, 1521, and 1525.

53

38 BRN 3, 55 referring to 1 Cor 14:38. Erasmus' comments can be found in LB VI 733E–F. It is not clear whether St Paul was simply defying an opponent ('If he refuses to recognize this, then let him refuse') or proclaiming that he would be rejected by God. Theophylactus was an eleventh-century Byzantine exegete.

54

39 *Petri Lombardi sententiae in IV libris distinctae* (Rome: Grottaferrata 1971) bk 1, dist 5, cap 1–2 (pages 87–8). Latomus' argument (BRN 3, 56) was that Peter (c 1100–1160) bishop of Paris and author of the most influential theological textbook of the Middle Ages, had made his key discoveries without a knowledge of Greek.

55

40 LB V 77C–D. Several passages in Plato – eg *Phaedo* 61A, *Gorgias* 484B – convey this general idea. Other references are to Augustine, Prologus in *De doctrina christiana*, in PL 34 36. 1 Corinthians 12–14 passim.

41 Wisdom of Solomon 1:4

42 *Institutio oratoria* 6.2.26

56

43 Romans 5: 21 and 5–7 passim
44 *Adagia* II iii 41 (LB II 497B)

APOLOGY AGAINST THE DIALOGUE OF LATOMUS,
BOOK 2

1 BRN 3, 53–84. See translator's introduction 35, on the difficulties raised by
the 'old theologian' in this book.

57

2 BRN 3, 59. Erasmus distorted the meaning of 'quasi hominem,' which Latomus clearly intended to mean 'as a man (rather than a boy).'
3 The 'one man' is probably Lefèvre d'Etaples and the reference to *Apologia ad
Jacobum Fabrum Stapulensem* (5 August 1517), rather than to Dorp and *Epistola Apologetica ad Martinum Dorpium* (1515). Erasmus had pursued his argument with Lefèvre for some months, whereas his relations with Dorp had
been cordial. For the texts see LB IX 2–50: for background CWE 4 Ep 496
(Dorp friendly); CWE 5 Epp 597, 794 (anxiety over debate with Lefèvre).
4 Aristotle names opponents in *Metaphysics* VI 6 (1031 a 15f). Plato's dialogues
Protagoras, Gorgias, Parmenides, Meno, and *Sophistes* criticized sophists.

58

5 *De pueris instituendis* (CWE 26 297–346) contains only general advice and
Erasmus may be thinking of the more specific recommendations he had
made in the *De ratione studii* (CWE 24, esp 669), or of the poem *Institutum
hominis christiani*; see C. Reedijk *The Poems of Erasmus* (Leiden 1956) 304–13.

59

6 Comic portrayals of the Olympians in dialogues such as 'Zeus tragoedicus'
(Loeb edition, vol 2, ed A. Harmon; New York 1919), had earned Lucian
this nickname.
7 On Erasmus' translations from Lucian, most of which were executed with
More's collaboration in England during the first decade of the sixteenth
century, see E. Rummel *Erasmus as a Translator of the Classics* (Toronto 1985)
50–69.
8 The second, sixth, and ninth satires of Juvenal (fl c 80–130 AD) dealt with
sexual themes. His contemporary Martial and the earlier elegiac poet Catullus (d c 55 BC) were condemned by moralists for their overt sensuality. The
Arabic philosopher and commentator Averroes (1126–78) questioned the
immortality of the individual soul and held that matter was eternal, thus
undermining the concepts of a creation and a last judgment. The early
second-century Roman writers Suetonius (*Vita Neronis* ch 16) and Tacitus
(*Annales* bk 15, ch 44), both alluded to Nero's persecution of Christians after
the burning of Rome and condemned the sect. Pliny the Elder (c 23 AD–79
AD), lawyer, naturalist, and military commander, asserted in his *Naturalis
historia* (7.55.188–90) that man was an animal like any other and that all

speculation about immortality was 'childish fantasy.' His death in the erup-
tion of Vesuvius is described by his nephew Pliny the Younger in *Epistolae*
6.16.

9 CWE 26 338f. The *Facetiae* of Poggio Bracciolini (1380–1459) were a series of
occasionally scurrilous anecdotes completed about two years before his
death and widely circulated thereafter: see L. Sozzi 'Le "Facezie" e la loro
fortuna europea' in *Poggio Bracciolini, 1380–1980 – VI centenario della sua
nascita* (Florence 1982) 235–259.

10 The comment on confessors' manuals was a shrewd blow: the *Confessionale*
of the Dominican Antoninus of Florence, of which seventy-one fifteenth-
century editions are known, gave details of carnal sins from 'mollities'
down to 'bestialitas,' as well as descriptions of the canonically acceptable
positions in sexual intercourse. On the general theme see S. Ozment *The
Reformation in the Cities* (Yale 1975) 20–30. Plato's attitude to poets is stated
in *Republic* 3, 398A 5–9.

11 An echo of *Adagia* III i 87, LB II 739A (*Nihil est ab omni parte beatum*).

60

12 On Marullus see CEBR II 398–9. Classical affectations, whether in literature
or life-style, often attracted charges of paganism which are now regarded as
groundless. On the notorious case of the Roman Academy see A. Dunston
'Paul II and the Humanists' *Journal of Religious History* 7 (1973) 287–306.

13 On the poets concerned see G. Raby *History of Christian Latin Poetry from the
Beginnings to the Close of the Middle Ages* (Oxford 1953) 17–20 (Juvencus);
47–71 (Prudentius); 168–70 (Paulinus). Erasmus stressed the need to stimu-
late younger children in *De pueris instituendis* (CWE 26 336).

14 See n5 above: again, the specific reference seems to be to *De ratione studii*
(CWE 24 669). The recommendation comes from Quintilian *De institutione
oratoria* 1.8.5.

61

15 PL 34 (1861) 992–3
16 PL 22 141 (*Life of Jerome*); PL 23 398–491 (*Apologia adversus Rufinum*)
17 LB V 82 especially C–D

62

18 BRN 3, 62. Allusion to Augustine *De doctrina christiana* 2.11 (PL 34 42)
'... Necessaria est linguarum cognitio.'

63

19 Reference throughout this section is to *De doctrina christiana* 2.12–15 (PL 34
43–6). The quotation is from col 45.

64

20 PL 34 173–484 (*De genesi*), PL 36–7 (*Enarratio in Psalmos*)

66

21 In his *Praefatio pio lectori* (LB VI unpaginated introduction to the volume),

Erasmus disowned the role of commentator and added 'In regiis et qui verrunt et qui coquunt honesti habentur.'

22 Paul discusses the 'gift of tongues' in 1 *Corinthians* 14. Erasmus deals with the function of language in *De recta pronuntiatione* (CWE 26 369–475). George of Trebizond (1396–1468) was a Greek émigré who worked at the curia under Nicholas V and became professor of Greek at Padua in 1463: see J. Monfasani *George of Trebizond* (Leiden 1976), and *Collectanea Trapezuntiana* (New York 1984) 729–34 for a detailed bibliography on the translations of Chrysostom's *Homiliae in Matthaeum* (Paris 1962) 89.

67

23 F. Fournier, introduction to Le Cerf edition (Paris 1962) 89

24 A probable reference to the lost *De principiis* of Origen, condemned by Jerome c 400 and known only from his fragmentary translation, and that of his opponent Rufinus. It contained controversial doctrines on the Trinity and on free will.

68

25 BRN 3, 69. The quotation is precise, as Erasmus claims, though no mention is made of his name. Latomus was attempting to divide theology into two fields, 'crassior' (cruder) and 'subtilior' (more refined). Secular piety was equated with the first, and was to be kept out of the universities, which investigated the second.

26 LB V 84, especially E–F, and 106C

69

27 No texts on the natural sciences were specified by the old theologian at BRN 3, 69f. Erasmus probably took it as read that a general grasp of the eight books of Aristotle's *Physics* was intended.

70

28 BRN 3, 69–71 outline the old theologian's syllabus. For more details see ch 97 and n49 below.

29 LB V 105D

71

30 For Erasmus' aversion to writers such as Scotus and Holcot see bk 1, ch 2, and notes. William Durand (1230–96) was an eminent canonist and author of a compendium of liturgical knowledge entitled *Rationale divinorum officiorum* which was widely distributed in the later Middle Ages.

31 Horace *Odes* 2.1.7

72

32 Reference to *Adagia* I ii 18, CWE 32 163–4 (*Muti magistri*)

33 BRN 3, 70, referring to PL 22 43–5 (*Life of Jerome* ch 6). Same volume, 540–5, Ep 53, for the letter to Rufinus

34 The allusions seem to be to Bernard of Clairvaux (1090–1153), who urged his fellow Christians to colonize waste areas of mountain and forest, and to

Anthony of Egypt (allegedly c 250–356), the ascetic who returned from his hermitage to combat the influence of Arianism in Egypt.

35 Ambrose definitely used Origen's ideas in devotional works such as *De bono mortis*: see *Fathers of the Church* 65 (Catholic University of America Press 1972) 70–113. Augustine *Confessions* 6.3.4 mentions hearing Ambrose's sermons.

73

36 Jean Gerson (1363–1429), chancellor of the University of Paris, leading conciliarist, and one of the most respected theologians of his day. He asserted the superiority of the council over the pope at Constance in 1415. The reference is to his treatise *De libris legendis a monacho* ch 6 in *Oeuvres complètes* 9 (Paris 1972) 613.

37 Seneca *Controversiae et Suasoriae* ed M. Winterbottom (2 vols, Loeb Classical Library, New York 1974); *The Minor Declamations of Quintilian* ed M. Winterbottom (Berlin and New York 1984). Declamations were short exercises, intended to demonstrate the essentials of rhetorical technique. The mention of 'ten days' probably alludes to *Institutio oratoria* 2.1 where Quintilian recommends that boys should pass to rhetoric 'as soon as they are able.'

74

38 *De doctrina christiana* 6.6, in PL 34 93

39 See ch 53 above, and notes.

40 *Origines Vier Bücher von den Prinzipien* ed H. Gorgemanns and H. Karpp (Darmstadt 1976)

75

41 Denys l'Aréopagite *La hiérarchie céleste* ed R. Roques (Editions le Cerf: Paris 1958)

76

42 BRN 3, 73. Erasmus' presentation of Latomus' argument is overstated; all that Latomus claimed was that 'the argument with the Epicureans on the immortality of the soul would have been impossible unless Paul had discussed what the soul was, whence it came, and what its powers were.' See *Acts* 17:16–31, especially 31, where Christ is specifically called 'man.' For Christ's instructions to the twelve apostles not to reveal that he was the Messiah, see Luke 9:21.

43 Presumably the *Disputationes Tusculanae*

44 Echo of *Adagia* I ii 4, CWE 31 148–9 (*Clavum clavo pellere*)

45 *Acts* 2: 14–36

77

46 BRN 3, 74, perhaps alluding to LB IX 102B. I have inserted quotation marks in the passage extracted from Latomus' dialogue, though they are not contained either in LB or the Basel text of 1540. The argument is that philosophical questions may be relevant to understanding passages such as John 20.

47 Prov 26:27

48 BRN 3, 74. The allusion is evidently to Pico's studies at the Universities of
Bologna, Ferrara, and Padua between 1479 and 1482, and to his widely pub-
licized debate with Ermolao Barbaro on eloquence and wisdom. V. Branca
ed *Hermolai Barbari epistolae, orationes et carmina* I (Florence 1943) 100–9; CEBR
III 81–4.

78

49 The list is so exhaustive that not all of the members are identifiable: on
Scotus and Holcot see bk I, ch 2, above and notes; on Aquinas, Alexander
of Hales, and Bonaventure, bk I, ch 5, and notes; on Nicholas of Lyra, bk I,
ch 30, and notes; on Gerson see n35 above. Pierre d'Ailly (1350–1420) was
Gerson's immediate predecessor as chancellor of the University of Paris, an
influential Nominalist philosopher, and (with Gerson), a defender of conciliar power at Constance in 1415. William of Paris is probably Guillaume de
St Thierry (d 1148), a Cistercian opponent of Abelard's critical theology.
'Amarchanus' is definitely Maurice O'Fihely (c 1460–1513), Franciscan, Scotist, and professor of theology at Padua from 1491: he was archbishop of
Tuam from 1506, and author of the definitive commentary on Scotus. William of Ockham (1300–49), defender of the spiritual ideals of the Franciscans against John XXII, represented the critical philosophy of 'Nominalism'
against the 'Realism' of Scotus. Erasmus rightly saw that thinkers of the
most diverse views were represented in a list which reflected current tastes
in academic theology.
50 *Ratio seu methodus* (LB V 132F–138C) and *Adhortatio ad christianae philosophiae
studium* (same volume 143D) are possible references.

79

51 Swabian noble and Dominican (1206–80), who taught in Cologne and Paris
and did much to prepare the way for Aquinas' reconciliation of Christian
and Aristotelian thought.
52 LB V 137A cites contemporary practice at Cambridge and Louvain as
examples of the proper pursuit of scholastic debate.
53 BRN 3, 76

80

54 BRN 3, 80. Latomus attacked 'sophists' for using their professional skills for
ostentation and profit. His mention of a doctor hinted at Matthaeus Adrianus, professor of Hebrew at the Collegium Trilingue of Louvain and a
known spendthrift: see translator's introduction 33.

81

55 Echo of *Adagia* I viii 4, CWE 32 4 (*Pilo non facio*)
56 *Galatians* 2:21. Paul also cited Aratus in his speech to the Athenians (*Acts*
17:29).
57 Direct quotation from BRN 3, 81

82

58 The reference may be to *Miles gloriosus* 2.2.58, where Plautus speaks of the
Latin writer Naevius as 'barbaro poetae.'

59 *Fathers of the Church* 32 (Catholic University of America Press 1955), Augustine letters IV, trans Sister Wilfred Parsons, 141–190

83

60 An oblique reference to Edward Lee, who was studying Greek at Louvain and claimed to have made contributions to the *Novum instrumentum* which Erasmus failed to acknowledge. See CEBR II 311–14 for a detailed account of the quarrel.

DEFENCE OF THE DECLARATION ON MARRIAGE

Introductory Note

86

1 *Declamationes aliquot Erasmi Roterodami*. The others were the *Querela pacis*, the *De morte*, and the *Encomium artis medicae*.
2 In the *Paraphrasis in Elegantias Vallae* Erasmus makes a clear distinction between the rhetorician, the pleader of a case in court, and the declaimer. According to this definition, to give or write a declamation is to exercise oneself in speaking on a fictitious topic.
3 See ASD I-2 338.
4 For the history of this treatise see CWE 25 1–6. The translation of the *epistola suasoria* is contained on pages 129–45.

87

5 'Atensis probavit omnia' (Ep 1125:118, 13 August 1521). In the letter to Botzheim, Erasmus maintains that he was suborned by his colleagues and even driven to his death by their machinations. (Allen I 31–6).

The Defence of the Declamation on Marriage

89

1 Professor of theology at Louvain since 1506 and leading administrator of the university. In the *Catalogus lucubrationum* Erasmus claims that he was pleading the theologian's cause more than his own, 'magis illius causam agens quam meam,' Allen I 23.
2 His name was Jan Robyns, who may well have been the unnamed licentiate who Erasmus says was spreading lies about him (Ep 946:4n).
3 Erasmus questions the Latinity of the word *licentiatus* recently introduced in place of the earlier term *licentia*.
4 *Adagia* I iv 3

90

5 A disputation held on any subject whatever, as signified by the medieval Latin coinage
6 Disputations held by the candidate before three doctors on the night preceding the awarding of the doctorate in theology

7 In the dialogue of this name, Euthydemus and Dionysodorus confute their pupils to the applause and amusement of the onlookers. Euthydemus compares the initiation into learning to the mystery religions, 277DE.

8 A novel written in the second century AD, which gives an elaborate account of the author's initiations into various mysteries

9 A Paris divine and philosopher then in Louvain. Erasmus expressed admiration for his verse paraphrases from the Bible (Ep 456) and his prose style, which combined scholasticism with humanism.

10 Erasmus reiterates that others suborned him and drove him to his death, since he was fitted neither by age nor health to undergo such a trying experience, *Catalogus lucubrationum* Allen I 22.

11 CSEL 76 349. In the prologue Jerome confesses that he attempted an explanation of the prophet before he knew the relevant history. He quotes 1 Cor 13:11, 'When I was a child, I spoke as a child, etc.'

91

12 Mock-epic poem long attributed to Virgil

13 A parody of Homer written in the fourth century BC

14 Froben wrote that the little book arrived at the press at an opportune moment since he was about to celebrate the marriage of a dear relative. Allen Ep 604:10n identifies the bride as Anna Schabler, who was to be married to Bruno Amerbach. Froben describes the work as a youthful diversion that Erasmus had written to exercise his skill.

15 CWE 25 145–8

16 Erasmus is probably referring to the strong strain of misogyny in ancient literature beginning with Hesiod and extending through the early church Fathers. The first half of Juvenal's sixth satire is a violent diatribe against marriage, which St Jerome used in his *Adversus Jovinianum*.

17 *Summa theologica* II-II, 154, art 2

92

18 He is made to praise injustice in the *Republic*, 358E–362C.

19 CWE 25 130. Erasmus is referring here, of course, to his essay in *De conscribendis epistolis*, which he mentioned previously on page 91.

20 Peter Lombard *Sentences* 4.33

21 Origen *In Genesim homilia* V, PG 12 190–4

93

22 In a private conversation according to Erasmus in Allen Ep 1967:160–3.

94

23 Urged by several friends, Jerome recanted some of his harsher views against matrimony in the letter to Pammachius, *Letters* 58.

24 In the first part of the *De bono coniugali* he defends the sacredness and dignity of marriage, but in the latter part he predicates its inferiority to perpetual continence.

25 Member of the Donatist sect excommunicated by his own followers. His original saying was *quod volumus sanctum est* 'holiness is whatever we wish

it to be,' which Erasmus here negates. The phrase is quoted by Augustine in epistle 93.43 (PL 33 328); cf *Adagia* IV vii 16.

26 Matt 19:12
27 1 Cor 7:25

95

28 Jan Lengherant of Binche in Hainault, a member of the 'collegium strictum' of theology at Louvain, elected dean on 28 February 1517. Cf Henry de Vocht (ed) *Literae ad Craneveldium* (Louvain 1928) 3, 195.
29 King of Macedonia 413–399 BC. The story is told in Plutarch *Moralia* 177 B; cf Erasmus *Apophthegmata* LB IV 238B.
30 Matt 6:22; Luke 11:34
31 *Adagia* II iii 29, taken from Pliny *Naturalis historia* 7.40
32 Published in quarto by Martens, May 1519. Cf CWE 42 xxi. Erasmus complains also to Jan Becker of Borssele (Ep 952) that the work was delayed because of the troubles in Louvain. In this same month of March he composed an apology against a dialogue of Jacobus Latomus.

ACTS OF THE UNIVERSITY OF LOUVAIN AGAINST LUTHER

Introductory Note

98

1 CWE 6 281, 393 (Epp 933, 980). See *Acta* 25–35.
2 *Erasmi opuscula: A Supplement to the Opera omnia* ed Wallace K. Ferguson (The Hague 1933) 310. *Axiomata* line 30; *Consilium* lines 159–65. See K. Brandi *Charles V* (London 1954) 112–24.

99

3 *Acta* 66
4 Craig R. Thompson *The Colloquies of Erasmus* (Chicago 1965) 488–99. M. Lowry *The World of Aldus Manutius* (Oxford 1979) 76–8
5 Ferguson, introduction 312. His note to line 25 stresses the strong resemblance of the account of Baechem's sermons to that in Ep 1153 (18 October 1520), and his commentary on the *Axiomata* (336–7) notes seven direct verbal resemblances to *Acta*.
6 *Opuscula* 332–4

100

7 *Acta* 55–7. *Axiomata* 17–19
8 Ep 1156. See Ferguson's introduction 341–2, and entry on Faber in CEBR II 4–5.
9 In his notes on editions (350), Ferguson mentions printing errors such as 'insensus' for 'infensus' which are likely to have derived from hurried reading of a manuscript.
10 Ep 1199. Nicolaus Paulus considered Faber the author: see *Opuscula* 344–5.

Acts of the University of Louvain Against Luther

101

1 The charges against Aleandro are a skilful mixture of fact, innuendo, and falsehood. The rumour of Jewish extraction is based on his association with the Spanish émigré Moses Perez, who taught Aleandro Hebrew and was baptized 'Girolamo' in 1499. Aleandro prepared the Greek edition of Plutarch's *Moralia* for Aldus in 1507, had been active in teaching Latin to Venetian nobles in Venice and Padua over the previous decade, and lectured with great success in Paris in 1512–13. The charges of loose living and self-advancement gain some confirmation from the pursuit of patronage reflected in his letters and from his own admission of contracting venereal disease after a liaison in 1500. See entry in CEBR I 28–32; H. Omont *Journal Autobiographique de Jérôme Aléandre*, Notices et extraits des manuscrits de la Bibliothèque Nationale XXXV (Paris 1896) 37; J. Paquier *Lettres familières de Jérôme Aléandre* (Paris 1909). The burning of Lutheran books at Louvain on 8 October 1520 brought the first open breach between Erasmus and Aleandro.

2 Jacob of Hoogstraten (d 1527), Dominican and inquisitor from 1510 for the archbishoprics of Cologne, Trier, and Mainz, bore the chief responsibility for the prosecution of Reuchlin. He was dismissed from his inquisitorial office in April 1520, but restored on September 6 – a prospect alarming to Erasmus, who had observed Hoogstraten's collaboration with Baechem as early as 19 October 1519 (Ep 878). See entry in CEBR II 200–2, and *Opuscula* 318 n5. In 'beast' he may be making a vague reference to the beast of the Apocalypse.

102

3 See CEBR I 403, on Dorp's conciliatory attitude at this time. The reference is to his *Oratio in praelectionem epistolarum divi Pauli* 27 September 1519.

4 Erasmus here clarifies an aim that shows in all the *Opuscula* – that of playing for time by questioning both the authenticity of the bull and the manner of its being presented. Godschalk Rosemondt (d 1526), a theologian who had spent all his teaching life at Louvain and was rector for the half-year from August 1520, was treated with some caution by Erasmus who looked to him for protection from the attacks of Baechem (see next note). CEBR I 81–3, *Opuscula* 319 n13

5 The close coincidence of the account given here with that contained in Ep 1153 provides one of the principal items of evidence cited by Ferguson for attributing this tract definitely to Erasmus. Nicolaas Baechem of Egmond (Edmondanus d 1526), Louvain theologian and Carmelite, was an early critic of Erasmus' *Novum instrumentum* (Epp 483, 948) and one of the first to link his name with Luther's (Ep 1033). Erasmus' attempts to have him silenced are traced in detail in CEBR I 81–3. Erasmus is probably suggesting that Luther's ideas on human depravity derive from Augustine and Bernard, and those on papal power from the conciliar theorists Gerson and Cusanus.

103

6 On Dorp see n3 above. Peter Schade's *Oratio de variarum linguarum cogni-*

tione paranda, delivered at Leipzig in 1518, had sparked the controversy with Latomus. See introduction to *Apologia.*

7 H. de Jongh *L'Ancienne faculté de théologie de Louvain* (Louvain 1911) 237–8. The allusion is to a dispute on 30 August 1520, over the precedence of doctors of civil and canon law over masters of theology. The lawyer mentioned was Jean de Mera.

8 The Spanish Cardinal Bernardino López de Carvajal (d 1522). See A. Pacheco's entry in CEBR I 274–5. *Opuscula* (322, nn56–7) notes that the bull made use of the proclamations of the Universities of Cologne and Louvain against Luther – hence the suspicions expressed here by Erasmus.

9 The three men named are (1) Tommaso de Vio (Cajetanus 1469–1534), eminent canon lawyer and defender of papal power who, as papal legate to Maximilian, demanded Luther's submission at Augsburg in 1518. Erasmus' attitude to him softened after 1521. CEBR I 234–42. (2) Karl von Miltitz, Saxon, papal chamberlain and nuncio to Germany after Cajetan (*Opuscula* 323 n66). (3) Marino Caracciolo (1469–1538), Neapolitan, papal nuncio to the empire in 1517, when his mission to deliver the Golden Rose to Elector Frederick the Wise overlapped with those of Cajetan and Aleandro. CEBR I 265–5

10 It is not quite clear whether Erasmus was thinking of Pfefferkorn, the Jewish convert who instigated the prosecution of Reuchlin, as being also responsible for encouraging Julius II to 'destroy the world': the sense of the whole passage may be distorted by hyperbole. On Pfefferkorn see J. Overfield 'A new look at the Reuchlin affair' *Journal of Medieval and Renaissance History* 8 (1971) 167–207. CEBR III 767

11 Another hyperbole: Aleandro's reputation for learning in Padua was sufficient to earn him the dedication of Aldo's edition of Homer (1504), and his success in Paris won him the rectorate of the university in 1513: E Paquier *Jérôme Aléandre* (Paris 1900) 53.

104

12 Remacle d'Ardenne, Cologne lawyer (1480–1524), who as secretary to Charles V implemented the burning of books in Brabant during October 1520. *Opuscula* 324 n78

13 See nn2, 5, 9, above. The historical reference is to the 'Second triumvirate' signed by Antony, Octavius, and Lepidus near Bologna in November 43 BC. The pact divided the Roman world among the three warlords, and led to a purge of over 2000 republican sympathizers. *Cambridge Ancient History* X 19–22

14 Jan Driedo of Turnhout (d 1535), professor of theology at Louvain and at various times dean and rector of the theology faculty. A supporter of the Collegium Trilingue, he represented the moderate opinion which Erasmus hoped would give Luther 'brotherly advice.' But the refutation mentioned here was never published. CEBR I 405–6.

105

15 Cajetanus *De indulgentiis* (8 December 1517). Silvester Mazzolini di Priero (d 1523), Dominican and Master of the Papal Palace, published *In Praesump-*

tuosas Martini Lutheri conclusiones de potestate papae in February 1518.
Thomas Radinus (1488–1527), a German Dominican teaching in Rome, published *Ad principes et populos Germaniae* in August 1520. The Franciscan
Augustine Alveldt (d 1535), taught in Leipzig and published *De apostolica
sede* on 5 May 1520. CEBR I 38, and *Opuscula* 327 nn124–5

MINUTE COMPOSED BY A PERSON
WHO SERIOUSLY WISHES PROVISIONS TO BE MADE
FOR THE REPUTATION OF THE ROMAN PONTIFF
AND THE PEACE OF THE CHURCH

108
1 Cf *Acta* 79–80, *Axiomata* 1

109
2 This whole passage has obvious resemblances to *Acta* 110–30. See n15 on
  that text for references to Mazzolini (Prierias) and Aldveldt (Augustinus).
  Mazzolini's position as Master of the Papal Palace lent some substance to
  Erasmus' charge of advancing his personal interests.
3 Luther's stance in the debate with Eck at Leipzig in July 1519 had been
  condemned by the Universities of Cologne and Louvain. But (*Acta* 93–9)
  Louvain had stopped short of condemning his position on papal power. For
  the general background see R. Bainton *Here I Stand* (New York/London
  1950) 110.
4 The difference between the tone of the bull and Pope Leo's known character is mentioned in Epp 1156:85–9, 1167:399–400.

110
5 *Acta* 105
6 *Acta* 138–40
7 *Axiomata* 37–9. For the thought cf *Apologia in Latomum* II 44, LB 6 91A.

111
8 The same warning is used in Ep 1156:53, and helps to confirm Erasmus'
  authorship of this piece. The allusion is to the Hussite rising in Bohemia
  after the execution of Hus himself in 1415; see R. Betts *Essays in Czech History* (London 1969). The comparison of Luther and Hus had been given pro-
  minence by Eck at Leipzig.
9 *Axiomata* 37
10 Erasmus hoped that contacts such as Pace, More, and Peutinger at these
  courts would enable him to exert some indirect influence. See Epp 1118 and
  1156, and introduction.

112
11 *Axiomata* 30. The rising of the Spanish 'Communeros' was gathering force in
  the late summer of 1520; K. Brandi *Charles V* (London 1954) 143.

MANIFEST LIES

Introductory Note

114

1 *Apologia in eum librum quem ab anno Erasmus Roterodamus de confessione edidit ... per Godefridum Ruysium Taxandrum. Eiusdem liber de carnium esu ante biennium per Erasmum Roterodamum enixus* (Antwerp: S. Cocus 1525)

2 Allen Ep 1608:4–8

3 Erasmus describes the meeting in CWE Ep 1196:36–102.

4 Allen Ep 1603:38–40

5 Ep 1582 of July 1525

6 Cf E. Rummel *Erasmus and His Catholic Critics* (Nieuwkoop 1989) I ch 1, 4.

7 Gl Kgl Saml 96 Fol; cf Rummel *Catholic Critics* II 28 and 'Manifesta Mendacia: Erasmus' reply to "Taxander"' *Renaissance Quarterly* 43–4 (1990) 731–43. For a transcription of the text cf Rummel 'An unpublished Erasmian apologia in the Royal Library at Copenhagen' *Nederlands Archief voor Kerkgeschiedenis* 70–2 (1990) 210–29. The text with full critical apparatus will eventually appear in ASD. In the present translation lacunae in the text as well as illegible and undecipherable words have been indicated by elision marks. These gaps, which are on the whole negligible and concern only isolated words, do not affect the context.

8 Cf C. Reedijk 'Three Erasmus Autographs in the Royal Library at Copenhagen' in *Studia Bibliographica in Honorem Herman de la Fontaine Verwey* (Amsterdam 1966) 327–49. He suggested that the apologia was directed against Zúñiga (338 n2); later H.J. de Jonge conjectured that the arguments were addressed to Masson (ASD IX-2 43).

9 Cf Rummel *Catholic Critics* II 121. Pio's second attack on Erasmus appeared posthumously in 1531. After some deliberation Erasmus decided to publish a reply, a decision for which he was much criticized.

10 Allen Ep 1717:7–15

11 Allen Ep 1747:49–51

115

12 This protégé of Jacques Masson engaged in a controversy with Erasmus in 1529. Cf Rummel *Catholic Critics* II 14–22.

13 Allen Ep 2205:194–99. 'Bucenta,' a pun on 'Vincentius,' means 'cowherd.'

Manifest Lies

116

1 Cf Taxander sig Ai v: 'I recently wrote ... against certain insane assertions and concerning matters that were challenged and called into question by the famous Erasmus of Rotterdam – matters that have already been decided by the council of the church, indeed by Christ himself.'

2 Published Basel: Froben and Antwerp: Hillen 1524 (text in LB V 145–70); it

concerned the practice of confession, as indicated by the subtitle *De modo confitendi* ('On the Manner of Confessing,' used below 116).

3 Edward Lee (d 1544) published a critique of Erasmus' New Testament in 1520. Erasmus answered with a *Responsio* (Antwerp: Hillen 1520, text in LB IX 123–284). For an account of Erasmus' controversy with Lee see Rummel *Catholic Critics* I 95–120.

4 LB IX 255C–D

5 LB IX 262D–E

6 First published Antwerp: Hillen 1525 and again in his *Opera omnia* (Louvain: Gravius 1550), where the passage to which Erasmus alludes here appears on fol 89v.

7 Published with *De quaestionum generibus* (Antwerp: Hillen 1525) and in *Opera omnia* (Louvain: Gravius 1550), where Masson deals with the origin of confession at fol 113v.

8 *Exomologesis* LB V 145B

117

9 Cf Taxander sig Ai v: 'certain insane assertions ... impiety against the church, the immaculate bride of Christ ... scurrilous blasphemy.'

10 Taxander sig Aii v

11 *Spongia* ASD IX-1 164

12 For example, at sig Aii v: 'Luther, a disciple not unworthy of such a teacher'

13 Jan Briart of Ath (1460–1520), vice-chancellor of the University of Louvain, had attacked Erasmus' *Encomium matrimonii*; Erasmus in turn clarified his position on marriage in his reply, *Apologia pro declamatione in laudem matrimonii* (*The Defense of the Declamation on Marriage*). See above 85–95.

14 *De interdictu esu carnium* (Basel: Froben 1522), text in ASD IX-1 19–50

15 Cf Taxander sig Aiii r–v.

118

16 Diego López Zúñiga (d 1531) carried on a lengthy controversy with Erasmus over his New Testament edition. Cf H.J. de Jonge's introduction to the text of Erasmus' first apologia, ASD IX-2. Erasmus explains his views on warfare at LB IX 370B–D.

17 *Institutio principis christiani* (*The Education of a Christian Prince*) (Basel: Froben 1515). The English text is in CWE 27 205–88. It contains a section 'On Starting War' (282–88).

18 Taxander sig Aiii v

19 Nicolaas Baechem Egmondanus, a member of the faculty of theology at Louvain, with whom Erasmus had a number of confrontations. Cf Rummel *Catholic Critics* I 135–43, II 4–7. Erasmus presumably calls this a slight misrepresentation because he had called Baechem 'such a showman' (*talis histrio*, Allen Ep 1153:88), but not an 'impudent showman,' as Taxander said.

20 Cf Taxander sig Aiv v: '... and this happened to Vincentius and Latomus, truly the most learned theologians.' Vincentius Theoderici is one of the authors hiding behind the pseudonym 'Taxander.' Cf introduction 114 above.

21 Taxander sig Aiv v
22 Ibidem sig Av r
23 Ibidem

119
24 Ibidem sig Avii r
25 In his *Exomologesis* Erasmus had listed the advantages and disadvantages of confession, as practised in his time.
26 Taxander sigs Aviii v–Bi r; he is referring to Erasmus' account in *Exomologesis* LB V 154A–B.
27 Cf Ep 1299 of 1522. On his continued efforts to defend the work against detractors see C.R. Thompson *Colloquies* 623–4.
28 Taxander sig Biv r, quoting Erasmus' *Exomologesis* LB V 155B–C. The passage was also attacked by Masson *Opera omnia* fol 109v.

120
29 Taxander sig Bv v–Bvi r: 'He criticizes a priest, who was about to say mass, when he noticed that he had bits of sugar between his teeth; Erasmus criticizes him because out of reverence for the precepts of the church he hesitated, unsure whether he was allowed to celebrate mass. "I laughed at the stupidity of the pious man," he says. What pious men praise and admire in the old man, Erasmus derides. Is it right to laugh at a man who respects the decrees of the holy Catholic church?' Taxander is referring to a passage in Erasmus' *Exomologesis* LB V 158D.
30 Taxander argues that neglect of the rule (which states that one must not take food or drink before going to communion) might lead from minor to greater infractions, to the point where even drunk people would not be afraid to approach the table of the Lord and 'the divine word will be heard at public banquets' (sig Bvi r).
31 Taxander sig Bvi v: 'Concerning confession ("general confession," as they call it) it is foolish to argue.'
32 Erasmus erroneously put 'page 26' instead of 'page 28.'
33 Taxander sig Bvi v
34 LB V 150D
35 Taxander sig Bvii r. Taxander meant 'counsel,' 'advice.' Erasmus alludes to this passage in Taxander in *Scholia* added to *De esu carnium* in 1532; *Constat autem virginitatem ... non fuisse praecepti sed consilii tantum* ('It is an established fact that virginity was a matter, not of precept but of counsel,' ASD IX-1 72).
36 Taxander sig Bvii r

121
37 LB V 159C
38 Taxander writes: 'The insanity of this old scholar is astonishing' (sig Bvii r).
39 Taxander sig Ci r
40 Ibidem sig Cii r
41 *Exomologesis* LB V 157A–B

122

42 Cf Taxander sig Fvi r: 'that man who begrudges us the light of divine piety and attempts to extinguish the lantern of confession' (quoted by Erasmus below 124).

43 Taxander sig Cvii r

44 Ibidem sig Cvii v

45 Ibidem; Taxander is referring to the arrangement in *Exomologesis* LB V 147C–160B.

123

46 Cf Taxander sig Cviii r: 'In his letter to Barbier he wrote ... that Ath wanted Erasmus to add [to his *Annotations*] that confession was instituted by Christ. "For this dogma," Erasmus said, "as its truth was not yet clear to me, I was unwilling to take responsibility."' Taxander is quoting Erasmus' Ep 1275:32.

47 Taxander (sig Cviii r) quotes *Ratio seu methodus compendio perveniendi ad veram theologiam* Holborn 205; Erasmus added the qualifying sentence at Holborn 206.

48 Taxander sig Cviii v, citing *Ratio* Holborn 205

49 The scholastic teacher John Duns Scotus (d 1308)

50 Taxander at sig Diii v: 'Therefore the pope has the power to empty purgatory, but not at his nod.' Erasmus wants to emphasize that 'at his nod' was not his, but Taxander's formulation.

51 Erasmus erroneously put 'page 49.' The reference is to page 59, ie Taxander sig Dvi r.

52 Cf *Annotations* LB VI 503C–F.

53 Taxander sig Ei r, referring to the story of the leper at Matt 8:4 and Erasmus' explanation of the passage in his reply to Lee, LB IX 257A–E

54 Cf LB IX 257B.

55 Taxander sig Ev v

56 Erasmus quotes Jerome as his source for this expression, cf *Adagia* II iv 33.

124

57 Taxander sig Fv r: 'None of the popes, however, instituted confession, as Erasmus asserts.'

58 The canonist Panormitanus (1386–1445); cf Allen Ep 2787:40–41 note, which gives a reference to *In iv et v Decret. libros* (Lyons 1586) 249–59.

59 Taxander sig Fiv r: 'Interpret this as a reference to the annual confession, which we are told to make at Easter.'

60 Taxander sig Fv v, loosely quoting Erasmus' apologia against Lee LB IX 255B

61 Taxander sig Fv v, presumably referring to *Ratio* Holborn 206

62 Gal 2:11–14

63 Taxander was no doubt referring to Matt 16 (sig Fv v). Inverting numbers was a common printing mistake.

64 Taxander Fvi r

65 Ibidem

66 Taxander sig Fvi r, quoting Erasmus' apologia against Lee, LB IX 256D: 'In saying this I cite, not my belief, but the opinion of others.'
67 Taxander sig Fvi r
68 Taxander Gi r

125

69 Ibidem: 'Boys are taught from those *Colloquies*, in which he clearly denies that confession is instituted by Christ, where he discredits indulgences with remarkable cunning ...; the whole apologia [against Lee] ... is nothing but an attempt to do away with confession.'
70 An error in numbering: Erasmus has jumped a decade. He repeats this mistake below, cf note 78.
71 LB IX 258E, quoted by Taxander sig Gi v. Erasmus was referring to a paid audience.
72 Taxander sig Gii r: 'that unfortunate Christian liberty, which he dreams up'
73 The point of Erasmus' remark is somewhat obscure. Taxander says: 'How Hutten – formerly called "the Star of Germany" – is berated in the *Spongia!*' (sig Gii r)
74 Taxander sig Gv r: 'Panormitanus is praised because he denies confession; Thomas is disdained because he is a monk and supports confession.' Cf above note 58.
75 Taxander sig Gv r
76 It is unclear to which passage Erasmus is referring.
77 In Taxander's book a new section begins here. It is entitled *Appendix in librum Erasmi Roterodami De esu carnium.*
78 An error in numbering. Erasmus has jumped a decade.

126

79 Taxander sig Gvii r concerning *De esu carnium* ASD IX-1 24
80 *De modo orandi* ASD V-1 154
81 *Virginis matris apud Lauretum cultae liturgia* (text in ASD V-1 95–109)
82 Taxander sig Gvii v
83 Taxander sig Gviii r: 'What Erasmus sowed, Luther reaps ... Luther goes on preaching what Erasmus taught.'
84 Ibidem
85 Taxander did not quote Erasmus verbatim, but it is clear that he was referring to *Exomologesis* LB V 167F: 'Holy Writ teaches nothing about indulgences.'
86 Taxander sig Gviii r
87 LB VII 647C–D

127

88 Taxander sig Gviii v
89 Ibidem
90 Taxander sig Hi r, referring to Matt 26:8
91 Ibidem
92 Cf Epp 1499:27–8 (for Erasmus' communications with Adrian), 1418 (to Clement VII and 1410 (to Lorenzo Campeggi).

93 Erasmus added the last clause as an afterthought, squeezing the line into the narrow space between 'others' and the next heading.
94 Taxander sig Hi r
95 Taxander sig Hi v
96 Taxander sig Hii v, referring to ASD IX-1 26
97 Ibidem, referring to the same passage in ASD IX-1 26

128
98 Taxander sig Hii v
99 Taxander sig Hiii r
100 For Erasmus' comments on prolix prayers cf his *Annotations* LB VI 35F and *De modo orandi* ASD V-1 140.
101 Cf LB VI 35F.
102 Taxander concludes his argument: 'In these works Erasmus gives clear proof of his faith and he persecutes the church and agrees with Luther's positions' (sigs Hiii r–v).
103 Taxander sig Hiii v: 'I wish Erasmus were as concerned about Luther's ventures as he professes himself to be.'
104 ASD IX-1 26
105 Taxander sig Hiv r: 'He tries to prove this with deliberate lies.'
106 Taxander sig Hv r
107 For a similar remark see Erasmus' *Scholia* on *De esu carnium*: 'If ... they were exhorted with fatherly counsel, more people would fast voluntarily than are fasting now under compulsion by the law' (ASD IX-1 89).

129
108 Taxander sig Hvi r
109 ASD IX-1 30
110 Erasmus omits the page number. The reference is to Taxander sig Hvi v.
111 ASD IX-1 28, cf Taxander sig Hvii r.
112 Taxander sig Hvi v. He furthermore alleges that Erasmus wanted marriage for priests and monks legitimized 'in order to enjoy the privilege himself.'
113 From this point onward Erasmus no longer numbers his replies.
114 Taxander sig Hvii r
115 Ibidem
116 Taxander sig Ii r

130
117 Ibidem
118 Ibidem
119 Jean Gerson (1363–1429), a distinguished theologian at the University of Paris.
120 Taxander sig Iii r
121 Taxander sig Iiii r
122 Taxander sig Iv v; Erasmus had obtained a dispensation for health reasons.
123 ASD IX-1 46

131

124 The book was dedicated to Lee, 'eminent theologian, exceptionally learned
   in the two languages, almoner to Henry VIII, king of England' (sig Ai v).
   The dedicatory letter, which occupies the first ten pages of the book, is
   dated Louvain, 13 February 1525.

WORKS FREQUENTLY CITED

SHORT-TITLE FORMS
FOR ERASMUS' WORKS

INDEX

WORKS FREQUENTLY CITED

This list provides bibliographical information for publications referred to in short-title form in introductions and notes. For Erasmus' writings see the short-title list following (pages 176–9).

Allen   P.S. Allen, H.M. Allen, and H.W. Garrod eds *Opus epistolarum Des. Erasmi Roterodami* (Oxford 1906–47) 11 vols, plus index volume by B. Flower and E. Rosenbaum (Oxford 1958). Letters are cited by epistle and line number.

ASD   *Opera omnia Desiderii Erasmi Roterodami* (Amsterdam 1969–   )

ARG   *Archiv für Reformationsgeschichte*

Bentley *Humanists and Holy Writ*   Jerry H. Bentley *Humanists and Holy Writ: New Testament Scholarship in the Renaissance* (Princeton 1983)

BHR   *Bibliothèque d'Humanisme et de Renaissance*

Brecht   Martin Brecht *Martin Luther: His Road to Reformation, 1483–1521* (Philadelphia 1985)

BRN   *Bibliotheca Reformatoria Netherlandica* ('s Hertogenbosch 1903)

CCSL   *Corpus christianorum, series Latina*

CEBR   *Contemporaries of Erasmus: A Biographical Register of the Renaissance and Reformation* ed P.G. Bietenholz and T.B. Deutscher (Toronto 1985–7) 3 vols

CSEL   *Corpus Scriptorum Ecclesiasticorum Latinorum*

CWE   *Collected Works of Erasmus* (Toronto 1974–   )

de Jongh   H. de Jongh *L'Ancienne Faculté de Théologie de Louvain* (Louvain 1911)

Holborn   *Desiderius Erasmus Roterodamus: Ausgewählte Werke* ed Hajo Holborn and Annemarie Holborn (Munich 1933; repr 1964)

LB   J. Leclerc ed *Desiderii Erasmi Roterodami opera omnia* (Leiden 1703–6) 10 vols

More   Thomas More *The Complete Works* (New Haven 1963–   )

NAKG   *Nederlands Archief voor Kerkgeschiedenis*

Opuscula   W.K. Ferguson ed *Erasmi opuscula: A Supplement to the Opera omnia* (The Hague 1933)

Pastor   Ludwig von Pastor *The History of the Popes from the Close of the Middle Ages* ed and trans R.F. Kerr et al, 6th ed (London 1938–53) 40 vols

PL   J.P. Migne ed *Patrologiae cursus completus ... series Latina* (Paris 1844–64) 221 vols

Reedijk *Poems*   C. Reedijk ed *The Poems of Desiderius Erasmus* (Leiden 1956)

Rogers   Elizabeth Frances Rogers ed *The Correspondence of Sir Thomas More* (Princeton 1947)

RQ   *Renaissance Quarterly*
Rummel *Catholic*   Erika Rummel *Erasmus and His Catholic Critics*
  Critics   (Nieuwkoop 1989) 2 vols
Scrinium Erasmianum   *Scrinium Erasmianum* ed V. Coppens (Leiden 1969) 2 vols
Thompson *Colloquies*   Craig R. Thompson ed and trans *The Colloquies of Erasmus*
  (Chicago and London 1965)
de Vocht CTL   Henry de Vocht *History of the Foundation and the Rise of*
  the Collegium Trilingue Lovaniense, 1517–1550
  Humanistica Lovaniensia 10–13 (Louvain 1951–5) 4 vols
de Vocht MHL   Henry de Vocht *Monumenta Humanistica Lovaniensia: Texts*
  and Studies about Louvain Humanists in the First Half of the
  16th Century Humanistica Lovaniensia 4 (Louvain 1934)

Titles following colons are longer versions of the same, or are alternative titles. Items entirely enclosed in square brackets are of doubtful authorship. For abbreviations, see Works Frequently Cited.

Acta: Acta Academiae Lovaniensis contra Lutherum *Opuscula* / CWE 71

Adagia: Adagiorum chiliades 1508, etc (Adagiorum collectanea for the primitive form, when required) LB II / ASD II-4, 5, 6 / CWE 30–6

Admonitio adversus mendacium: Admonitio adversus mendacium et obtrectationem LB X

Annotationes in Novum Testamentum LB VI

Antibarbari LB IX / ASD I-1 / CWE 23

Apologia ad Caranzam: Apologia ad Sanctium Caranzam, or Apologia de tribus locis, or Responsio ad annotationem Stunicae ... a Sanctio Caranza defensam LB IX

Apologia ad Fabrum: Apologia ad Iacobum Fabrum Stapulensem LB IX

Apologia adversus monachos: Apologia adversus monachos quosdam hispanos LB IX

Apologia adversus Petrum Sutorem: Apologia adversus debacchationes Petri Sutoris LB IX

Apologia adversus rhapsodias Alberti Pii: Apologia ad viginti et quattuor libros A. Pii LB IX

Apologia contra Latomi dialogum: Apologia contra Iacobi Latomi dialogum de tribus linguis LB IX / CWE 71

Apologiae contra Stunicam: Apologiae contra Lopidem Stunicam LB IX / ASD IX-2

Apologia de 'In principio erat sermo' LB IX

Apologia de laude matrimonii: Apologia pro declamatione de laude matrimonii LB IX / CWE 71

Apologia de loco 'Omnes quidem': Apologia de loco 'Omnes quidem resurgemus' LB IX

Apologia qua respondet invectivis Lei: Apologia qua respondet duabus invectivis Eduardi Lei *Opuscula*

Apophthegmata LB IV

Appendix respondens ad Sutorem LB IX

Argumenta: Argumenta in omnes epistolas apostolicas nova (with Paraphrases)

Axiomata pro causa Lutheri: Axiomata pro causa Martini Lutheri *Opuscula* / CWE 71

Carmina varia LB VIII

Catalogus lucubrationum LB I

Christiani hominis institutum, carmen LB V

Ciceronianus: Dialogus Ciceronianus LB I / ASD I-2 / CWE 28

Colloquia LB I / ASD I-3

Compendium vitae Allen I / CWE 4

[Consilium: Consilium cuiusdam ex animo cupientis esse consultum] *Opuscula* / CWE 71

De bello turcico: Consultatio de bello turcico (in Psalmi)

De civilitate: De civilitate morum puerilium LB I / CWE 25

Declamatio de morte LB IV

Declamatiuncula LB IV

Declarationes ad censuras Lutetiae vulgatas: Declarationes ad censuras Lutetiae vulgatas sub nomine facultatis theologiae Parisiensis LB IX

De concordia: De sarcienda ecclesiae concordia, or De amabili ecclesiae concordia (in Psalmi)

De conscribendis epistolis LB I / ASD I-2 / CWE 25

De constructione: De constructione octo partium orationis, or Syntaxis LB I / ASD I-4

De contemptu mundi: Epistola de contemptu mundi LB V / ASD V-1 / CWE 66

De copia: De duplici copia verborum ac rerum LB I / ASD I-6 / CWE 24

De immensa Dei misericordia: Concio de immensa Dei misericordia LB V

De libero arbitrio: De libero arbitrio diatribe LB IX

De praeparatione: De praeparatione ad mortem LB V / ASD V-1

De pueris instituendis: De pueris statim ac liberaliter instituendis LB I / ASD I-2 / CWE 26

De puero Iesu: Concio de puero Iesu LB V / CWE 29

De puritate tabernaculi: De puritate tabernaculi sive ecclesiae christianae (in Psalmi)

De ratione studii LB I / ASD I-2 / CWE 24

De recta pronuntiatione: De recta latini graecique sermonis pronuntiatione LB I / ASD I-4 / CWE 26

Detectio praestigiarum: Detectio praestigiarum cuiusdam libelli germanice scripti LB X / ASD IX-1

De taedio Iesu: Disputatiuncula de taedio, pavore, tristicia Iesu LB V

De vidua christiana LB V / CWE 66

De virtute amplectenda: Oratio de virtute amplectenda LB V / CWE 29

[Dialogus bilinguium ac trilinguium: Chonradi Nastadiensis dialogus bilinguium ac trilinguium] Opuscula / CWE 7

Dilutio: Dilutio eorum quae Iodocus Clithoveus scripsit adversus declamationem suasoriam matrimonii

Divinationes ad notata Bedae LB IX

Ecclesiastes: Ecclesiastes sive de ratione concionandi LB V

Elenchus in N. Bedae censuras LB IX

Enchiridion: Enchiridion militis christiani LB V / CWE 66

Encomium matrimonii (in De conscribendis epistolis)

Encomium medicinae: Declamatio in laudem artis medicae LB I / ASD I-4 / CWE 29

Epigrammata LB I

Epistola ad Dorpium LB IX / CWE 3 / CWE 71

Epistola ad fratres Inferioris Germaniae: Responsio ad fratres Germaniae Inferioris ad epistolam apologeticam incerto autore proditam LB X / ASD IX-1

Epistola ad graculos: Epistola ad quosdam imprudentissimos graculos LB X

Epistola apologetica de Termino LB X

Epistola consolatoria: Epistola consolatoria virginibus sacris LB V

Epistola contra pseudevangelicos: Epistola contra quosdam qui se falso iactant evangelicos LB X / ASD IX-1

Epistola de esu carnium: Epistola apologetica ad Christophorum episcopum Basiliensem de interdicto esu carnium LB IX / ASD IX-1

Exomologesis: Exomologesis sive modus confitendi LB V

Explanatio symboli: Explanatio symboli apostolorum sive catechismus LB V / ASD V-1

Expositio concionalis (in Psalmi)

Expostulatio Iesu LB V

Formula: Conficiendarum epistolarum formula (see De conscribendis epistolis)
Hymni varii LB V
Hyperaspistes LB X

In Nucem Ovidii commentarius LB I / ASD I-1 / CWE 29
In Prudentium: Commentarius in duos hymnos Prudentii LB V / CWE 29
Institutio christiani matrimonii LB V
Institutio principis christiani LB IV / ASD IV-1 / CWE 27

[Julius exclusus: Dialogus Julius exclusus e coelis] *Opuscula* / CWE 27

Lingua LB IV / ASD IV-1A / CWE 29
Liturgia Virginis Matris: Virginis Matris apud Lauretum cultae liturgia LB V / ASD
    V-1

Manifesta mendacia CWE 71
Methodus (see Ratio)
Modus orandi Deum LB V / ASD V-1
Moria: Moriae encomium LB IV / ASD IV-3 / CWE 27

Novum Testamentum: Novum Testamentum 1519 and later (Novum instrumentum
    for the first edition, 1516, when required) LB VI

Obsecratio ad Virginem Mariam: Obsecratio sive oratio ad Virginem Mariam in
    rebus adversis LB V
Oratio de pace: Oratio de pace et discordia LB VIII
Oratio funebris: Oratio funebris Berthae de Heyen LB VIII / CWE 29

Paean Virgini Matri: Paean Virgini Matri dicendus LB V
Panegyricus: Panegyricus ad Philippum Austriae ducem LB IV / ASD IV-1 / CWE 27
Parabolae: Parabolae sive similia LB I / ASD I-5 / CWE 23
Paraclesis LB V, VI
Paraphrasis in Elegantias Vallae: Paraphrasis in Elegantias Laurentii Vallae LB I /
    ASD I-4
Paraphrasis in Matthaeum, etc (in Paraphrasis in Novum Testamentum)
Paraphrasis in Novum Testamentum LB VII / CWE 42–50
Peregrinatio apostolorum: Peregrinatio apostolorum Petri et Pauli LB VI, VII
Precatio ad Virginis filium Iesum LB V
Precatio dominica LB V
Precationes LB V
Precatio pro pace ecclesiae: Precatio ad Iesum pro pace ecclesiae LB IV, V
Progymnasmata: Progymnasmata quaedam primae adolescentiae Erasmi LB VIII
Psalmi: Psalmi, or Enarrationes sive commentarii in psalmos LB V / ASD V-2, 3
Purgatio adversus epistolam Lutheri: Purgatio adversus epistolam non sobriam
    Lutheri LB IX / ASD IX-1

Querela pacis LB IV / ASD IV-2 / CWE 27

Ratio: Ratio seu Methodus compendio perveniendi ad veram theologiam (Methodus for the shorter version originally published in the Novum instrumentum of 1516) LB V, VI

Responsio ad annotationes Lei: Liber quo respondet annotationibus Lei LB IX

Responsio ad collationes: Responsio ad collationes cuiusdam iuvenis geronto-didascali LB IX

Responsio ad disputationem de divortio: Responsio ad disputationem cuiusdam Phimostomi de divortio LB IX

Responsio ad epistolam Pii: Responsio ad espistolam paraeneticam Albert Pii, or Responsio ad exhortationem Pii LB IX

Responsio ad notulas Bedaicas LB X

Responsio ad Petri Cursii defensionem: Epistola de apologia Cursii LB X

Responsio adversus febricitantis libellum: Apologia monasticae religionis LB X

Spongia: Spongia adversus aspergines Hutteni LB X / ASD IX-1

Supputatio: Supputatio calumniarum Natalis Bedae LB IX

Tyrannicida: Tyrannicida, declamatio Lucianicae respondens LB I / CWE 29

Virginis et martyris comparatio LB V

Vita Hieronymi: Vita divi Hieronymi Stridonensis *Opuscula*

Index

In this index references to the text and to the notes are separated by a slash. References to the notes are identified by the number of the page on which the reference occurs and by note number.

Aachen xli, xlii
Abraham 92
Accursius 48 / 152 n29
Adrianus, Matthaeus xx, xxi, 33, 35, 36 / 138 n24, 158 n54
Aeschines 8, 44
Ailly, Pierre d' xxxi, 78 / 158 n49
Alaard of Amsterdam 34
Albert, elector of Brandenburg xxxviii, xli, xlii, xliv, xlv
Albert the Great 77, 79 / 158 n51
Alcalá, University of 32 / 137 n21, 148 n1
Alciato, Andrea 152 n29
Aleandro, Girolamo xxi, xxxix, xl, xlii, xliv, 33, 87, 101, 103, 104, 105, 269 / 141 nn51, 53, 148 n4, 162 n1, 163 n11; relations with Erasmus 99, 100; and burning of books 102
Alexander the Great (Life of) 40 / 150 n12
Alexander of Hales 39, 78 / 149 n7, 158 n49
Alphonso the Magnanimous, king of Naples 150 n14
Ambrose, St xiv, 25, 26, 40, 43, 53, 65, 70, 71, 72, 81, 95 / 157 n35
Amerbach brothers xxiv / 91 n14, 138 n24
Ammonio, Andrea xvi, 86 / 135 n10

Anderlecht xlviii
Antoninus, St, archbishop of Florence 155 n10
Antonius, St 72 / 156 n34
Antwerp xiv, xv, xvi, xxvi, xxix, xxx, xxxix, xlix, 5, 7, 101 / 136 n17
Apelles 14
Apologia in Latomum, date of composition 34–6
Apostolius, Michael 141 n51
Apuleius 90
Aquileia 51 / 143 n23, 153 n36
Aquinas. See Thomas Aquinas
Arabic language 41 / 147 n98
Aragon xvi
Aratus, Phenomena 150 n9, 158 n56
Archelaus 95
Aristotle xxxi, 4, 8, 15, 17, 25, 26, 43, 44, 57, 59, 61, 65, 75, 76, 77 / 147 n113, 154 n4
Armagh, Maurice of 78 / 158 n49
Ate xxxii
Atella 144 n34
Atellanes 11
Ath xxxii
Athanasius, St 27
Augsburg xliv, xlv, 100
Augustine, St xiv, 25, 26, 28, 40–1, 43, 45, 52, 53, 54, 55, 58, 61, 62, 65, 67, 70, 71, 72, 73, 77, 79, 81, 82, 94, 95, 102, 104, 111 / 143 n22, 150 n13,

151 n18, 153 n40, 155 nn18, 19; on importance of languages 62; ignorant of Hebrew 63–4; as rhetorician 81
– works of: *De doctrina christiana* 10; *Confessions* 25 / 147 nn97, 108; *De bono coniujali* 94/ 160 n24
Augustinians xxi
Augustinus (Alveldt) 105, 109, 287 / 164 nn1, 15
Averroes 59, 61 / 154 n8

Bade, Josse (printer) 5 / 134 n6
Baechem, Nicolaas xxviii, xxix, xxxii, xxxiii, xli, xliii, xliv, 102, 104 / 141 n54, 161 n5, 162 nn2, 4, 166 n19
Baer, Ludwig xlvii
Baldus degli Ubaldis 39, 48 / 149 n6
Barbaro, Ermolao 158 n48
Barbier, Pierre 134 n9, 168 n46
Barlandus, Adrianus xviii, xxi, 32, 33, 36 / 138 n25, 148 n1
Bartolus of Sassoferrato 39, 48 / 149 n6
Basel xiv, xv, xxii, xxiii, xxiv, xxvii, xlvii, xlviii, l, 5, 33, 80 / 138 n24, 139 n39, 140 n44, 147 n116, 151 n19
Basil, St 14, 24, 26, 27, 44 / 151 n18
Batt, Jacob xi
Béda, Noël xxvii, 87
Bérault, Nicolas xlvii
Bergen, Antoon van ix, x
Bergen, Hendrik van ix, x, xi, xii
Bernard of Clairvaux, St 72, 102 / 156 n34
Berquin, Louis de 87
Beveren, Nicolaas van 30
Bintius (Jan Lengherant of Binche) 95
Blount, William, Lord Mountjoy xi, xxxiv, xlviii, 14, 86 / 133 n2
Boece, Hector 142 n1
Bohemia xlv
Bologna xiii / 147 n98
Bombace, Paolo xvii, xxiv, xlvii
Bonaventure, St xxxi, 39, 78 / 149 n7, 158 n49
Bordeaux xix, xx, 32

Borssele, Anna van, the Lady of Veere x, xi
Borsele, Jan Becker van 161 n32
Botzheim, Johann von 142 n1
Brabant ix
Brabant, Council of xxv
Briart, Jean, dean of Louvain theological faculty and university vice-chancellor xvi, xvii, xviii, xix, xxv, xxxi, xxxii, xxxiii, xxxiv, xxxv, xxxvi, xlviii, 35, 86, 87, 89, 90, 93, 95 / 135 n10, 136 n13, 145 n69, 148 n10, 166 n13, 168 n46
Bruges xvi, xxiii, xxxix, xliv, xlviii
Brussels xii, xvi, xviii, xxxvii, xxxviii, xxxix, xli, xlviii
Budé, Guillaume xxii, 48 / 137 n21, 149 n39, 152 n29
Bullock, Henry 32 / 148 n1
Burgundy, court of xii, xvi, xxxvii, xxxviii, xxxix, xl, xli, xliii, xlv, xlviii
Burgundy, Nicholas of 147 n118
Busleyden, François de, archbishop of Besançon xi, xii, xx
Busleyden, Gilles de xx, xxi, 33
Busleyden, Jérôme de, archdeacon of Cambrai xii, xix, xx, 32 / 137 n22, 138 n26

Caesar, Julius 13
Cajetan, Cardinal (Tommaso de Vio) 103, 105 / 163 nn9, 15
Calais xxxviii
Camarina 11, 24
Cambrai ix
Cambridge xiii, xiv
Cambron 139 n35
Campania 144 n34
Campeggi, Lorenzo, Cardinal xxxvi, 127
canon law 147 n98
Canterbury xxxviii
Capito, Wolfgang xxvii, xxxvi / 138 n24, 140 n47
Caraffa, Gianpietro, Cardinal, Pope Paul IV 135 n10
Carmelites xxviii
Carmina Priapeia 59

Carraciolo, Marino 103 / 163 n9
Carvajal, Bernardino López de,
    Cardinal 277 / 137 n12, 163 n8
Castile xvi
Catherine of Aragon xxxviii
Catholicon 15
Catullus, Gaius Valerius 59 / 154 n8
celibacy 117, 129
Chaldean, study of 41, 50
Charles, Prince, archduke of
    Burgundy, king of Spain, Holy
    Roman Emperor xv, xvi, xix,
    xxxvii, xxxviii, xxxix, xli, xlii, xliii,
    xliv, xlv, xlvi, xlviii, xlix, 32, 98,
    111 / 134 n9, 135 n11, 140 n49, 141
    n52
Chrysostom. *See* John Chrysostom
Cicero, Marcus Tullius xi, 8, 12, 26,
    44, 48, 60, 76, 83 / 144 n46, 145
    n70, 147 n106
Circe xxxii
Cisneros, Jiménez de, Cardinal 32 /
    137 n21
Claymond, John 137 n21
Clement V, Pope 41, 42 / 147 n98
Clement VI, Pope 143 n18
Clement VII, Pope 127
Clichtove, Josse 87
Colet, John ix, x, xiii, xxii / 134 n8
Collège de France 137 n21
College of San Ildefonso 137 n21
Collegium Trilingue (Louvain) xix,
    xxi, xxii, xxv, xxx, xliv, 32–3, 34, 35,
    36 / 137 n21, 138 n26
Cologne xviii, xxiii, xxxvii, xl, xli,
    xlii, xliii, xlv, 98, 99, 100, 103, 109 /
    163 n8
Cologne, University of xvi / 135
    nn10, 12
Complutensian Polyglot (Bible) xv /
    137 n21
Cop, Guillaume 48 / 152 n28
Copenhagen, Royal Library of xlix,
    114
Corpus Christi College, Oxford 137
    n21
Corunna xxxvii
Cratander, Andreas 99

Croy, Charles de 139 n35
Croy, Guillaume de, Cardinal xxi,
    34 / 148 n8, 149 n3
Croy, Robert de 139 n35
Cusa, Nicholas of 102
Cyprian, St, bishop of Carthage 21,
    52, 60, 71, 81, 95, 126 / 153 n37

Damasus, Pope 52
Davus 13
Decretals 45
Delft, Gillis van 90, 95 / 140 n43
Deloynes, François 32 / 148 n1
Demonax 49 / 152 n31
Demosthenes 8, 43, 44 / 143 n16
Desmarez, Jean xii, xvi, xvii, xviii,
    xx, 30, 86
Deventer ix
*Dialogus bilinguium ac
    trilinguium* xxxii, xxxiii
Diana, temple of at Ephesus 146 n86
Didymus 72
Dionysius Areopagiticus 75, 123 /
    157 n41
Doctrinale of Alexandre de Ville-
    Dieu 145 n57
Dominicans xxviii, xxix, xlix, 114,
    115, 131
Donatists 82
Dorp, Maarten van xii, xiv, xv, xvi,
    xvii, xviii, xix, xxii, xxxii, xxxiii,
    xlviii, 2, 3, 4, 5, 7, 10, 11, 13, 16, 17,
    18, 22, 24, 25, 27, 29, 30, 86, 90, 95,
    102, 103, 114 / 133 n3, 136 nn13, 15,
    16, 17, 142 n7, 143 n10, 146 n77, 154
    n3, 162 n3
Dover xxxviii
Durand, William 71, 78 / 156 n30

Eck, Johann Maier von xxiii, xxxvi,
    34, 36, 109
Egmond xxviii
Egmond family xxi
England x, xi, xiii, xiv, xv, xvi,
    xxxviii, 24 / 134 n8
English 11
Epicurus 76
Episcopius, Nicholas 151 n19

Erasmus, Desiderius: first residence in
Louvain xii; in Italy xiii; returns
to England from Italy xiii–xiv;
second residence in Louvain xiii,
xvii; in Basel 1514–16 xiv–xv; first
association with the Froben
Press xiv–xv; completion of the
first edition of the Greek New
Testament xv; councillor to Prince
Charles xv; dispensation from Leo
X xvi; hostility of Louvain
theologians to *Praise of Folly* and
Greek New Testament xviii–xix;
involvement with the founding of
the Collegium Trilingue xix–xxii;
prepares second edition of Greek
New Testament xxiii–xxv; dispute
with Lee xxv–xxvii; controversies
with Baechem and Theoderici
xxviii–xxix, 102; the controversy
over *De laude matrimonii* xxxiii–
xxxvi; and the beginning of the
Lutheran crisis xxxvi–xl; turns
away from Luther xlvii; departure
from Louvain xlviii; controversy
with Taxander xlix–li; controversy
with Dorp 2–6; defence of the
Moria 7–22; at the University of
Louvain 32–3; on the Collège de
Montaigu 34; personal dislike of
Aleandro 99; and Elector Frederick
99–100; on pronunciation 152 n25
Erasmus, works of
– *Acta Academiae Lovaniensis contra
Lutherum* xl, 98
– *Adagia* xi, xiii, xiv, xxxix, 20 / 144
nn33, 39, 145 n70, 146 nn81, 83, 88,
93, 147 nn103, 114, 168 n56
– *Adagiorum collectanea* 133 n2
– *Annotations on the New
Testament* x, xiv, xxiv, li, 29, 32–3,
42, 53, 58, 66, 126 / 168 nn46, 52,
170 n100
– *Antibarbari* x
– *Apologia ad Jacobum Fabrum
Stapulensem* xxiii
– *Apologia adversus debacchationes
Sutoris* 140 n41

– *Apologia contra Latomi dialogum* xxx
– *Apologia de 'In principio erat
sermo'* xxviii
– *Apologia de loco 'Omnes quidem
resurgemus'* xxix
– *Apologia in Latomum* xxxii, 35–6
– *Apologia pro declamatione de laude
matrimonii* xxxiv / 140 n43
– *Apologia ... qua respondet duabus
invectivis Eduardi Lei* xxvii / 134
n9, 138 n29
– *Appendix de scriptis Clichtovei* 87
– *Auctorium selectorum
epistolarum* xxiv
– Augustine, St, *Works* xlviii
– *Axiomata Erasmi pro causa Martini
Lutheri* xlii, xliii, xliv, 98
– Basil, St, *Works* xiii
– *Catalogus lucubrationum* 89 n1, 90
n10
– *Colloquia* xxvi, li, 119, 124, 125 /
141 n51
– *Consilium cuiusdam ex animo
cupientis esse consultum et Romani
pontificis dignitate et christianae
religionis tranquillitati* xl, xliv, xlv,
98
– *Declamatio de morte* 2
– *Declamatio in genere suasorio de laude
matrimonii* 140 n42
– *Declamationes aliquot* 86 n1, 140
n42
– *De conscribendis epistolis* 86, 91 / 92
n19
– *De copia verborum ac rerum* xiii
– *De laude matrimonii* xxxiii
– *De libero arbitrio* 1, 128
– *De orando Deum* li, 125, 128 / 169
n80, 170 n100
– *De pueris instituendis* 58, 60 / 154
n5
– *Dilutio eorum quae Jodocus Clithoveus
scripsit adversus Declamationem Des.
Erasmi Roterodami suasoriam
matrimonii* 88
– *Disticha Catonis* xiv, xvii, 3 / 142
n3
– *Enarratio in primum psalmum* 5

- *Enchiridion militis christiani* xii, 4, 9 / 140 n47, 144 n25
- *Encomium matrimonii* 2, 86 / 166 n13
- *Encomium medicinae* 151 n22
- *Epistola apologetica ad Dorpium* xv, xviii
- *Epistola de esu carnium* l / 166 n14, 169 n79, 170 n107
- *Epistolae ... ad diversos* xlviii
- *Epistolae aliquot eruditorum* xxvi
- *Exomologesis: De modo bene confitendi* li, 116, 119, 120 / 169 n85
- *Institutio christiani matrimonii* 88
- *Institutio principis christiani* xv, li / 144 n26, 166 n17
- Jerome, St, *Works* xiii, xiv, xv, xix, 2, 4, 7
- John Chrysostom, St, *Works* xiii
- *Julius exclusus* 144 n48
- Libanius, translation of xii
- Lucian, dialogues of xiii, xx
- *Lucubratiunculae aliquot* xii
- *Manifesta mendacia* xlix, l, li
- New Testament xiii, xiv, xv, xviii, xix, xxii, xxiv, xxv, xxvii, xxviii, xxix, xxx, xxxvii, xlviii, 2, 3, 4, 5, 7, 29, 32 / 137 n21
- *Opera omnia* (1540) 6 / 143 n18
- *Opuscula aliquot Erasmo Roterodamo castigatore* xvii / 142 n3
- *Opuscula Erasmi* xxvi
- *Panegyric to Duke Philip* xii, 9 / 133 n4, 144 n27
- *Paraphrases* li
- *Paraphrasis in Elegantias Vallae* 86 n2
- *Paraphrasis in duas Epistolas Pauli ad Corinthios* xxxiv, 87
- *Paraphrasis in Epistolam Pauli ad Galatas* 95
- Plutarch, translations of xiii
- *Praise of Folly (Moria)* xiii, xv, xviii, xix, 2, 3, 4, 5, 7, 9 / 136 n20, 142 n6, 145 n65, 146 n77, 147 n116
- *Prologus in supputationem calumniarum Bedae* 87
- *Purgatio ad expostulationem Hutteni* 141 n53
- *Ratio seu methodus verae theologiae* xxx, li, 33, 34, 39, 43, 53, 55, 61, 68, 70, 79 / 168 nn47, 61
- Seneca, edition of xiii
- *Spongia* li, 117
- *Virginis matris ... liturgia* 169 n81

Erfurt xxvi
Euclid 46
Eugenius IV, Pope 150 n14
Euripides 43
Eustochium 14 / 145 n54

Faber, Johannes xliv, xlv, xlvi, 100
fasting 117, 128, 129, 130
feast days 117, 125, 127, 128
Feltre, Vittorino da 151 n21
Field of the Cloth of Gold xxxviii
Fisher, Christopher xiii / 134 n6
Fisher, John, bishop of Rochester xiii, xxii, xxvii
Fisher, Robert xxxiv
Florizoon, Adriaan, Pope Adrian VI ix, xii / 133 n1, 135 n12, 139 n35
Flushing xxxviii
Foxe, Richard, bishop of Winchester 32 / 137 n21, 138 n31
France xi, 10 / 139 n39
Francis I, king of France xvi, xxxvii, xxxviii, xxxix, xlviii / 137 n21, 141 n49
Franciscan order 24
Frankfurt xv, xxiii
Frederick the Wise, elector of Saxony xxxvii, xxxix, xlii, xliii, xliv, xlv, 99, 100
Froben, Hieronymus 151 n19
Froben, Johann xiv, xv, xxiii, xxiv, xxvii, xxxvi, xlviii, 32, 36 / 136 n17, 140 n44, 153 n37
Froben press xiv, xv, xlviii / 136 n17, 140 n44

Gaguin, Robert x
Galen 44, 45 / 151 n22
Gallus, Alexander 15
Gattinara, Mercurino xxxviii–xxxix, xliv
Gaza, Theodorus 44 / 151 n21

Geldenhouwer, Gerard xxii, xxxix
Gellius, Aulus 144 n28
Germany xi, xiv, xxi, xl, xlv / 139 n39
Gerson, Jean xxxi, 72, 73, 78, 95, 102, 130 / 157 n36
Ghent xvi
Gillis, Pieter xiv, xvi, xvii
Gillis van Delft xxxiii, xxxiv
Glareanus, Henricus xxii
Gouda xii
Gourmont, Gilles de (printer) xxvi
Gratian, *Decretum* 35, 40, 41 / 150 nn12, 14
Gregory Nazianzen, St 24, 72
Grimani, Cardinal xiii, xxiv
Grocyn, William xxii
Grunenberg, Johann 36
Gryllus xxxii

Hainault xxxii
Halewijn, Joris van 86
Hebrew language 147 n98
Hebrew literature xxi
Heliodorus, bishop of Altinum 145 n55
Henry VIII, king of England xiii, xxxviii, xliv, xlvi, xlviii / 171 n124
Hermans, Willem x, xi, xii, xx
Herodotus 43
Herostratus 146 n86
Hesiod 43
Hilary, St 26, 43, 50, 70, 95 / 151 n17
Hillen, Michaël (printer) xxv, xxvi, xxvii, xxix / 136 n17
Hippocrates 44 / 151 n20
Holcot, Robert 38, 71, 78 / 149 n4, 156 n30, 157 n49
Homer 8, 43, 58–9, 60, 91
Hoogstraten, Jacob of xxxvii, xli, 87, 98, 101, 104, 105 / 135 n12, 162 n2
Horace (Quintus Horatius Flaccus) 9, 71 / 143 n24, 144 nn44, 50
Hugh of St Victor 49, 58 / 152 n32
Hussites xlv
Hutten, Ulrich von xlii, 84, 125
hydra 24

Iliad 143 n15
indulgences 126
Ingolstadt xxiii
Isidore of Seville 78
Isocrates 44
Italians 11
Italy xiii, xxi, 10 / 134 n8

Jerome, St xi, xxxi, 8, 11, 14, 15, 20, 21, 22, 24, 25, 26, 27, 40, 41, 44, 45, 52, 53, 54, 61, 64, 67, 71, 72, 74, 75, 79, 81, 82, 123, 126 / 143 nn21, 22, 23, 144 n37, 145 n54, 146 n87, 147 nn96, 100, 151 n24; on language of Gospel according to St Matthew 50; use of Hebrew 51, 82 / 153 n34
– works of: Commentary on Abdios 90, 94, 95; *Adversus Jovinianum* 91 n16
Joachim, elector of Brandenburg xlvi
John Chrysostom, St 24, 26, 27, 44, 49, 50, 51, 52, 66, 68, 75 / 152 nn32, 33, 156 n22
Jonas, Justus xxvi
Jovinian 45
Julius II, Pope xiii, 103
Jupiter xvii
Juvenal (Decimus Junius Juvenalis) 12, 15, 59 / 154 n8
Juvencus 60 / 155 n13

Karlstadt, Andreas 34, 36

Lactantius, Firmianus 21, 60, 95
Lady Margaret Beaufort professorship of divinity (Cambridge) xiii
Lascaris, Janus xxi, 33 / 148 n4
Latimer, William xxii, 32 / 148 n1
Latomus, Jacobus (Jacques Masson) xxix, xxx, xxxi, xxxii, xxxiii, xlix, 32, 34–5, 36, 37, 38, 39, 65, 66, 69, 76, 77, 78, 81, 84, 87, 98, 104, 114, 116, 117, 118 / 95 n32, 139 n35, 142 nn62, 64, 148 n8, 149 nn3, 15, 150 n10, 151 n17, 156 n25, 157 n42; on ancient and modern theologians 39; Latin style of 40; frivolous approach of 42–7, 48–9;

on study of language 43–4, 62; on
study of Scripture 53–5; second
book of 56; on pagan
literature 58–61
– works of: *De trium linguarum et
studii theologici ratione* 34–6
LeBreton, Guillaume 24 / 147 n95
Lee, Edward xxiii, xxiv, xxv, xxvi,
xxvii, xxix, xxxii, xxxiii, xlviii, 87,
116, 125, 131 / 138 nn29, 30, 32, 33,
159 n60, 166 n3, 168 nn53, 60, 169
nn66, 69, 171 n124
Lefèvre d'Etaples, Jacques xviii, xxiii,
xlviii, 28, 29, 32, 34, 36 / 138 n28,
154 n3
Legenda sanctorum 145 n59
Leipzig, Greek studies in 32, 33, 35,
99
Leipzig debates xxxvii
Leo X, Pope x, xiii, xvi, xxiv, xl, xlii,
xliii, xlv, xlvii, xlix, 108–9 / 164 n4
Leoni, Ambrogio 48 / 152 n28
Leoniceno, Niccolò 48 / 152 nn22, 28
Lepidus, Marcus Aemilius 104 / 163
n13
Le Sauvage, Jean, chancellor of
Burgundy xvi, xxxix / 135 n11
Letters of Obscure Men xviii
Licentius 61
Lily, College of the (Louvain) xii,
xvii
Linacre, Thomas 48 / 152 n28
Lips, Maarten xxiv, 34
Listrius, Gerardus 30 / 147 n116
Livy (Titus Livius) 144 n34
Lombard, Peter xxxi, 52, 54, 67, 78,
95, 104 / 153 n39
Lot, daughters of 92
Louis II, king of Hungary xlvi
Louvain ix, xii, xiii, xiv, xv, xvi, xx,
xxi, xxii, xxiii, xxiv, xxv, xxvi, xxvii,
xxviii, xxix, xxxii, xxxiii, xxxvi,
xxxvii, xxxix, xl, xli, xliii, xliv,
xlviii, li, 5, 114, 131 / 133 n1, 134
nn6, 9, 137 n21, 141 n54, 142 n3
Louvain, University of ix, xii, xvi,
xxvii, xxviii, xxx, xxxi, xxxii, xliii,
xlix, 2, 4, 13, 14, 16, 32, 34, 36, 47,

86, 89, 98, 100, 101, 103, 104, 109 /
135 nn10, 12, 138 n29, 139 n35, 163
n8
Low Countries x, xi, xii, xv, xvi,
xxxvii, xxxviii, xxxix, xliv, xlviii /
135 n12, 141 n49
Lucerne 145 n59
Lucian 16, 43, 58–9, 60 / 145 n64, 150
n12, 154 n6
Lucretius (Titus Lucretius Carus) 7
Luke, St 75, 76
Lupset, Thomas xxviii / 138 n31
Luther, Martin xxiii, xxviii, xxix,
xxxvi, xxxvii, xxxviii, xxxix, xl, xli,
xlii, xliii, xliv, xlv, xlvi, xlvii, xlviii,
xlix, l, 33, 36, 84, 98, 99, 100, 102,
104, 105, 106–7, 108, 109, 110, 111 /
139 n35, 140 nn46, 47
– works of: Ninety-five
Theses xxxvi; *Resolutiones
disputationum de virtute
indulgentiarum* xxxvi; *On Christian
Liberty* xlvi; *On the Babylonian
Captivity of the Church* xlvi; *To the
Christian Nobility of the German
Nation* xlvi
Lycaeum 81
Lyra, Nicholas of 49, 52, 58, 232 /
152 n32, 158 n49
Lysias 44

Macrobius 144 n28
Mainz 145 n59
Mammotrectus 15
Man, Abbot Meynard 3, 5, 30
Manutius, Aldus xiii, xxxix
Marchesinus, Johannes of Reggio 145
n59
Marck, Erard de la, bishop of
Liège xliv / 140 n48
Marcus Antonius 8, 104 / 163 n13
Margaret of Austria 141 n49
Martens, Dirk (printer) xii, xiv, xviii,
xxi, xxv, xxvi, xxx, xxxiv, 5 / 138
n27, 140 n42, 142 nn3, 7
Martial (Marcus Valerius
Martialis) 59 / 154 n8
Marullus 60 / 155 n11

Mary Tudor xxxviii
matrimony 118, 122
Mauritszoon, Jacob xii
Maximilian I, Holy Roman
    Emperor xxxvii, xliv
Medici, Giovanni de', Cardinal. *See*
    Leo X, Pope
Medici, Lorenzo de' 143 n20
Meghen, Pieter 134 n8
Melanchthon, Philippus 34 / 148
    n6
mendicant orders xxviii, xxix, xxxix,
    xli, xlii
Mera, Jean de 163 n7
Miltitz, Karl von 103 / 163 n9
Montaigu, Collège de 34 / 148 n8
More, Thomas xiii, xviii, xxiv, xxvii,
    xxxvi, xxxviii, xxxix, xlviii, 2, 10,
    32 / 136 n15, 138 n31, 141 n56, 142
    n4, 148 n2, 152 n30, 154 n7
Mosaic law 119
Mosellanus, Petrus (Peter
    Schade) xxix, xxx, xxxvii, 32, 33,
    34, 35, 84, 103 / 148 n6; as 'Peter'
    in Latomus' dialogue 40, 42 / 150
    nn10, 15
Moses 56, 101
Muses xxxii, 11

Naples 145 n61
Nastätten xxxii
Nazarenes, Gospel of the 50
Nepos, Jacobus xxiv
Nepotianus 14 / 145 n55
Nesen, Conrad xxxii
Nesen, Wilhelm xxxii, 36 / 140 n40,
    149 n15
Neuenahr, Count Hermann von xxii,
    xlii
Neve, Jan de, of Hondschoote xvii,
    xviii, 30
Nicholas V, Pope 151 n21, 156 n22

Ockham, William of xxxi, 15, 78 /
    158 n49
Octavius, Gaius 104 / 163 n13
Origen 25, 26, 50, 51, 52, 53, 67, 68,
    69, 70, 72, 74, 75, 79, 81, 92 / 143

n23, 146 n79, 153 n35, 156 n24, 157
    nn35, 40
Orléans xx
Ovid (Publius Ovidius Naso) 61
Oxford, University of v, ix / 147
    n48

Pacquet, Jacques 135 n12
Padua, University of 103 / 158 n48
Panormitanus (Nicholas de
    Tudescis) 41, 124, 125, 360 / 168
    n58, 169 n74
Parc, Premonstratensian abbey of 134
    n6
Paris x, xi, xiii, xx, xxi, xxvi, xxxii,
    xxxiii, xxxiv, xxxix, 87, 103, 109 /
    147 nn98, 112
Paris, William of 78 / 158 n49
Paul, St 12, 14, 17, 20, 39, 55, 56, 76,
    125, 228 / 375 n56; as
    rhetorician 81
- works of: First Epistle to the
    Corinthians 53 / 150 n9, 153 nn38,
    40, 156 n22; sermon in Athens 75 /
    150 n9
Paula, St 145 n54
Paulinus 60, 72 / 155 n13
Pelagius 74
Persius (Aulus Persius Flaccus) 144
    n41
Peter, St 76, 124
Petrarch 8
Peutinger, Konrad xliv, xlv, 100 /
    164 n16
Pfefferkorn, Johann 103 / 163 n10
Philip, archduke of Burgundy xii,
    xx / 133 n5
Philippi, Johannes (printer) xi
Pico della Mirandola 77 / 158 n48
Pilate, Pontius 35, 43 / 151 n17
Pindar 43
Pio, Alberto 114
Pirckheimer, Willibald xv, xxii / 134
    n10
Piso 8
Plato 8, 9, 11, 19, 48, 55, 57, 59, 90,
    92, 197 / 145 n67, 146 nn75, 90, 150
    n13, 153 n40, 154 n4, 155 n10

Plautus, Titus Maccius 82 / 143 n14, 158 n58
Pliny the Elder (Gaius Plinius Secundus) 59, 66 / 144 n33, 145 n64, 154 n8
Pliny the Younger (Gaius Plinius Caecilius Secundus) 16 / 154 n8
Plutarch xxxii, 43, 61 / 144 n45, 146 n85, 161 n29
Poggio Bracciolini 8, 15, 59, 95 / 145 n60, 155 n9
Poliziano, Angelo 8, 48 / 143 n20, 149 n6, 152 n29
Pompeius Festus 149 n2
Pontano, Giovanni 15, 59, 95 / 145 n61
pope, powers of the 123, 125, 126, 127, 129
Poppenruyter, Johann 47 / 152 n27
prayer 128
Prierias, Silvestro (Mazzolini) xxxvi, 105, 109 / 163 nn1, 15, 164 n2
Prudentius 60 / 155 n13
Ptolemy 46
Pucci, Antonio xxiv
purgatory 123
Pyrgopolinices 8 / 143 n14
Pyrrhus, king of Epirus 144 n45

Quintilian (Marcus Fabius Quintilianus) 12, 19, 55, 60, 73 / 144 n46, 155 n14, 157 n37
quodlibetica 90

Remacle d'Ardenne 278 / 141 n52, 163 n12
Remigius of Auxerre 49, 50 / 152 n32
Rescius, Rutgerus xxi, 33
Reuchlin, Johann xv, xviii, 32, 104 / 135 n12
Rhenanus, Beatus xiv, xxiv / 140 n44
Riario, Cardinal xiii, xxiv
Robijns, Jan xxi / 89 n3
Rome xiii, xli, xlvi
Rosemondt, Godschalk xliii, 102 / 141 n54, 162 n4
royal lectureships (France) 137 n21

Rufinus 8, 45, 61, 74 / 143 n23
Ruistre, Nicholas, bishop of Arras xii

St Donatian's College (Louvain) xii, xx, xxii, xxvi
Saint-Omer ix
St Paul's School (London) xiii
St Peter's (Louvain) ix, xviii, 30
saints, veneration of 118, 120, 126, 127, 128
Salamanca 147 n98
Sallust (Gaius Sallustius Crispus) 8 / 143 n17
Scala, Bartolomeo 8 / 143 n20
Schets, Erasmus 135 n11
Schürer, Lazarus 139 n39
Schürer, Matthias 142 n7
Scotist 24
Scotus, John Duns xxxi, 15, 38, 39, 52, 71, 72, 75, 77, 78, 81, 104, 123 / 149 n4, 150 n7, 156 n30, 158 n49
Scribonius Largus 144 n42
Sélestat 139 n39
Seneca, Lucius Annaeus 8, 60, 61, 73 / 157 n37
Septuagint 51–2 / 153 n34
Sermons on Luke 67
Silenus 20
Simonides 21
Socrates 8, 11, 16, 47
Sophocles 43
Spain xii, xv, xvi, xix, xx, xxxvii, xlviii, 112
Spalatinus, Georgius xlii, xliii, 99 / 141 n55
Spaniards 11
Standish, Henry, bishop of St Asaph 146 n94
Standonck, Jan 34 / 139 n35
Stercke, Jan xx
Steyn, monastery of xiv
Stoa 81
Strasbourg 142 n7
Suetonius, Gaius Tranquillus 15, 59 / 144 nn47, 49, 154 n8
Switzerland 139 n39
Symmachus 51 / 153 n36
Syriac language 147 n98

Tacitus, Cornelius 15, 59 / 154 n8
Tartarus xvii
Taxander, Godefridus Ruysius
    (pseudonym) xlix, li, 114, 115, 118
Terence (Publius Terentius Afer) 143
    n14, 144 n53, 146 n88
Theoderici, Vincentius xxix, xlix, l,
    114, 118; called 'Bucenta' 115 / 165
    n13
Theocritus 43
Theodotion 51 / 153 n36
Theophylactus 53 / 153 n38
Thersites 8 / 143 n15
Thessalians 21
Thibault, Jan (printer) xxv, xxx
Thomas Aquinas, St xxxi, 20, 39, 49,
    50, 58, 72, 75, 77, 78, 79, 82, 95, 104,
    125 / 92 n20, 146 n77, 149 n7, 152
    n32, 158 nn49, 51, 169 n74
Thraso 8 / 143 n13
Thucydides 43
Titelmans, Franz 115
Todischus, Thomas 105 / 164 n15
Torino, University of xiii / 145 n66
Torresani, Andrea 99 / 151 n22
Trebizond, George of 66 / 156 n22
Tunstall, Cuthbert xxiv, xxxiii, xlviii,
    86 / 136 n43, 138 n31
Turnhout, Jan Driedo van 104 / 163
    n14
Tychonius 94

Ulysses xxxii
Utenheim, Christoph von, bishop of
    Basel l, 117

Valla, Lorenzo xviii, 8, 28, 29, 49 /
    134 n6, 152 n32
Vatinius 8
Venice xxi, xxxix
Vespasian (Titus Flavius
    Vespasianus) 13
vesperiae 90
Victorinus 81
Vienne, Council of 41 / 147 n98, 150
    n15
Vigilantius 8
Villinger, Jacob xliv
Virgil (Publius Virgilius Maro) 60, 91
Vives, Juan Luis 34

war 118
Warham, William, archbishop of
    Canterbury xxxviii
Wartburg, castle of xlvi
Wentford, Roger xxii
Wickman, Pieter xlviii
Wimpfeling, Jacob xv
Wittenberg 36
Wolsey, Thomas, Cardinal xxii,
    xxxviii, xlviii
Worms xliii, xliv, xlvi, 99

Xenophon 43

York, Margaret of 35

Zúñiga, Diego López xlix, 114, 118 /
    166 n16
Zwingli, Huldreich 100

This book

was designed by

ANTJE LINGNER

based on the series design by

ALLAN FLEMING

and was printed by

University

of Toronto

Press